INTEGRATING POSTMODERN THERAPY AND QUALITATIVE RESEARCH

This book integrates postmodern theories of therapeutic research and practice to demonstrate how these approaches can be effectively integrated into methods of data collection and analysis.

Drawing from theories of counseling, and marriage and family therapy, the book thoroughly explores the similarities between therapy and qualitative research. Chapters consider therapies that offer a humanistic "way of being," such as collaborative language systems, narrative therapy, and solution-focused brief therapy, and identify complementary philosophies and traits that can be used to guide the qualitative researcher's practice. Transcripts and vignettes of the author's practice as both a therapist and a researcher further help to illuminate how readers might enrich their processes of research and data analysis.

Suitable for use in graduate-level qualitative research courses, as well as an adjunct to marriage and family therapy courses, *Integrating Postmodern Therapy and Qualitative Research* innovatively encourages readers to reflect on and develop their personal practice and approach to analyzing key information.

Dr. Carlos Perez is an associate professor and chair of the Department of Psychology and Counseling at Lubbock Christian University. He is a licensed professional counselor, a licensed marriage and family therapist, and a certified family life educator. His research efforts focus on issues of masculinity and marital infidelity.

"The journey of qualitative inquiry is like the therapeutic process. Both are tricky and complicated, and both lead to rich rewards. In these chapters, Dr. Carlos Perez offers important guidance on how to help researchers be better thinkers and better people, and this will result in better scholarship."
—*Jason B. Whiting, PhD, LMFT, author of* **Love Me True: Overcoming the Surprising Ways We Deceive in Relationships**

"*Integrating Postmodern Therapy and Qualitative Research* is a landmark text that emphasizes being with participants and being for conversation rather than the traditional question-driven approach. Dr. Perez's articulation of the trustworthiness of the researcher is novel, and a good reminder that it is from this starting point that qualitative research should ensue rather than be pursued. Through postmodern therapies, epistemological and philosophical reflection, and systemic thinking, he invites the person-of-the-researcher to examine critically their own way of being, their biases, and ultimately what is to be gained from research. This book embodies the ethics of qualitative research that both seasoned and beginner researchers should read." —***Josh R. Novak, PhD, LMFT, assistant professor of marriage and family therapy; director of the Relationships and Health Lab, Auburn University***

"Counselors and marriage and family therapists typically develop as therapists before they establish their identity as researchers. With this in mind, Dr. Carlos Perez summarizes three models of marriage and family therapy and offers a map for postmodern therapists as he considers how to integrate those frameworks into a qualitative methodology. Dr. Perez addresses common questions around the nuances of self-disclosure and positioning of the researcher. Students, therapists, and beginning researchers will gain insight into how the fundamental tenets of each model can be organized into a feminist-informed, postmodern approach to scholarly inquiry." —***Sara E. Blakeslee Salkil, PhD, LMFT, IMFT-S, assistant dean; graduate programs program coordinator, Online Marriage and Family Therapy, Abilene Christian University***

INTEGRATING POSTMODERN THERAPY AND QUALITATIVE RESEARCH

Guiding Theory and Practice

Carlos Perez

NEW YORK AND LONDON

First published 2021
by Routledge
52 Vanderbilt Avenue, New York, NY 10017

and by Routledge
2 Park Square, Milton Park, Abingdon, Oxon, OX14 4RN

Routledge is an imprint of the Taylor & Francis Group, an informa business

© 2021 Carlos Perez

The right of Carlos Perez to be identified as author of this work has been asserted by him in accordance with sections 77 and 78 of the Copyright, Designs and Patents Act 1988.

All rights reserved. No part of this book may be reprinted or reproduced or utilised in any form or by any electronic, mechanical, or other means, now known or hereafter invented, including photocopying and recording, or in any information storage or retrieval system, without permission in writing from the publishers.

Trademark notice: Product or corporate names may be trademarks or registered trademarks, and are used only for identification and explanation without intent to infringe.

Library of Congress Cataloging-in-Publication Data
A catalog record for this title has been requested

ISBN: 978-0-367-27711-6 (hbk)
ISBN: 978-0-367-27708-6 (pbk)
ISBN: 978-0-429-29741-0 (ebk)

Typeset in Bembo
by Nova Techset Private Limited, Bengaluru & Chennai, India

This work is dedicated to my wonderful wife, Ali, whose support is the soul of this book. I cannot ask for a better conversation partner. And to Noah, my inspiration.

CONTENTS

List of tables and figures ix
Preface xi

1 What is a therapist? What is a researcher? 1
2 Epistemology and philosophy 29
3 Postmodern therapies and approaches 45
4 The collaborative researcher 61
5 The narrative interviewer 81
6 The solution-focused researcher 95
7 Hierarchy and self-disclosure 113
8 On writing 125

Appendix A 139
Appendix B 149
Appendix C 161
Index 185

LIST OF TABLES AND FIGURES

Table 1.1	The counseling therapist	8
Table 1.2	The marriage and family therapist	16
Table 1.3	The researcher	22
Table 2.1	Epistemology continuum	33
Table 6.1	The postmodern researcher	110
Figure 8.1	Analysis trialogue	133

PREFACE

I am primarily trained as a marriage and family therapist. In my education, I also received training in teaching and research. Texas Tech University, where I received my doctorate, trains its students well in all three areas. It was during my doctoral training where I grew fond of qualitative research. I have practiced therapy, teaching, and qualitative research since then.

As a therapist

I consider myself a postmodern therapist. I am drawn particularly to the ideas of Harlene Anderson and Michael White: the not-knowing stance, the co-construction of knowledge, the power dynamics of the therapist–client relationship, the power of politics, and the way we as therapists are a part of the meaning-making process with clients. In my practice, I try to be as egalitarian and feminist as possible, eliminating hierarchy where I can and treating clients like the experts. In therapy, I try to be as mindful as possible of my influence on the process of therapy itself. I know and understand that as a therapist, my position comes with some sort of influence onto the conversation. Therefore, I try to be as transparent as possible about my own life, the way I do therapy, and my thoughts during the interactions in therapy.

I believe in multiple realities and that people struggle in their own construction of their reality. The process of construction, being socially created, is a part of the therapy process as it relates to my approach to therapy. I am mindful of myself, the client's reality, and the context of their struggles. Therefore, it is my job to help clients understand the multiple influences they are subject to and to deconstruct those realities.

With this awareness, I also espouse the experiential approach to therapy, the ideas and practices of Carl Whitaker, Irvin Yalom, and Virginia Satir. I try to be myself, open, and genuinely and spontaneously led by the process of therapy and not by my own will placed onto the process. Even though theory drives practice, at some point a therapist should let go of theory and be themselves in the process; theory is for beginners. Specifically, with the tradition of experiential therapy, the existential encounter is very important to therapy. Many therapists have expounded on this idea, and Carl Whitaker believed that one's actual presence in therapy is where change happens in therapy. I try to use my own presence when working with clients, using my own intuition, what wisdom I have, and the collaboration between us in order to create a space for change.

As a researcher

As a researcher, I fall on the subjectivist part of the epistemological continuum, with a philosophical interpretive framework of postmodernism and social constructivism. I believe that when I am researching, alongside participants, whatever data produced is a product of our relationship, a co-construction. I believe there are multiple realities constructed through lived experiences. Therefore, the relationship between myself and participants is an effort to understand one's reality. Even among the data collected, there are multiple, subjective ways of understanding and interpreting.

My efforts to engage in research are an attempt to situate myself in the process of gathering and analyzing data. The qualitative researchers themselves are a central part of the research process. I strongly believe that if researchers do not understand and recognize this, they are doing the entire process and the participants a disservice. Therefore, I intentionally situate myself with the offerings of my own interpretation and collection of data as only one source of understanding and interpretation. There are many more perspectives and understandings than the one I may offer.

The combining of therapy and research

The idea for this book began in class. I teach a qualitative research course at the undergraduate level, which involves a lot of introductory concepts in qualitative research. To my students, it is no secret that I am also a practicing therapist. Therefore, conversation commonly lands in that area of interest. With qualitative research, in my class specifically, conversation is paid to the personal qualities of a qualitative researcher. I pay specific attention to the human aspect of qualitative research.

I acknowledge my bias. Being a postmodern, humanistic therapist, I realize that my approach to therapy is seen in other areas of my work, namely, research.

I also make this known to my students. I am also transparent about my fondness of qualitative research, more so than quantitative research. I understand and appreciate quantitative research and all the strengths it offers. I prefer qualitative research because of the humanistic way I practice it. I love learning from and being with people. I personally believe qualitative research has the strongest possibility of offering the richest data from people's experiences. It is the experience of one's life that is the foundation of research and therapy.

I believe both the researcher and the therapist share the aforementioned qualities and characteristics. Both are experts in inquiry. Both love to learn about people from people. Both understand that a person's experience is unique, worthy of analyzing, and worthy of helping. I think therapy and qualitative research are different means to the same end: people.

My education in therapy and research trained me to view the two as separate endeavors. I have been a part of countless conversations about the ethics of research and therapy; therapy is not research, and research is not therapy. It's an ethical dilemma to combine the two. I disagree.

If the qualitative researcher approaches a participant's life with questions, curiosities, and potentially personal information, I argue that the researcher *needs* to have some sort of therapeutic awareness, presence, and process. The space in which one asks intimate questions is very precious to me. To approach that space in qualitative research without the qualities of a therapist, I believe, is borderline irresponsible. Therefore, more training programs should be blurring the two.

Data

During the course of writing this book, I sought specific individuals with experience in qualitative research, and counseling or therapy. I interviewed them after divulging my personal stance on merging the two worlds. Most qualitative researchers in the field of marriage and family therapy already practice their research with a "base" of a therapy or counseling. Their conversations will provide extra thoughts that will parallel with the arguments of this book. Their insights will also shed light into an area that has not been explored: how a researcher *is* during the process of research, interviewing, analyzing data, and presenting that data.

A concept that I am expounding on is the area of trustworthiness of data. In the past, researchers have focused on defining trustworthiness of data as centered on participants: member checking, multiple interviews, and cross-examining data with participants. True to the postmodern concept of co-construction of knowledge, the researcher, then, is also a part of the trustworthiness of data. Since the argument of this book is that the researcher is a part of the co-construction of data, there then needs to be a way in which researchers also use themselves as a source of trustworthiness. The postmodern philosophies and characteristics of a therapist will be examined to further pursue the idea of the *trustworthiness of the researcher*.

How this book is organized

Each chapter is intended to be read as a separate focus. The overarching theme of this book is the integration of postmodern therapy into qualitative research. Therefore, different chapters will cover different postmodern therapies, with emphasis on certain characteristics of a postmodern therapist. The three therapies that will be discussed include collaborative language systems, narrative therapy, and solution-focused brief therapy. The actual practices of the therapies will be of less importance to this book. Instead, the beliefs, philosophies, characteristics, and "ways of being" of the therapist will be reviewed, along with how they can be integrated into qualitative research.

The first three chapters will focus on setting up the frame of thought to combine therapy and research. With the hope that this book will reach more than only researchers and therapists, the definitions of therapy, what a therapist is, what postmodern therapy is, and who the researcher and therapist are will all be answered as well as I can present them.

The second half of this book will dive into the specific postmodern therapist: collaborative language systems, solution-focused brief therapy, and narrative therapy. The chapters will emphasize the therapy's tenets, philosophies, and apply them to the qualitative researcher and their practices. This integration is not intended to propose a set of methods or systematic approaches to qualitative research. Instead, the proposed integration applies to all methodologies. Postmodern therapy can benefit all qualitative research approaches.

There is a certain way of being curious that is the central focus of this book. This is the sort of curiosity that originates not from us, but one driven by conversation. Curiosity in the practice of therapy and research, when espousing the constructivist epistemology, means being curious about our participants' lives. They begin our process of being curious. As they share, disclose, and think out loud, our curiosity is sparked, and therefore questions asked. As we ask questions, they share more. And as they share, we emerge with new curiosities. The participant leads with their lives and stories, in which our curiosities follow.

The postmodern theories of therapy presented in this book all take on forms of this curiosity. At the heart of therapy and qualitative research, I argue, is *curiosity*. Both the therapist and researcher are experts at being curious.

Ultimately, this book is for the qualitative researcher, the researcher who is looking to expand their approaches to therapy by examining herself or himself. My hope is that this book will help researchers adopt different philosophies and views of people, and therefore approaches to their research; question how they approach research and analysis; and gain insight into their own way of being and researching. In reading this book, the researcher will question what research is and expand their definition into a way of being rather than something done. The research never ends, just like our sense of curiosity. There will always be something to be curious about, and therefore always something to research.

I want this book to be about therapy and qualitative research, but more than that, I want it to be about you, the reader. Through reading what's to follow, my hope is that you reflect on it, become introspective, and learn something about yourself. If you are not a therapist, it's OK. There is something here for you, too. If you are not a qualitative researcher, that's also OK. There is something here for you to. Even if you are not a part of the scientific or academic world, it's OK. I hope you find something in here that speaks to you, who you are as a person, and how you can view people differently as a person that wants to know about people.

This book is about therapy and research, but more than that, it's about people; the desire to know people, be curious, and foster a questioning attitude that is shown in research, therapy, and in our interactions.

1
WHAT IS A THERAPIST? WHAT IS A RESEARCHER?

Introduction

The question stands: What is a therapist? What do they do? Also, what is a qualitative researcher? What does a researcher do? These are difficult questions to answer. Even though this is not a review of therapy or counseling, the field itself requires some overview in order to answer what a therapist is and, more important, who the therapist is. The same holds true for a review of qualitative research and who the researcher is. So that an idea of each can be reached, and so that the person of the therapist and researcher can be studied, a brief history of how I conceptualize both professions will be visited.

The counseling therapist

Psychoanalysis

Counseling and therapy both arguably originated from the early workings of Freud and Jung, who are still influential today. The early workings of psychoanalysis were practiced by exploration, where the therapist was considered to be an interpreter, exploring inner workings of the unconscious and inner conflict found in inherent drives. The analysis of dreams was also practiced, interpreting dreams as inner conflict, projected emotions, and unconscious processes (Sharf, 2018).

Countertransference played a big role in determining the process of the therapist. The psychoanalyst believed that transference and countertransference were a projection of unconscious feelings onto the therapist, and the therapist onto the client, which greatly hindered the therapeutic process (Gabbard, 2004). The view of transference and countertransference has changed in recent decades, but the psychoanalyst was concerned with the interpretations that came from such projected feelings. The traditional psychoanalyst was considered a neutral presence, allowing the patient to project their unconscious conflict onto and toward the therapist. However, as the practice grew, empathy became an important factor.

The common misconception of a psychoanalyst is a cold, uncaring person who sits and analyzes their patients. As psychoanalysis grew in practice, its approach evolved into object relations and more relational aspects of client. Therapists' practice also grew into taking a relational approach to their clients (Rigas, 2012). Using a relational approach, the empathy and the relationship between the therapist and client became key (Ornstein, 2011). This approach called for a different sort of therapist; rather than being the traditional analyst whose main focus was interpreting and diagnosing, the therapist was concerned with patients' feelings, their needs for nurturing, and allowing feelings of transference to develop in order to empathize with them. Although not often emphasized, the psychoanalyst was largely considered a person that valued relationships and genuine feelings between themselves and the patient.

Carl Jung

Carl Jung was one such therapist. Also interested in the unconscious, dream interpretation, and the function of one's personality, Jung introduced a personal component of psychoanalysis with his view of archetypes and the way one's personality develops. Fascinated with severe psychological disturbances, Jung also gave room for his own humanity to be used in the therapy process. Jung argued that one's own psyche was an issue of learning within the therapist themselves; if the doctor cannot evaluate their own psyche, then the patient will not be able to as well (Jung, 1961).

Jung's concept of the wounded healer was essential to his approach to his patients. His practice included self-reflections of his own pain, relationships, and experiences, which he used to connect with his patients; he was able to better understand the psyche of his patients having been able to understand his own. He also believed that the best way to analyze patients was to be consciously and continuously aware of one's own personal wounds. Jung was one of the first in the field of counseling and therapy to present the counselor with the phenomenon of the use of self in the therapist practice. His archetypal work was also brought out of his own study of himself, mainly his relationships to other psychoanalysts. This started a wave of counseling outside of psychoanalysis in which the personhood of the counselor and therapist was essential to the process of counseling and therapy.

Alfred Adler

Carl Jung started a wave of counseling that was heavily influenced by philosophical thought that Alfred Adler followed. Jung studied Kant's philosophies as they pertained to the development of a person, one's being. Adler followed this line of influence, also being heavily influenced by Kant, Nietzsche, Marxian ideas of socialism, and Vaihinger's philosophies of "as if." Although influenced by Freudian practices of analysis, Adler sought more importance in the social aspect of an individual as well as disagreeing with Freud's theory of the unconscious (Ansbacher & Huber, 2004). Therefore, Adler was concerned with a style of life, meaning how his patients adapted to obstacles in their lives and therefore the way they created solutions. He largely focused on the tasks of style of life within different stages of life.

In giving large focus to the social aspect of patients' lives, Adler sought to conduct himself in therapy from a place of mutual trust and respect (Dreikurs, 1967). His efforts in practicing a respectful, trusting relationship were shown in his collaboration with his patients' goal setting: if his goals for his patients did not align with theirs, Adler readjusted so they could both be in similar positions of progress in therapy. The Adler approach to therapy was one of the first in which therapists collaboratively aligned themselves with their clients' goals. Being heavily influenced by the philosophy of Marxian, social order, the therapists paid careful attention to their place of power within the therapeutic relationship, encouraging patients to progress throughout therapy.

Existential therapy

Existential therapy was a branch of psychotherapy that dealt with problems relating to what it means to be a human being. It was a philosophical approach that veered from the psychoanalytic approach in that it focused on certain themes found within a client's life, and what those themes meant to them in their problems. Existential therapy continues to grow today into other areas of counseling, being integrated in many forms of therapy. However, at its inception, existential therapy was philosophical by approach, taking from philosophical thoughts of Kierkegaard, Nietzsche, Husserl, and Heidegger. One of the biggest influences on existential therapy was the idea of meaning, as taken from Victor Frankl, asking what it is to be human: Who am I? Who will I be? Where do I come from? This approach to therapy also called into question *how* we are in relationship with the external world, our selves, and with spiritual aspects of our being.

This approach to therapy also produced a different sort of therapist from the psychoanalyst. Being heavily influenced by philosophy and experiences, the existential therapist also thought about such things in relationships with their clients. The therapists themselves were philosophers. However, this is one of the first approaches where therapists overtly sought out a genuine caring relationship with their clients, true to the philosophy and ontology of *being* with their clients. Existential therapists sought to be their true authentic selves with their clients and formed an authentic love for their clients as well.

Person-centered

Carl Rogers

Whereas the existential therapist was one of the first to consider the personhood of the therapist, being existentially attuned to their relationship with their clients, Carl Rogers was one of the first to label such efforts into specific counseling techniques. Along this development of therapy came person-centered therapy, where Rogers presented an overt practice of caring for clients instead of diagnosing or forming traditional treatment plans. Rogers believed in congruency and conditionality in his practice, where when an individual experiences conditional regard, they began to formulate their sense of self based off their conditions in which they experience validation and love. Therefore, an individual experiences incongruities with who they really are and who they are being for their conditions in which they experience love and acceptance. The aim of therapy was for an individual to be a fully functioning person, meeting their own needs for positive regard (Rogers, 1969).

In order for clients to reach their fully functioning sense of self, Rogers's approach consisted of a genuine therapist, practicing unconditional positive regard, accepting clients for who they are. His own personhood was the driving force of therapy, being non-directive and practicing genuineness (Bozarth, 2012). Even though during this time the personhood of the therapist was being considered and practiced, Rogers created a new type of therapist, the first of which where the therapist was a real person that was allowed to show how they cared for their clients, intentionally referring to it as a humanistic approach to therapy.

Gestalt

Along the same humanistic practices was Gestalt therapy. Developed by Fritz Perls, this approach, considered Experiential in theory, helped an individual become aware of themselves and others, developing a complete self. This included bodily and psychological attunement by the client: awareness of their mind and body while being responsible for their emotions, conflict with others, and how they attuned to each (Sharf, 2018). Although similar to the person-centered approach in their presence with clients, Perls's relationship efforts differed slightly.

Like the Rogerian therapist, a Gestalt therapist will pay careful to their relationship with their clients. As one works toward awareness, completeness, and attunement, the therapist does so with the client, within the workings of their relationship. This belief comes from Buber's I–thou work (Buber, 1965), where the relationship and dialogue are a vehicle to understand the client, not to have something intervened onto them. In such a relationship, the therapist is genuine, focused on the client's needs in a two-way client/therapist relationship (Sapriel, 2012).

Experiential therapy

Experiential therapy was one of the first to intentionally use the therapeutic relationship as a vehicle for change. Where Carl Rogers used himself as a catalyst for therapy, approaching his client with unconditional positive regard, Fritz Perls used the relationship between himself and his clients to practice their awareness of the relationship in the present therapeutic moment. He labeled this approach a *dialogical relationship*, where both the therapist and the client are fully aware of themselves and the other person at the same time. Even though Perls's approach to therapy was more direct than the Rogerian approach, the conversation at hand was mutually involving of both parties. This level of awareness was only experienced and intentionally sought by the therapist in therapy.

Cognitive and behavioral therapy

In the recent decades, the field of counseling became interested in scientific, empirically based approached to therapy. The field became interested in proving that counseling worked. With this interest arose behavior therapy, based on classical and operant conditioning. The approach focused on behaviors, how they are shaped among problems, and how they are extinguished. In this approach, behaviors were modified, reinforced, and therefore the presenting problems became resolved through modifications in behavior. Psychological testing and testing methods were common with this approach.

This wave of the counseling field produced a different sort of therapy and therapist. Where before, Carl Rogers and Fritz Perls were concerned with the experiences of their clients, and themselves as therapists, behavioral therapists were more in tuned to outcomes and testing for measured behaviors. The behavioral therapist was one who also performed the desired behavior for the client seeking to change theirs. The therapist was considered a model for change, mimicking and guiding such desired behavioral changes.

Albert Ellis

Similar to behavior therapy was Albert Ellis and his approach, rational emotive behavior therapy. Ellis sought to bridge philosophical approaches like existential therapy, humanistic approaches like client-centered therapy, along with the practice of behavioral therapy. Driven by hedonistic philosophy, seeking pleasure over pain, and ethical humanism, valuing human interest over deity, he also sought to value the person within the client, believing we are separate from our action. He focused on irrational beliefs that lead to irrational emotions, which lead to problems. Ellis challenged irrational beliefs and therefore worked on changing the way clients thought in order to change the way they feel (Ellis, 1973).

Such an approach to therapy also produced a unique sort of therapist. Ellis was one of the first to articulate the need for advanced empathy from the therapist, being attuned to their own selves and the need for communicating such beliefs in relationships. He believed it was the responsibility of the therapist to be philosophically inclined toward the basics of communication. Once again, with this approach of therapy came a therapist that needed the skill of humanistic qualities as they are placed onto the relationship with their client.

Aaron Beck

Cognitive therapy, developed by Aaron Beck, helped clients understand the way they developed maladaptive thoughts and how those thoughts influenced their feelings and behaviors. Similar to behavioral and rational emotive therapy, cognitive therapy also sought to understand the thoughts behind behaviors. Cognitive therapy was one of the first approaches to strongly utilize questionnaires and empirical measurements and is still widely empirically studied.

The cognitive therapist took the position of an expert, being able to utilize such empirical measurements, study clients and outcomes, and bring tools into therapy for clients. Even though done collaboratively, where the client's data collaborates with the therapist's tools, the cognitive approach has traditionally been seen as an evidenced-based approach to therapy, being able to prove it works and that clients change.

The recent decades of cognitive, rational emotive, and behavior therapy produced a certain kind of "scientific" therapist, different from psychoanalysis and Rogerian approaches. This wave of therapy produced therapists interested in proving their efficacy in therapy, trained to diagnose, measure, test, and develop plans for treatment that targeted specific presenting issues.

Postmodern/constructivist approaches

In the more recent decades came the constructivist approaches to counseling, which will be expounded on in the following chapter. The constructivist approach to therapy was based on the belief that clients construct their own lives through their experiences, contexts, and relationships. To this end also arose the feminist approach to therapy. Feminist therapy concerned itself with a person's experiences with gender, politics, power, and how they create difficulties in their lives. Also based in constructivist thought, the feminist therapist believed in the client's construction of gender and their experiences of oppression. Feminist therapists also take on a multicultural approach to therapy in that gender is experienced differently in different cultures, therefore the experience of gender oppression is also different in each culture.

This era of therapy created a different sort of therapist than each previous era. Constructivist therapists were different in that they did not believe in diagnosing, labeling clients, or assuming their experiences. Rather than being a therapist with knowledge of dysfunctions, diagnoses, and therapeutic treatments, the constructivist therapist was concerned with learning from the client and using their own descriptions of their experiences to guide the therapy process. This will be discussed further in the following chapter.

The most recent trend in therapy is the integrative approach, where therapists choose which approaches of therapy suit their personality, clients, and what each approach has in common. Therapists may combine two or more approaches and use them in a way that is tailored to their clients and the process of therapy. I argue that this era of therapy is producing a specialized therapist, one where the personality of the therapist can be made known through their integration of therapies, and in how each is used. With a plethora of therapeutic options, clients and therapist benefit in that the therapist is equipped with what best fits them (Table 1.1).

The marriage and family therapist

The field of counseling and therapy has significantly evolved over the previous decades. Marriage and family therapy, specifically, has changed since the days of Erikson, Bateson, Haley, and the Millan Research Institute group, where the field arguably began. During the decades of 1940 to 1960, the field of family therapy was developed by different practitioners with different backgrounds and philosophical thoughts. Therefore, the evolving definition of a therapist is also quite difficult to establish. With the evolution of the field, the definition of what a therapist is can largely rely on how the therapist chooses to identify themselves and their theoretical orientation. With so many approaches to therapy and various schools of thought, what a therapist is, *who* the therapist is, can be quite diverse. What follows is a brief view of the history of marriage and family therapy with special attention paid to the evolution of the therapist as well.

Systems and schizophrenia

Marriage and family therapy evolved from Freudian practice in group therapy and Bertalanffy's general systems theory (Nichols & Davis, 2017). From the psychoanalytic influence, many moving parts were happening within a similar time frame. With a relational component to Freud's work, Nathan Ackerman approached group therapy with the mind of "what causes the group to change as it develops." Ackerman focused on the relationship dynamics of a group, which started the trend in systemic thinking and relational focus.

During this time, Gregory Bateson was studying trends in communication according to Marxian philosophy. Bateson, along with his colleagues (Bateson, Jackson, Haley, & Weakland, 1956), was one of the founders of applying cybernetics to human systems, studying the communication dynamics between people and explaining it through systemic language. His theory toward schizophrenia started

TABLE 1.1 The counseling therapist

	Influencer/philosophies	Beliefs/theory	Practice	The therapist
Freudian psychoanalysis	Physics, chemistry, biology, philosophy, psychology	Drives and instincts, structure of personality; id, ego, superego, levels of consciousness	Countertransference between therapist and patient, interpretation of unconscious conflict, interpretation of dreams, unlocking defense mechanisms	Neutral, allowing the patient to transfer onto the therapist; empathetic presence, nurturing relationship
Carl Jung psychoanalysis	Philosophy, theology, anthropology, science, mythology	Levels of consciousness, archetypes, personality functions	Individuation, conscious realization of the psychological, uniqueness of self; integrating conscious and unconscious leads to fullness	Humanity is essential, the doctor must analyze their own psyche, awareness of change within the therapist
Alfred Adler	Kant, Nietzsche, Marxian, Vaihinger	Social aspect of the individual, style of life and obstacles within, inferiority and superiority	Assessing social aspects including family, birth order, insight and interpretation	Mutual respect and trust for patient, mutually align goals together, readjust according to patient resistance

(Continued)

TABLE 1.1 (*Continued*) The counseling therapist

	Influencer/philosophies	Beliefs/theory	Practice	The therapist
Existential therapy	Kierkegaard, Nietzsche, Husserl, Heidegger, Frankl	*How* we are in relationships, "Who am I?" spiritual and relational focus	Finding themes in client's life, what do problems mean in their lives	Genuine caring relationship, *being* with clients, being true authentic self with clients
Carl Rogers's person-centered therapy	Humanistic, believing in people and relationships, existential	Individuals are incongruent and not fully functioning in their conditional regard	Unconditional positive regard, accepting clients,	Being a real person with clients, showing love and care toward clients
Gestalt therapy/experiential	Humanistic, existential, experiential, Buber	Awareness, complete self, responsible for emotions and conflict with others	Mature, grow, self-responsibility	Genuine person, dialogical relationship, I–thou, empathic and supportive
Cognitive, behavioral	Operant conditioning, classical conditioning	Cognitive distortions, automatic thoughts	Seek behavioral change, change in thoughts	Collaborative, catalyst for helping clients understand their behaviors/thoughts
Rational emotive	Existential, humanistic, hedonistic, ethical humanism	Focus on irrational beliefs, irrational emotions	Challenging client's beliefs to change the way they feel	Directive, teacher collaborative
Constructivist/postmodern approaches	Feminism, social-construction, language, power, gender	Individuals construct their experiences, victims of destructive narratives, how one experiences power and gender	Deconstruct, non-diagnosing, client is the expert	One-down, learner of the client's story, client guides the therapist

a wave of studying families and their dysfunction. During that time, studying schizophrenia and communication was a common thing among family therapists.

It was during this wave of therapy, in the 1950s, that the therapist began to focus on the family and its impact on individual members. Because of the schizophrenia research, therapists realized that the family's function played a role in the course of schizophrenia itself (Metcalf, 2011). The *systemic* view of families strongly emerged with this practice. Therapists realized that a family's interaction was more influential over individuals than previous psychoanalytic therapists realized.

In this era of communication and schizophrenia, John Bowlby also began to focus his work on family treatment (Bowlby, 1949). He decided to treat children and their parents together, interpreting that each family member offered some contribution to the problem. From there, Ackerman took the initiative to start "family treatment" (Nichols & Davis, 2017). During these phases of the field, others were also practicing forms of relational treatment: Wilfred Bion studied group functioning and process/content (Bion, 1948), Kurt Lewin studied equilibrium and field theory (Lewin, 1951), David Levy studied maternal overprotectiveness (1943), and Frieda Fromm-Reichmann studied the schizophrenogenic mother (1948), to name a few.

During these initial phases of marriage and family therapy, the therapist was seen as an inventor and analyst. The therapist was also a philosopher, heavily influence by the philosophies of Maturana, Kant, George Kelly, Jean Piaget, among others. Therapists during this period questioned what it meant to live in a system, and questioned the reality of individuals and families and how they were living. Still heavily influenced by Freudian thought, the therapist philosophized about what a "problem" was; did it live within one's mind, or did it come from other living systems found within a biological framework of living systems? What was the role of a family in such problems and was that a bigger, connected entity that also needed to be pursued?

From these initial thinkers in family therapy, the therapists themselves also began to evolve. Where at first the therapist was known as an originator of practice, leaders in new treatment, the next decades produced a more specialized, "expert" therapist. Whether it was their knowledge of symptoms, systems, relationships, or problematic patterns, the following decades introduced a therapist that introduced the family to solutions according to the systemic dysfunction the family brought to therapy. As the expert, the therapist worked to disrupt problematic sequences, establish or weaken boundaries, and rearrange a family's systemic functioning, all from the position of "knowing" the etiology of the family's problems.

Palo Alto influence

From 1950 to 1960, the Palo Alto group was very influential to the field: Gregory Bateson, Don Jackson, Jay Haley, and John Weakland. From this group came other influential thinkers and therapists that also adopted a form of its systems thinking.

In 1956, the group published its double bind theory, which offered a systemic understanding of communication and family dynamics around schizophrenia. Their concepts of homeostasis, communication, and cybernetic function of a family largely impacted approaches to treatment and other therapists.

Murray Bowen

One of those therapists influenced by the Palo Alto group was Murray Bowen, also studying schizophrenia from his own theoretical framework. To this day, therapists still ascribe to the Bowen family systems model of therapy. Bowen was one of the first therapists to take a multigenerational perspective in family and individual functioning. His concept of differentiation of self was foundational to family therapy in formulating "problems" within both the individual and family level. Bowen was also one of the first therapists to give attention to the therapist themselves. He gave detail on how therapists should compose themselves in therapy: as an objective third party that intentionally should not become triangulated in the process.

Bowen's contribution to therapy, and therefore the therapist, was one of emotional importance. His theory of emotional units, a family functioning as one emotional system, included the therapist. But his approach was one of caution. His effort as a therapist was *not* to become emotionally entangled in the family's emotional atmosphere. If the therapist became too emotionally involved in the family, the therapist would hinder the therapeutic process and the family would not be able to reach its truest emotional capacity. Therefore, the therapist was responsible for remaining "differentiated," being a part of the system while still remaining separate from it, and not letting his level of involvement be influenced by the family's emotional state (Bowen, 1978). The therapist was the guiding force behind this process, which the family learned from the way the therapist comported themselves in therapy.

This was one of the first times in the field of therapy that the therapist bore this level of emotional responsibility to the family. However, the influence from the Bateson and the Mental Research Institute (MRI) group remained: the therapist was seen as the expert. In Bowen's theory, the therapist was the emotional expert as well as the expert in systems and functioning.

Carl Whitaker and Virginia Satir

In the same study of emotionality, Carl Whitaker stands out. His approach to therapy was different than most, even today. Whitaker's approach to therapy consisted of the belief that individuals are cut off, frozen in their emotional states. He believed that the root of all psychological problems was emotional suppression (Nichols & Davis, 2017). Therefore, his approach to therapy was to engage in emotion, and that started with himself. His aim in therapy was to offer support and emotional provocation in order to get his clients in touch with their feelings. He used his own personhood, his own unconscious to run therapy, which is still considered somewhat deviant today.

Whitaker's influence was big in the following decades into 1960–1980. I believe him to have started a wave of therapy in which therapists were very creative and forthcoming in their approaches to problems and solutions. Whitaker's emotional approach to therapy, and his way of being, impacted the way therapists conducted themselves and their therapy. Emotionality from the therapist became more acceptable. Emotions themselves became an area of focus in treatment. And the relationship between the therapist and client became a point of focus.

Virginia Satir also joined the emotional, experiential form of therapy. Also influenced by the Palo Alto group, she conceptualized families as one emotional whole. Her approach, similar to Whitaker's, consisted of emotional connection and fostering empathy within family members. She was one of the first therapists to make family treatment include as many family members as possible, up to 15 family members at a time, giving special attention to each emotional aspect of the family.

Creativity at work

This wave of therapy of emotional environment combined with systems influence gave way to a new wave of therapy; one where therapists were very creative in their approaches. The schizophrenia research days were coming to a slow in 1960–1970. Instead, therapists sought to put their own personal interpretation of system thinking to their own style of treatment.

Monica McGoldrick and her work with genograms is an example of therapists providing their own personal touch to therapy. To help families see tangible areas within themselves, the genogram represented relationships by symbols, patterns, and shapes (McGoldrick, Gerson, & Petry, 2008). It was a benefit to the therapy process when families were able view their patterns, relationship discord, and functioning within the larger family.

Jay Haley and Cloe Madanes were part of a crucial wave of therapy in the field of marriage and family therapy. Originally out of the MRI group, Haley's approach to therapy expounded on paradoxical interventions, ordeals, and directives. His strategic approach was also influence by Bateson's study of communication but was also heavy in systems theory in the way families maintain a problem through positive feedback loops. His approach was to change the system in order to alleviate the problem. However, this work was heavily influenced by his own way of conceptualizing hierarchy, power, and communication. Where the MRI group believed there was no normal way of functioning for a family, Haley strategically implemented his own thoughts of healthy functioning onto the family through his directives and paradoxical interventions. Even though the approach is loved or not so loved by therapists, his creativity is unmistakable.

Salvador Minuchin (1974) was also in the wave of therapists that heavily subscribed to a systems theory practice. His approach to family therapy and his creativity in his systems thinking was made evident in his structural conceptualization of a family. A family, with its different subsystems, behaves in accordance to its hierarchical structure. "Problems," then, are a result of an incongruent hierarchy. If the therapist changes the structure of a family, they resolve the presenting complaint. Minuchin was one of the first therapists to give attention to the therapeutic intervention known as *joining*. In this technique, the therapist spends a conscious effort to become relatable to the family, win their trust, and be involved in the system. As the therapist becomes trusted by the family, they can then effectively intervene. Effective change is largely brought about because of the therapist's ability to *join* with the family. It's a technique that focused on the therapist's ability to empathize, be warm and loving, and to be a personable presence to the family. This intervention became one of the turning points of the therapist's work, in my opinion.

During this time, the therapist was still influenced by the original works of the Palo Alto and MRI groups: thinking systemically and conceptualizing therapy is circles rather than lines. Rather than thinking linearly (A causes B), therapists believed in influences, not causes; they focused on interactions, not blame. They also started to place themselves within the family system. The term *homeostasis* was popular in thinking of the functionality of families; family members will continue to interact and influence one another in order to maintain the family's homeostasis, or its normal mode of functioning. For the therapist, it was their role to disrupt a family's homeostasis, which placed them in the system of the family. Their involvement was a part of the circular interactions of the family.

At the same time, in the decade of 1960–1970, it was also becoming more acceptable for the therapist to be "involved" with the family, even on an emotional level. This was seen in Carl Whitaker and Virginia Satir, both practicing experiential therapy. They believed in a therapist that was free from theory and a regimented way of conducting therapy. The therapist was genuine, themselves, and free to be as spontaneous as possible, relying on the therapist's personality to be the conductor of therapy, and not the theory the therapist espoused. This way of doing therapy relied on the "existential encounter," which will be visited in the following chapters. When the therapist and client were as free as possible to be themselves, the connection becomes genuine and a catalyst for change. This way of doing therapy began the wave of including emotions in therapy.

Sue Johnson

As a result of the influence of emotions and systems thinking, Sue Johnson (2004) made one of the most significant contributions to therapists with emotion-focused therapy. Richard Schwartz (1995) also included both experiential and systems thought with his approach, internal family systems therapy. The two models of therapy took on the experiential, emotional focus of Carl Whitaker with the systemic understanding of family functioning. Emotions and interactions were equally important in this wave of therapy. This was one of the first models of therapy where the therapist intentionally sought to uncover hurt, betrayal, or emotional abandonment within a family. Also influenced heavily by Bowlby's work, attachment theory became a common theoretical approach within this installment of therapy.

Once again, this new installment of therapy produced a new kind of therapist. The evolvement of the therapist during this time was one of heavy emotional engagement. The emotion-focused therapy approach, along with internal family systems, required the therapist to be a part of the system and also to be emotionally engaged. The emotional composure, stamina, and tolerance of the therapist were crucial to these approaches. These therapies required something more from the therapist than only knowledge of systems, patterns, or dysfunction. It required the therapist to *be* a certain kind of therapist and person. The emotional attunement of the therapist was a large part of the therapy process, as was practiced by Whitaker and Satir.

Constructivism and postmodernism

With so many different options and approaches to therapy, the field of counseling and marriage and family therapy found itself in an era of questioning. With a plethora of therapeutic options, what is the best way to treat clients? What is the most effective approach? What works the best? Marriage and family therapy specifically took a turn when the wave of constructivism and postmodernism hit, which will be expounded on in the following chapter. The constructivist wave of therapy forced therapists to focus on other issues at hand: feminism, culture, politics, destructive social narratives, and power. What did it mean for a family to be oppressed by gender roles? What was the gender narrative that was affecting family life? How does one *deconstruct* the oppressive narrative of gender? Outside of the systemic influence, during this wave of therapy, the therapist tended to play the role of advocate, learner, and, more important, the non-expert.

Postmodernism and constructivist approaches to therapy were taken on by Michael White's narrative therapy, Harlene Anderson's collaborative language systems, and Steve de Shazer and Insoo Kim Berg's solution-focused brief therapy (more on these specific approaches in the following chapters). Once again, the postmodern wave of therapy produced a different type of therapist, where the therapist takes on certain characteristics and treats therapy, and therefore clients, differently than the previously mentioned waves of therapy. Postmodern therapists believe in clients' construction of their own experiences, therefore making clients experts of their own lives. One of the biggest shifts of the therapist in this wave was that this approach took the therapist away from being the expert in therapy. Instead, the therapist became a learner of the client. The therapist believed that there were certain parts of the client's lives that they did not know, which became a stance taken by postmodern therapists, *not-knowing*.

The postmodern therapist also took on the practice of not diagnosing. Most postmodern therapists believe in non-normality, meaning there is no normal or correct way of functioning. When problems people take on cause them to function differently, a postmodern therapist will see to correcting the influence of the problem on the person rather than fixing or diagnosing the client. More on this in the following chapter.

Continuous evolution

The fields of counseling and marriage and family therapy have greatly evolved in the recent decades. Therapist and counselors, now more than ever, are concerned with issues of family violence (Avis, 1992), multiculturalism (McGoldrick, Pierce, & Giordano, 1982), gay and lesbian rights (Laird & Green, 1996), and issues regarding families and technology (sex, internet use, child pornography), of which literature that focuses on therapy issues and a family's use are sparse. Other trends like medical family therapy and brain imaging in therapy are also cutting edge.

Throughout these waves of therapy, the definition and therefore role of the therapist also evolved. The therapist was once considered an expert analyzer in the time of Freud. The therapist focused on dysfunctions, diagnosis, and worked as the facilitator of change. That role evolved to be a group facilitator, an expert in systems, a family structurer, and a postmodern non-expert. The definition of the researcher has also evolved, in fact, in similar ways to the definition and practice of a therapist.

When answering what a therapist is, the answer in continually evolving. The field of mental health is entering a time where tailored treatments are in abundance, and the therapist is more so specialized in a treatment in addition to having a widespread of knowledge. The same can be said of the evolution of a researcher (Table 1.2).

What is a researcher?

Within the world of academia, the researcher was credited with the stamp of the scientist. Researchers were known for their expertise in discovery, answering questions with solidified answers supported by empirical data. This became the way of truth; this is how we came to know what we know. If it could be measured, it could be discovered. Still today, this form of knowledge exists. Professors and researchers try to claim their hypotheses as true or prove other's to be untrue with the support of their data. The scientific method was, and still is, the way of "traditional" research. The role and the definition of the researcher, then, was to discover, prove, validate, hypothesize, and test.

TABLE 1.2 The marriage and family therapist

	Therapists	Theory of therapy	Beliefs	The therapist
Systems	MRI group, Palo Alto group, Bateson, Haley, Jackson, Weakland	Systems family therapy, MRI approach, communications theory	Cybernetics, dysfunction lies within systemic interactions, communication is inevitable, fix metacommunications, homeostasis	Philosopher, systemic thinker, direct, expert in cybernetic communications
	Bowen	Bowen family systems therapy	Balance of individuality within the system, emotionality within logic, multigenerational, emotional unites, differentiation of self	Emotionality of the therapist, remaining separate from the system, differentiation
	Haley	Strategic family therapy	Dysfunction lies in faulty communication, symptom communicates a function, feedback loops	Expert, direct, strategic in interventions, his own beliefs of "normal functioning"
	Salvador Minuchin	Structural family therapy	Dysfunction lies within structure of the family, systemic, fix the structure, fix the problem	Join the system first, become involved, challenge beliefs, adapt to the family environment in treatment
Joining	Carl Whitaker, Virginia Satir	Experiential therapy	Problems are rooted in emotional suppression, Does not rely on theory, therapist is the leader in change, emotionally connection is key	Emotionally involved, emotionally dynamic in therapy, expressed own emotions, hugged, cried
	Sue Johnson	Emotion-focused therapy	Attachment (Bowlby), experiential, systemic, heal attachment injuries through connective experiences	Emotionally attuned to clients, express emotion, provocative in inviting emotion, emotional stamina of the therapist

(Continued)

TABLE 1.2 (Continued) The marriage and family therapist

	Therapists	Theory of therapy	Beliefs	The therapist
Postmodern	Harlene Anderson	Collaborative language systems	Change through conversation, mutual engagement, power of language, social constructionism, natural dissolution of "problems"	Not-knowing, mutually engaged with client, suspending beliefs and preknowledge
	Michael White, David Epston	Narrative therapy	Power of narratives, social construction of power and privilege, indoctrinated into destructive narratives	Humanistic, people have what it takes to live preferred stories, help people live out those stories, political activist against problematic narratives, not-knowing
	Steve de Shazer, Insoo Kim Berg	Solution-focused brief therapy	Power of language, world of solutions, resources within individuals, do what works, little theory	Engaged in solutions, belief in the process of conversation, mutually invested, not-knowing

When qualitative research became a form of inquiry, the role and definition of the researcher evolved into something different from the traditional scientific researcher trying to prove their hypotheses. Just like the role of the therapist evolved from Freudian analysis to Harlene Anderson and postmodern not-knowing, so did the researcher.

Qualitative research has become a global effort in studying complex issues and interpreting issues that affect daily life and functioning: educational issues, social challenges, relationship dysfunction, health care, political science, women's studies, economics, and social work, just to name a few (Denzin & Lincoln, 2011). With such a large span of issues and challenges, the definition of qualitative research is also quite difficult to establish.

Qualitative research spans different concepts and traditions that are often overlapping and related to each other. Concepts and assumptions like foundationalism, positivism, postfoundationalism, postpositivism, poststructuralism, postmodernism, and posthumanism are all different philosophical and epistemological approaches that are sometimes used by different researchers espousing different beliefs. Again, difficult to establish one definition, the practice itself has also seen different eras.

According to Erickson (2011), qualitative research has seen at least eight historical moments in its evolution. These moments span from 1900–1950 during traditional, scientific research methods, to 1950–1970 when the modern age of the researcher was respected, to 1970–1986 when genres of research and approaches blurred, to 1986–1990 when issues of representing researcher participants accurately arose, to 1990–1995 during the postmodern wave of researching, to 1995–2000 that considered postexperimental philosophies, to 2000–2010 when different research methods were in competition with one another, and then to 2010 and beyond where the future of research is to be defined. Like the field of therapy and counseling, history and moments influence the way we approach our work with people. Each moment in history asked certain things of researchers, and therefore the evolution of their practices and the researcher themselves.

As the researcher evolved, they themselves began to have a primary place in the research process. Epistemologies and ontological assumptions became important to researching. More than researcher bias, the idea of how one believes and sees the world will influence the way they ask questions slowly became important to the research process. This thought became an important part of research in general, but qualitative researchers have taken a stronger hold on this practice given the political and social needs of the researcher.

The researcher

Therefore, to define qualitative research, and too the researcher, is to consider the moment in history in which they are being defined. I believe qualitative research to be a practice of observation, philosophy, interpretation, and methods in which we show other's stories to the world.

To answer the question of what a researcher is can be difficult. However, the evolution of the researcher is undeniable. The researcher now is vast, able to research creatively, scientifically, qualitatively, or even artistically. Daly (2005) describes the qualitative researcher as someone that can artistically and scientifically study the human form. Lincoln and Denzin (2011) believe that to engage in qualitative research is to be a philosopher, while Bateson (1972) once thought a qualitative researcher not as a scientist, but as a theoretician, theorizing about the human condition.

Of the many different definitions of the qualitative researcher, one of my favorites is that the researcher is a bricoleur, or a handyman (or woman). As a researcher, and as a bricoleur, the researcher is left to their own devices, their own learnings and knowledge, resources and tools, in order to finish their product; their methods, then, are emergent, their process is continuously changing and taking on new forms as different tools and techniques are added to the process (Weinstein & Weinstein, 1991).

Relevant to the researcher, who is also a therapist, or the researcher in any helping profession, the arsenal to bricoleur from can expand into their research knowledge of methods and approaches, and also to their knowledge of therapy and inquiry. The researcher's methodological bricoleur is vast: interviews, self-reflection, art, manuscripts, film. The theoretical bricoleur is also vast: feminism, postmodernism, Marxian, social construction. And relevant to the current focus, the therapy bricoleur is also vast for the therapist/researcher: narrative therapy, collaborative language systems, solution-focused brief therapy.

Given so many philosophies, techniques, methods, politics, and even research methods, the definition of the researcher is once again difficult to establish. However, there is one common factor that all of these bricoleur options offer: the researcher themselves.

With the different history of qualitative research, the researcher has evolved to be an instrument of research itself. However, since the 1980s, considered the era of the crisis of representation (Denzin & Lincoln, 2011), researcher bias has largely been an issue with research itself. As is the case with quantitative and qualitative methods, research is ultimately done by a person or a group of people, whose conclusions are seldom unbiased. Even when quantitative researchers provide correlations, regressions, and other statistical analysis, their methods and interpretation of their data ultimately is on some level biased.

The idea of being involved in the research process took especially strong precedence in qualitative research. There is a level of subjectivity like no other in qualitative research, and the researcher is largely a part of that subjectivity. Even when a researcher claims to be of the positivist tradition, that they believe there is one solid truth out there and it is the researcher's job to represent it through their investigations, they are still a person using other people to promote, validate, prove, and support *their* own claim to their own truth they are seeking. I even argue that the reason for choosing a qualitative approach to research in itself offers some subjectivity or bias from the researcher.

Researchers themselves, from the evolution of the scientific method to the postmodern landscape of inquiry, have faced a unique challenge. Kenneth Gergen (2014) argues: "When research commences with an 'object of study' the result is an extension of existing traditions, and suppression of alter- native realities. The social imaginary is circumscribed" (p. 294). He further argues that the tradition of research has reached a limit on its progress and has reached a place of "equanimity," due to the plethora of pragmatism in its approaches. Even though the tradition of scientific research is long withstanding, scientific research itself is still largely unchallenged. Gergen, therefore, calls for a new approach to understanding and inquiry. What he proposes, from what I interpret, can be achieved through qualitative inquiry.

There are multiple reasons a researcher chooses qualitative research. Corbin and Strauss (2015) argue that researchers seek qualitative research when desiring to explore participant's inner experiences and meanings they associate; to explore areas not as widely researched; to understand variables and phenomena that can be later tested through quantitative measures; and to comprehensively study a certain phenomenon or experience within individuals or families. Ultimately, the researcher chooses qualitative research because they choose to ask questions that can only be answered through qualitive research methods (Corbin & Strauss, 2015). In doing so, I ague that qualitative researchers want the opportunity to connect with their participants, engage in conversation, be present with people, offer participants a chance to promote their voice, and understand the world through their participants' eyes.

The beauty of qualitative research is the possibilities of discovery. That discovery can come from different methods, beliefs, philosophies, and, of course, people. The researcher brings their own beliefs into the process, and therefore their own unique inquiry. How one views the world influences the way they ask questions. With so many possibilities of asking questions, different qualitative methods are available to bricoleur from. Some of the common qualitative methods are briefly mentioned in the following, with specific attention to characteristics of the researcher in each approach. Even though there are more approaches to research than mentioned, these are the most common among social sciences in which therapists and counselors are commonly trained.

Approaches

Creswell and Poth (2018) recognize qualitative research as a "legitimate mode of social and human science inquiry," (p. 6) not in comparison to quantitative research. Creswell, trained as a quantitative researcher, argues the limitations of inquiry because of the many modes of assumptions researchers carry.

Therefore, because of the researcher's limit on inquiry and their plethora of assumptions, he argues the importance of philosophical assumptions and how they are applied to the design and approaches to qualitative research.

As Creswell has aided our use of philosophical assumptions, Daly (2005) has given us great insight into epistemological stances and the widening role of the researcher. The researcher, now, is entering into a time of multiplicity, where one philosophical assumption used to inquire may not be another's. Therefore, one's questions can be transformed into several different questions depending on one's epistemology and methodological approach.

The following sections are brief descriptions of the five common approaches to qualitative research methods (also see Table 1.3). Even though brief, the emphasis here is on the researcher and not the approach itself.

Grounded theory

Corbin and Strauss (2015) and Kathy Charmaz (2014) expounded on the tradition of grounded theory in qualitative research. They believed that if they could gather enough people's experiences, they could generate a working theory based off their participants' sharings. If they had enough people that experienced the same phenomenon, they could substantially create an emerging theory, grounded in their experiences. Grounded theory research, then, seeks to generate a theoretical explanation for a process or action (Corbin & Strauss, 2015). This method of inquiry traditionally took on two schools of thought: one where interpretation was more objective and positivist in tradition, and one that was more subjective and constructivist in philosophy. Charmaz took on the tradition of the subjectivist, in where she believed that the researcher was a part of the development of the generated theory. Since the researcher was a part of the process of collecting data and gathering participants' experiences, they too were considered in the process. This co-construction of knowledge came from the postmodern school of thought, in where two people, together, formulate their known truths, or their way of knowing; knowledge is socially constructed. Therefore, the researcher was just as central to the emerging theory as the participants.

Charmaz (2014) argues that the grounded theory approach to inquiry aligns well with an objectivist assumption of a positivist paradigm. In such an approach, the researcher believes in an external, objective reality, which can be accurately known and represented. In this approach, the researcher also believes in unbiased data collection and representation: "Let the data speak for itself." In an objectivist grounded theory, there is a direct link between the researcher's data and theory, keeping out the researcher's preconceptions. The researcher, then, is a distant expert (Daly, 2005).

Regardless of the objectivist or constructivist approach to grounded theory inquiry, above all, the grounded theory researcher is a theorist. The researcher,

TABLE 1.3 The researcher

	Philosophy	Type of inquiry	Method	The researcher
Grounded theory	Objectivist, subjectivist, positivist, constructivist	Theoretically explain a process or action	Formulate theory from individuals' experiences	Theorist, philosopher, inquiring about experience,
Narrative inquiry	Anthropology, sociology, linguistics	Explore the life of an individual, story of experiences	Immerse in individual's stories, artifacts, pictures, journals, life history	Learner of stories, collaborator, co-storying, storyteller
Phenomenology	Existentialism, experiences of being	Meaning of lived experiences, universally experienced phenomenon	Asking experiential questions of *how* one experiences, and *what* one experiences, essence of experience	Bracketing, suspension of beliefs, philosopher, interpreter
Ethnography	Anthropology, sociology, structural functionalism, symbolic interaction	Examining culture-sharing group, patterns, beliefs	Immersed in day-to-day lives of group, observes, interviews	Interpreter, analyst of culture, advocate for the group
Case study	Psychology, social science, sociology, education	In-depth understanding of a case, explore issues or problems of a specific case	Interviews, observations, documents, audio visuals	Advocate, uncovering issues within a case, promoting change, taking action

both objectivist and constructivist, is one that knows the importance of people's experiences in formulating theories and therefore the need to research people for such scholarly endeavors.

Narrative research

When the researcher wants to explore the life of an individual, or the story of an individual experience, they might choose the narrative approach to research. The narrative approach offers specific procedures for exploring and analyzing stories told from participants (Chase, 2011). More than individual stories, the narrative researcher is also curious about social, cultural, family, linguistic, and other institutional narratives that influence individual experiences (Clandinin, 2013). With anthropological roots, the narrative researcher is also curious about the sociological, historical, and linguistic approaches to individuals and their stories (Chase, 2011). Narrative research is also found in development research, psychology, and sociology. Similar to the ethnographic researcher, the narrative researcher tends to immerse themselves in data from the individual, collected stories, artifacts, pictures, participants journals, or even objects important to their participant. The researcher, then, becomes an avid leaner of the stories told within all types of data. In the process of unraveling participant's stories, the researcher becomes a part of the storytelling process, and specific attention is on how the story unfolds between the researcher and participant (Reissman, 2008).

Phenomenological research

Phenomenology has strong philosophical roots. The phenomenological researcher is primarily a philosopher and existential thinker, with thought influenced from common philosophers: Heidegger, Sartre, and Merleau-Ponty.

Moustakas (1994) utilized the philosophical assumption of one's experiences as a means of inquiry. His role as a researcher became one of naivete. As he approached his participants, he "bracketed" out his own experiences as they related to his inquiry. Therefore, the definition of the researcher took a turn to one that is objectively apart from the research process, making data collection and analysis a process where the data itself takes its own shape based on the participants. It was the job of the researcher to provide a clear explanation of what they collected based on the experiences of the participants.

The basic curiosity of the phenomenological researcher is to reduce the individual experience with a phenomenon down to its universal essence, to grasp the very nature of the things being studied (Creswell & Poth, 2018). The researcher "begins with wonder at what gives itself and something that gives itself. It can only be pursued while surrendering to a state of wonder" (van Manen, 2014, p. 27). Of the many characteristics of the researcher, this approach calls for curiosity about not only *what* an individual experiences, but also *how* they experience that phenomenon (Moustakas, 1994).

Ethnography

The ethnographer is curious about an entire culture-sharing group, the many people that interact over time and how that group of people formulates its own culture. In the ethnography approach, the researcher describes and interprets the shared and learned values, believes, behaviors, and language with the group being studied (Harris, 1968). Ethnographic researchers have commonly been anthropologists, studying structures of society, with strong social theoretical orientations: structural functionalism, symbolic interaction, feminism, Marxism, critical theory, multicultural studies, and postmodernism (Creswell & Poth, 2018; Madison, 2011). The ethnographer is also curious about individual experiences, but as they pertain to the larger culture in which they are embedded. With a large amount of fieldwork and immersion into the culture itself, the ethnographer is also one that is curious about what it is like for participants to live in the culture they are studying.

According to the practices of the ethnography approach to inquiry, the researcher is one that presents a holistic view of the studied culture. The researcher presents a cultural portrait according to their interpretation of their findings, in which they might advocate or suggest changes for the culture (Creswell & Poth, 2018). Similar to the case study approach, the ethnographer is commonly one that will give voice to the studied culture.

Case study

Similar to ethnography, the case study researcher also aims to investigate how a culture works, but specifically as it pertains to a single case. A case can be a concrete entity, a specific person, a small group, or an organization (Creswell & Poth, 2018). Specific to the qualitative researcher is the ability to put parameters around their case; the researcher chooses how many, or how few, people to include in their case. Therefore, the researcher serves as the deciding factor of what the case will be. The case study researcher is one who is curious about specific issues or problems in a single case they are studying, for example, violence on a college campus. In a similar manner, the researcher is also curious about issues or concerns across multiple cases, for example, violence across multiple college campuses (Yin, 2014).

The case study researcher commonly takes the belief of a critical epistemology, meaning they are attempting to study people's experiences for the sake of revealing a deeper understanding of the case for the sake of the issues being studied (Creswell & Poth, 2018). The case study researcher, then, commonly acts as an advocate for their case, bringing to light problems, issues, or challenges that may be in need of change within their case.

Conclusion

The definition of a therapist is difficult to establish. There have been dozens of approaches to therapy and counseling within the last 60–70 years alone, and more specified approaches within the last decade. Therefore, the definition of *who* the therapist is remains just as difficult. Not intended to be a review of counseling and therapy theories, we have briefly outlined major theoretical approaches to counseling and models of marriage and family therapy so that we can understand the evolution of the therapist behind them.

The same applies for the qualitative researcher. We have briefly overviewed a short history of qualitative research in order to better understand the evolution of the researcher. Major qualitative researcher approaches to the social sciences were also overviewed by way of the researcher behind each approach.

Just as difficult a task is to define *who* the qualitative researcher is. The field of researcher expands into more than just therapy, but multiple areas of practice and traditions. Specifically, for the qualitative tradition of researcher, the practice has spanned into the works of education, nursing and medicine, social work, business, economics, biblical studies, and the focus of this book, therapy and counseling. Therefore, the overview of counseling and marriage and family theories, with the main focus on the therapist, is for all fields that practice qualitative research. My hope is to take these approaches to therapy and research and make them tangible for all researchers to use in their practices.

Having discussed the therapist and researcher, the following chapter will visit major philosophical assumptions within qualitative research. Most of the philosophical assumptions discussed pertain to social sciences, however, the efforts in such an overview is for all fields to gain from their offerings.

References

Ansbacher, H. L., & Huber, R. J. (2004). Adler-psychotherapy and Freud. *Journal of Individual Psychology*, 60(4), 333–337.

Avis, J. M. (1992). Where are all the family therapists? Abuse and violence within the families and family therapy's response. *Journal of Marital and Family Therapy*, 18(3), 223–233.

Bateson, G. (1972). *Steps to an ecology of mind: A revolutionary approach to man's understand of himself*. New York: Ballantine Books.

Bateson, G., Jackson, D. D., Haley, J., & Weakland, J. (1956). Toward a theory of schizophrenia. *Behavioral Sciences*. 1(4), 251–264.

Bion, W. R. (1948). Experience in groups. *Human Relations*, 1(3), 314–329.

Bowlby, J. (1949). The study and reduction of group tensions in the family. *Human Relations*, 2(2), 123–128.

Bowen, M. (1978). *Family therapy in clinical practice*. New York: Aronson.

Bozarth, J. D. (2012). "Nondirectivity" in theory of Carl R. Rogers: An unprecedented premise. *Person-Centered and Experiential Psychotherapies*, 11(4), 262–276.

Buber, M. (1965). *Between man and man*. New York: Macmillan.

Charmaz, K. (2014). *Constructing grounded theory*. Los Angeles: Sage.

Chase, S. (2011). Narrative inquiry: Still a field in the making. In N. K. Denzin & Y. S. Lincoln (Eds.), *The SAGE handbook of qualitative research* (4th ed., pp. 421–434). Thousand Oaks: Sage.

Clandinin, D. J. (2013). *Engaging in narrative inquiry: Mapping a methodology*. Thousand Oaks: Sage.

Corbin, J., & Strauss, A. (2015). *Basics of qualitative research: Techniques and procedures for developing grounded theory* (4th ed.). Los Angeles: Sage.

Creswell, J. W., & Poth, C. N. (2018). *Qualitative inquiry and research design: Choosing among five approaches*. Thousand Oaks: Sage.

Daly, J. K. (2005). *Qualitative methods for family studies & human development*. Los Angeles: Sage.

Denzin, K. N., & Lincoln, Y. S. (Eds.) (2011). *The Sage handbook of qualitative research*. Los Angeles: Sage.

Dreikurs, R. (1967). *Psychodynamics, psychotherapy, and counseling: Collected papers*. Chicago: Alfred Adler Institute.

Ellis, A. (1973). *Humanistic psychotherapy: The rational emotive approach*. New-York: McGraw Hill.

Erickson, F. (2011). A history of qualitative inquiry in social and educational research. In. K. N. Denzin & Y. S. Lincoln (Eds.), *The Sage Handbook of Qualitative Research* (pp. 43–60).

Fromm-Reichmann, F. (1948). Notes on the development of treatment of schizophrenics by psychoanalytic psychotherapy. *Psychiatry*, 11(3), 263–274.

Gabbard, G. O. (2004). *Long-term psychodynamic psychotherapy: A basic text*. Washington, DC: American Psychiatric Publishing.

Gergen, K. J. (2014). From mirroring to world-making: Research as future forming. *Journal for the Theory of Social Behavior*, 45(3), 287–310.

Harris, M. (1968). *The rise of anthropological theory: A history of theories of culture*. New York: T. Y. Crowell.

Johnson, S. M. (2004). *The practice of emotionally focused couple therapy: Creating connection*. New York: Brunner-Routledge.

Jung, C. (1961). *Memories, dreams, reflections*. New York: Pantheon Books.

Laird, J., & Green, R. J. (Eds.) (1996). *Lesbians and gays in couples and families: A handbook for therapists*. San Francisco: Jossey-Bass.

Levy, D. (1943). *Maternal overprotection*. New York: Columbia University Press.

Lewin, K. (1951). *Field theory in social science*. New York: Harper.

Madison, D. S. (2011). *Critical ethnography: Methods, ethics, and performance* (2nd ed.). Thousand Oaks: Sage.

McGoldrick, M., Gerson, R., & Petry, S. (2008). *Genograms, assessment and their intervention*. New York: W. W. Norton.

McGoldrick, M., Pearce, J., & Giordano, J. (1982). *Ethnicity in family therapy*. New York: Guilford.

Metcalf, L. (Ed.) (2011). *Marriage and family therapy: A practice-oriented approach*. New-York: Springer.

Minuchin, S. (1974). *Families and family therapy*. Cambridge, MA: Harvard University Press.

Moustakas, C. (1994). *Phenomenological research methods*. Thousand Oaks: Sage.

Nichols, M. P., & Davis, S. D. (2017). *Family therapy: Concepts and methods*. Boston: Pearson.

Ornstein, P. H. (2011). The centrality of empathy in psychoanalysis. *Psychoanalytic Inquiry*, 31(5), 437–447.

Riessman, C. K. (2008). *Narrative methods for the human sciences*. Thousand Oaks: Sage.

Rigas, D. (2012). When interpretations are not enough: Interactions between the analytic pair, an intersubjective approach. *International Forum of Psychoanalytics*, 21(3–4), 182–188.

Rogers, C. R. (1969). *Freedom to learn: A view of what education might become*. Columbus, OH: Charles E. Merrill.

Sapriel, L. (2012). Creating an embodied, authentic self: Integrating mindfulness with psychotherapy when working with trauma. In T. Bar-Joseph Levine (Ed.), *Gestalt therapy: Advances in practice* (pp. 107–122).

Schwartz, R. C. (1995). *Internal family systems*. New York: Guilford Press.

Sharf, R. S. (2016). *Theories of psychotherapy and counseling: Concepts and cases*. Boston: Cengage Learning.

van Manen, M. (2014). *Phenomenology of practice: Meaning-giving methods in phenomenological research and writing*. Walnut Creek, CA: Left Coast Press.

Weinstein, D., & Weinstein, M. A. (1991). Georg Simmel: Sociological *flaneur bricoleur*. *Theory, Culture, & Society*, 8, 151–168.

Yin, R. K. (2014). *Case study research: Design and method* (5th ed.). Thousand Oaks: Sage.

2
EPISTEMOLOGY AND PHILOSOPHY

Introduction

When we start the process of qualitative research, we commonly begin with a question, a curiosity we want to explore or desire to answer. When we venture into the process of research, we also establish our research methods: how we will gather data, and which approach we will use to ensure our quality and rigor of work. We establish our procedures and dive into the process. However, before we start, we must also consider our own views, beliefs, philosophies, and the way we know how to ask questions. Even as we collect and analyze data, there is still the question of how we know how to analyze. There is a world within qualitative research that must be addressed before beginning the entire process: the world of knowledge.

This book is intended to reflect upon such knowledge, moreover, to reflect on the person behind that knowledge. When considering how we know what we know, we begin to ask questions considering epistemology. To enter into this world requires an amount of philosophy, interpretation, and, what I think to be the most important, self-reflection. The following questions must be asked: How do I know what I know? Why do I analyze the way I do? Why do I choose to ask these questions? How do I know how to interpret another's reality? One central question this chapter poses is the relationship the researcher has with their knowledges and the research process altogether. As we will see, how we believe, what we believe, and the values we hold about knowledge all influence our relationship with the research process, specifically our data.

Qualitative research is rooted in such questioning. Philosophical interpretations, paradigms, and epistemologies are all a foundational part of the qualitative research process, and too, the researcher. At the basic definition of epistemology, there is the search for knowledge, the spirit of knowledge, or, my favorite, the spirit of discourse. I believe that the qualitative researcher needs to be familiar with the spectrum of epistemologies. These concepts do more than merely offer us insight into thoughts on how one construes knowledge; they invite us to reflect on our self, to study our own views of the world, and to understand our own analytical schemas and how they are seen in the research process. To study epistemology is to study ourselves. Epistemology and philosophy are important to research and therapy because how we see the world influences the way we ask questions.

Epistemology continuum

Epistemology is foundational to science and inquiry overall. How do we know what we know? How do we study and come to know what is researched? Epistemology gives path to inquiry (Daly, 2005). It is by way of epistemology that we being to ask questions. Once the researcher establishes their epistemological beliefs, their inquiry and methods can appropriately follow. There are two ends of a continuum that hold epistemological beliefs: objectivism and subjectivism. In between these two points of the continuum, many different philosophical beliefs and stances are held. In other words, within the continuum of knowledges (objective or subjective) are held the personal ways we display our beliefs.

Specifically, in qualitative research, a central concept the continuum communicates is the different relationships between the knower and the known, or between the researcher and the researched (Daly, 2005). On the objectivist end, there is a clear separation from the knower and the known; it is our job as researchers to go out and discover knowledge the best we can; test it, validate it, and objectively report measurable findings. Ultimately, as researchers, we are striving to know and understand. As objectivist researchers, we know there is a "truth" out there that exists, and research is a means by which that truth is discovered. A common objectivist belief is that concrete, measurable reality exists independently and separate from our thought processes.

What the objectivist epistemology means for researchers is the relationship they put themselves in with participants. Since the researcher is discovering truth as it exists in the world, the researcher and the researched become two separate entities: the researcher – the one searching for knowledge, truth, and trying to obtain and measure it; and the researched – the embodiment or holder of truth. From the positivist positioning, participants are viewed as data, where they provide us with a vehicle to discovering truth. We as researchers gather that data, then decipher the truths they contain, without influencing it. This relationship has been described as a one-way mirror; the researcher's biases do not influence any outcomes the participants may offer (Guba & Lincoln, 1994).

Several approaches and beliefs in qualitative research espouse the objectivist epistemology. These approaches aim to grasp and explain the essence of objective reality as it exists in the lives of participants without the influence of the research. For example, some researchers use phrases like "let the data speak for itself," where the researcher is only a reporter of the data; the data itself has and obtains agency, and that data itself has an independent reality that can be understood and examined by the separate, objective researcher. According to Daly (2005), qualitative researchers use objectivist practices when they use coding strategies such as *interrater reliability*, using multiple people to establish a set of codes that are used to analyze and arriving at a "correct" way to interpret data.

A qualitative researcher that leans toward the objectivist side of the epistemology continuum will treat the overall approach to inquiry differently than one that falls on the subjectivist side. The subjectivist philosophy of truth and knowledge, and how we obtain it, is also different. Subjectivist epistemology especially influences one's positioning in the researcher/participant relationship. The objectivist researcher will believe there is a clear separation from the researcher and the researched; the reality that exists in participants lives is completely separate from the researcher and the research process. On the other end of the continuum, the subjectivist believes there is no separation between the knower and the known, all knowledge is constructed, including what the knower/researcher adds to the conversation and research process. Truth and knowledge are something obtained by interpretation and social interaction. The subjectivist believes in constructivism and social constructionism, where our knowledge is made and obtained through social interactions, contexts, time, and place, but ultimately an interpreted reality by individuals. There is no single concept of truth to the subjectivist. Rather, truth is what we make of our own reality through our interactions and relationships. This has several implications for philosophical underpinnings in research.

Subjectivism heavily implies relationships for the qualitive researcher. The researcher is in relationship with their participants, and the participants are only that, *participants*. This is in contrast to the objectivist view that understands participants to be vehicles to truth and knowledge. The subjectivist believes that the researcher is just as much of the process of constructing knowledge and truth as the participant. They are both a part of the process, co-construction of knowledge and data. On the subjectivist side of the continuum, data exists in the space between the researcher and the participants. The term "bias" has no meaning to the subjectivist, as all procedures of inquiry are approached with values, meanings, realities, and experiences from the inquirer.

Knowledge, and therefore how we gather knowledge, is also a different belief on the subjectivist side of the continuum. Where the objectivist will pursue truth and knowledge as something obtainable, measurable, and accurately described without influence or bias, the subjectivist accepts that knowledge is interpretive, subject to differing viewpoints. Truth, knowledge, and how we come to know what we know are all a part of an ongoing process of change, contexts, relationships, and a cumulation of knowledges having gone before us.

I like to view these two opposite ends of the continuum as a range of possibilities, not a dichotomous choice. Between these two points of the continuum, the researcher is offered many possibilities of interpretation, approaches to research, and how they place themselves in relationships with research and participants. Approaches to qualitative research, and therefore the researcher themselves, also fall between the continuum of possibilities (Bengston, Acock, Allen, Dilworth-Anderson, & Klein, 2005). This presents us with gradients of objectivist and subjectivist philosophical interpretations (Daly, 2005), where the researcher can practice their beliefs through their research in many different ways. These possibilities between the ranges of objectivist and subjectivist epistemologies are commonly known as philosophical interpretations, or paradigms (Table 2.1).

Philosophies and interpretations

Where epistemologies are beliefs in how we obtain knowledge, truth, and how we know what we know, philosophical interpretations, or paradigms, are beliefs that situate ourselves within the range of epistemologies and a scientific beliefs system. Studying these philosophies and paradigms are beneficial to the researcher in that philosophies drive the way we ask questions, how we construct and interpret data, and how we approach the overall research process. Kuhn (1962) emphasized how shared beliefs are what makes paradigms, or common philosophical stances. When a community of scientists or researchers with similar beliefs come together, and when their beliefs are challenged, paradigms and theories evolve. Even though the following philosophical stances are held in common belief for qualitative research, they are to be considered influx. Kuhn also argued that theories and paradigms are a prerequisite to what we see. I argue that the qualitative researcher ought to study philosophy, as it also offers insight into what and *how* they see the world.

Daly (2005) and Creswell and Poth (2018) discuss common philosophical interpretations to qualitative research commonly used among the social sciences: positivism, postpositivism, social constructionism, postmodernism, transformative theory, critical race theory, queer theory, and feminist theory. These philosophies can be placed on the continuum of epistemologies to convey the different beliefs they hold. On one side of the continuum, we have the positivist philosophies (objectivism), and on the other side of the continuum, we can place the postmodern/interpretivist (subjectivist) beliefs (Table 2.1).

Positivism

On the objectivist side of the epistemology continuum we find the positivist philosophy. Positivism holds the philosophical belief that there is a world beyond ourselves that can be understood and explained. The root *posit*

TABLE 2.1 Epistemology continuum

Epistemology	Objectivist				Subjectivist
Philosophy	Positivism	Postpositivism	Constructivist/Social Constructionism	Critical	Postmodern
Beliefs	Objective explanation of reality	Limits to certainty of knowledge	Reality is created and interpreted through interactions Objective reality is subjectively experienced by individuals	The experience of the individual Power as lies in structure, gender, race, and class Social construct of power	Subjective reality Multiple perspectives No singular, objective reality
Practices	Objective representation of data Empirically measure and validate Minimize/extrapolate bias	Efforts to objectively represent reality Not completely graspable Measurements are imprecise Conclusions are tentatively reached Potential for bias Reflexivity	Interpretation of symbols, language, contexts Relies on conversation Co-create data Reflexivity Memoing Openness about their own experiences	Call to action Change for the sake of the oppressed individual experience Open with their own experiences of power Reflexivity	Deconstructing reality Accept conclusions as inconclusive Seeks to understand Little concern with bias Discovery of experiences through language Include as many voices as possible Reflexivity
Relationship with data	Separation between knower and known No relationship between the researcher and the researched	Researcher can never fully remove themselves from research Research process is somewhat influenced by the researcher	No separation between researcher and researched Both are involved in the data process Researcher is made known within the data itself	No separation between researcher and researched Agent of change	No separation Data is generated through the relationship between the researcher and the researched

communicates a belief in systematic observation in order to posit, put forth, objective explanations of the observed reality (Daly, 2005). The positivist belief also holds that reality is systematically organized with regularities, patterns, logic, and measurable experiences and behaviors (Packer, 2018).

Truth, according to the positivist, can be reached with rigorous methodologies, hypotheses, measures, controlled conditions, and formal theory that have been tested and validated. Positivists aim to empirically measure reality, minimize bias, and refining the accuracy of representing such realities. "In the process of representation, this involves keeping separate the processes of the researcher's perceptions from the realities that we seek to understand" (Daly, 2005, p. 29). Therefore, the relationship the positivist practices is quite separate from the research and the participant. I argue that this also presents a linear relationship, where one means leads to another, the researcher only being a means to representation and the participant being a means to providing data.

Some qualitative approaches to inquiry present themselves from a positivistic philosophical belief. Ground theory methods were first conceptualized as a positivistic means of theorizing. With systematic ways of analyzing data, interviewing, and zigzagging between data collection and analyzing (Creswell & Poth, 2018), the result was an objective, standardized theory that was constructed on participants' experiences. Charmaz (2014) notes that some grounded theory methods assume that there is an objective reality that be understood and accurately represented, and therefore theorized about. The result being an objective theory supported by the realities of the participants. In some qualitative studies, hypotheses can be put forth and the data is used to test their plausibility.

Some ethnographic studies also call for a positivistic approach. An ethnographer that espouses the critical approach of researching culture will also collect data in a systematic way that objectively represents the culture itself (emic). Researchers do include themselves in their own findings in how they perceived their participants (etic), but they largely try to represent their participants, serving as an objective representation for their participant's voices and experiences.

Postpositivism

A step over from positivism on the objectivist side of the epistemology continuum is postpositivism. A key belief in postpositivism is that there are limitations to certainty of knowledge. Even though there are efforts to refine measures and validate that studies are well received, in the social sciences specifically, the human element of research acknowledges that there are some limitations to achieving an accurate representation of reality. Like the positivist, the postpositivist believes in an objective reality that exists out there, separate from our minds, but that reality is not completely graspable.

The postpositivist also holds the same philosophical belief towards objective measurements: they are always somewhat imprecise and whatever researched conclusions are drawn, they are done so tentatively and up for interpretation (Phillips & Burbules, 2000).

Similar to the positivist, the postpositivist believes in and practices rigorous methodologies in order to offer accurate experiments of reality. However, the approach of researchers on this point of the continuum holds that researchers can never remove themselves fully from their investigations. Postpositivists will include in their writings their potential for bias as well as their efforts to minimize that bias. This may include practices like reflexivity, memos of personal experiences, or ways their procedures are checked by a third party. Although trying to be separate from their research, the postpositivist's influence is unquestionable.

Most ethnographic studies fall under this philosophical approach. Ethnographers aim to accurately represent the culture they are studying with the emphasis on the outsider perspective. The researchers are open to their "native" state in the culture and are also aware of how their own experiences my differ from that of the culture being studied. They strive to accurately depict the culture while acknowledging that the observations are done from the outsider's perspective. Even though they are separate from the culture, they are still within it and acknowledge the tension that lies within their presence in the research.

Social constructionism

Social constructionism is rooted in the idea that all realities are constructed. "According to this view, reality is that which is created in the liminal zone between a perceived external reality and a subjective meaning-making process" (Daly, 2005, p. 32). Truth, or how we come to know what we know, happens in the mind of the individual, influenced by the external world around them. Epistemologically, social constructionism and constructivism falls in the middle of the objectivist and subjectivist; there is an objective reality that exists, but it is lived through and subjectively experienced differently be each individual living in it (Gergen, 1985).

Key to the beliefs of the social constructionist researcher is the social aspect of truth and knowledge. This belief argues that our realities, how we come to know what we know, are largely constructed through social means: symbols, language, relationships, and socially available understandings of reality and what those realities mean. Meaning, then, is also socially constructed; social information is the process through which we give meaning to our realities. This process of social information is only made through interaction. What our lives mean to us, what we perceive as truth, our knowledge, they all exist and are made through interactions.

What this implies for the researcher is that the interactions between the researcher and the participant are the process of data itself. The interactions produce data. The researcher is not separate from the process according to this philosophy. In fact, the researcher is just as much involved in the process. The relationship between the researcher and participant hold the means through which data is collected and generated. A common phrase used in both therapy and postmodern thought is the co-construction of knowledge. As the researcher and participant interact, they not only co-create knowledge, they co-create data. Data, then, is created between two people, not derived from one individual.

The social constructionist researcher relies heavily on language and conversation. Be it interviews, group data, or observations, conversation is the medium for data collection. The emphasis is strongly placed on language because it is language that allows us to explore, communicate, and therefor interactively shape our reality. Language is what makes experiences experiences.

Where the positivist practices causal explanations, objective descriptions, and accurately reporting *what* participants experience, the social constructionist is more interested in *how* participants experience their reality. A constructivist positioning will assume that participants' interpretations of their own experiences are true and trust them as valid and reliable. Through the process of inquiry, by asking questions and formulating ideas or clarifications within the conversation, the researcher also becomes a part of the interpretation process alongside the participant.

There is a tendency for the researcher to slip into a positivistic practice, even within the social constructionist philosophy. It is common for the researcher to disappear in the results section of their study, and to represent the data "as is," in its truest form (Daly, 2005). Researchers that espouse the social constructionist philosophy will steer away from "letting the data speak for itself." They will make themselves known throughout the entire process of the study, especially in the written results. Since they are involved the co-creation of the data, they are also involved it how it is shaped, presented, and especially analyzed.

Critical paradigm

The critical paradigm also leans toward the subjective side of the continuum because the philosophy believes in the individual's perceptions of reality, specifically as they pertain to issues of societal structure, issues of race, class, or power in general. The critical paradigm is primarily one of a political undertaking in research. Critical theory philosophy is taken from the Marxist, where society is structured by class, race, ethnicity, and power. Because of such societal structures, the researcher that espouses the critical paradigm will also believe in the position of action, wanting to change and advocate for oppression as it exists in society's structural makeup.

With the strong emphasis on political power and change, the critical researcher frequently practices reflexivity in their work. With potential political challenges and opposing beliefs, the researcher is up front with what they believe in, how they are driving their research agenda and design, and any potential actions for change the research calls for. Aware of their influence on the process, and the co-construction of knowledge, the critical researcher makes efforts to be as transparent as possible throughout the research process. With the call for action, the researcher's beliefs and political and philosophical underpinnings are key ingredients of the research process, which is then made as overt as possible to the audience.

The feminist framework is also a product of the subjectivist side of the continuum under the critical paradigm. In the feminist framework, the researcher also believes in the value of participants experiences as they largely relate to the experiences of gender inequality. Experiences are central in the feminist framework since the researcher relies on participants to convey their interpretations of how they have been in positions of inequality. Like the critical paradigm, key to the feminist framework is philosophy of interpretation of experiences for the sake of change and taking action, to "do something" about issues of inequality.

The feminist framework draws on different pragmatics and contexts as it pertains to research (Olesen, 2011). Research topics can vary from women's diverse situations; women oppression; injustice in society; gender equality; nonexploitive relationships; or issues of power as they relate to gender, abortion advocating, domestic violence, or individual identity, just to name a few. As placed within the critical paradigm, the feminist researcher is called to "correct both the invisibility and distortion of the female experience" (Lather, 1991).

The feminist approach to research centers itself on the inquiry into how women experience gender and to acknowledge that gender is a social construct (Creswell & Poth, 2018). Like the critical paradigm, the researcher heavily practices reflexivity, communicating their own roles and positions and how that influences how they see a woman's experience (Avis & Turner, 1996).

Postmodernism

To the far side of the subjectivist side of the epistemological continuum lies the social constructionist and postmodern philosophies, which also believe in our way of obtaining knowledge through our social interactions. Under the influence of Kuhn's (1962) critique of the scientific method, postmondernism presented itself as a challenge to "how we know what we know." The researcher that falls into this philosophy will approach inquiry with the goal of deconstructing, or exploring origins of truth, where and how participants came to experience their experiences. On this side of the continuum, our curiosities lie more in how people experience certain phenomena rather than what they are experiencing, for example, How was it for you to go through a divorce? Where the objectivist believes in one objective truth and how one goes about to obtain it, the subjectivist, postmodern researcher believes that there is no singular, objective reality. There is an underlying skepticism about what we know to be true or that we can know anything at all with certainty (Rosenau, 1992). Therefore, the efforts to research are only seen as a way to understand and interpret issues that are tentative and changeable. The postmodern researcher is willing to accept conclusions and positions as inconclusive and a process that continues to seek to understand; subjects trying to understand subjects (Wilber, 1998).

Under the postmodern philosophy, and as a research practice, the same assumption holds true as the scientific challenge to obtaining knowledge; how do we know what we know, and perhaps there is more than one way to come to know what we know. As a researcher, there is little concern with objectivity, bias, and the efforts to minimize such interactions with the research participants. The research is more focused on the discovery of participants' truths and experiences. On this end of the epistemology continuum, there is no separation between the researcher and researched; they are both a part of the research process, manifested in their relationship.

Likewise, the postmodern researcher also believes in the changeability and fluidity of knowledge (Daly, 2005). This idea gives room for interpretations within contexts, personal experiences, and specifically *how* one comes to live and experience their reality. In order to grasp the process of changeability and fluidity of knowledge, and in order to rely on the interpretation of how one experiences their reality, the researcher must concern themselves with the power of language.

Postmodernism, and therefore postmodern researchers, makes efforts to understand, deconstruct, and explore one's experiences or truths; language is the vehicle to such understanding. It is by way of language that participants express their experiences and how researchers collect and analyze data. The co-construction to data is key to this process. Both the researcher and the participant are involved in language construction; language is generated through the interactions of the research process. Therefore, the interactions and languages shared between the participant and researcher become data generative.

The belief in power of language also gives rise to many voices in postmodern research. The researcher makes efforts to bring as many voices as possible to the research, which comes from the belief that there are multiple perspectives on any given topic, phenomenon, or issue being researched. When the researcher includes as many voices as possible, the experiences described become more compelling, and therefore the data is more compelling.

More than an area on the epistemology continuum, this philosophy becomes a way of believing in interaction for the researcher. This also is not a research "trick" or "gimmick" used to approach the process. The postmodern researcher, and thinker, believes in the generative process found in interaction. The postmodern researcher also believes in the power of language and how it's used to communicate truths and experiences. The researcher *believes* that language is what organizes and constructs experiences, and trusts in how an individual experience their truths.

Other methods have similar beliefs and practices found within them. For example, the phenomenological approach to qualitative research believes in *epoching*, or the suspending of one's beliefs of what reality is in order to truly study another's experiences. The same practice holds true for the postmodern researcher: the suspending of beliefs in order to trust and join in the generative process to collect and construct data *with* participants. Most narrative approaches to inquiry also espouse the postmodern philosophy. Both the participant and the researcher are a part of the storytelling process; co-authors. As the researcher inquires and asks questions about the participant's journey, the researcher joins them in their journey as it is retold and narrated.

More than other approaches, the postmodern researcher makes extreme efforts to practice reflexivity in their research and writing. Marcus and Fischer (1986) see the postmodern researcher as a crisis of representation, calling into question what authority the researcher has in representing and researching challenging issues. How accurate can the voice or the capacity of the researcher be researching issues and topics? Where and how does the researcher fit into what they are researching, and why? With such a crisis, the researcher seeks to be as transparent as possible with their beliefs, experiences, biases, and ways of thinking so that their process becomes as collaborative and open as possible to the audience and participant.

Other philosophical interpretations and paradigms exist along the epistemological continuum. For example, queer theory concerns itself with the way individuals experience their identity (Plummer, 2011). This philosophical approach explores the issues related to identity construction, how we "preform" gender in society, and how dominate culture shapes an individual's narrative of identity. Disability theories and their approach to research focus on the meaning of disability within the individual experiences and how it's socially constructed (Mertens, 2003). This approach questions the labels placed on individuals with a disability and how society furthers such labels.

Ontology

A nice complement to epistemology and philosophical assumptions is ontology, the study of the nature of being, or studying where a certain thing exists (Schwandt, 2015). Bateson (1972) argues that both epistemology and ontology cannot be separated when studying a living being. To research individuals and to philosophically consider their humanity is to also study ontology.

Qualitative research, and the study of individuals, is one that concerns itself with the nature of *how* one *is*. One's reality is something that is meaningful to them, and therefore, something that is ventured into to understand. This is a fundamental, ontological difference between quantitative and qualitative research. Quantitative research practices accuracy in understanding or portraying its subject's reality, through standardized measures, statistical techniques of analyzing, and validated questionnaires. This is an ontological assumption in itself; to measure one's reality is to believe that reality itself is measurable, patterned, and even objectively understandable.

Qualitative research approaches reality differently. The human experience, the nature of being, can only be understood by way of exploring what is meaningful to the one being researched. An ontological assumption behind qualitative research (there are many different ontological assumptions) is that human reality is subjective. Therefore, there is an ontological respect for how one creates their own reality (Prus, 1994). This ontological assumption gives way to the importance of interpretation in qualitative research. The researcher is an instrument of interpretation, not a holder of measured, objective findings. Ontologically, the researcher believes that the human experience is situational, contextual, and everchanging. Therefore, to study human subjects is to ontologically study things of subjective reality.

There are several common ontological assumptions as they pertain to the social sciences and the qualitative researcher. It is important that the researcher be familiar with different ontological assumptions of reality as they lead to different views and formulations of theoretical questioning (Klein & Jurich, 2004). As mentioned before, how we view the world will influence the way we ask questions.

Meaning

Meaning is essential to ontology. When researching individuals, humans who live in subjective realities, the qualitative research must ask themselves what *meaning* means. This question poses a practice where researchers think about how an individual creates their reality and how they come to create what it meaningful to them. This is not a question of how one decides what to believe in, or why they chose to live their lives in a way that's meaningful to them. Asking what *meaning* means takes into account the social, contextual, and relationship realities one lives in, and therefore how meaning emerges from different contexts.

Individuals have the capacity to reflect on their lives, question what is important to them, and decide which areas to invest in and which are the most valuable to them. Meaning is assigned to specific behaviors that individuals interpret as necessary. The process of choosing and living what is meaningful to an individual presents a common ontological assumption that humans live in a reality that is meaningful to them.

Symbolic

The ontology of symbolisms suggests that individuals live in a meaningful world that can only be accessed through meaningful interactions with others. Language is the vehicle for interaction, where language is seen as a symbolic representation of one's meaningful reality as it's shared with others. "Words are the currency of qualitative research" (Daly, 2005, p. 65). Language and words are the means by which people formulate experiences; their words construe and make their reality. As a researcher, the ontological assumption lies in the power of the symbolism in language and words insofar as that they represent how we live our reality.

Social

Our ability to live in and create our own reality is contingent on interactions with others. Meaning is created only through social exchange. Ontologically, the nature of being human is to be in relationships. Therefore, the researcher approaches the process of research believing in such a meaningful social exchange. Since an individual can only be understood in the contexts in which they live, it is through their interactions with multiple people and contexts that individuals become who they are. The postmodern view of this reality also believes in the power of interaction and its ability to create a meaningful reality.

Similar to the postmodern philosophy, there is a respect for individual's experiences, their contexts, and how they influence their lives; how they all create a meaning-making system that ultimately projects a sense of values, beliefs, and way of life. To believe in someone else's beliefs requires a mindful suspension of our beliefs. To ontologically study individuals requires the same efforts; putting aside our own contexts in order to fully respect that of those being studied. This practice of qualitative research calls openness to other realities that may be different from ours; to understand the complexities in which an individual creates their own meaning and how those have come to *be* in their lives.

I, and therefore the premise of this book, lean on the subjective side of the epistemology continuum. The following chapters will outline specific postmodern approaches to counseling and therapy, and support how they align with that of the qualitative researcher. Both postmodern therapy and qualitative research hold similar beliefs and practices. When combined, the qualitative researcher has more possibilities to produce rich data from their research process.

Conclusion

After having discussed what a therapist and researcher is, this chapter overviewed major epistemologies and philosophical assumptions within qualitative research. Both the therapist and researcher share similar qualities with regard to inquiry, specifically the postmodern therapist. The discussion of epistemology is important to the researcher because of the self-reflection required to understand from *where* we ask questions and which philosophies underlie our inquiry. This chapter also discussed certain ontological assumptions, or the study of *being*. This is also important to qualitative research in that we are mindful of one's reality, their living experiences, and the way one's reality is organized around how they *are*. Once again, both researcher and therapist are similar in that their inquiry is founded in ontological assumptions.

The next chapter will visit the conversation of postmodernism specifically as it pertains to therapy. In my opinion, postmodern therapy articulates well the qualities, characteristics, and personhood of the therapist. Outlining these qualities is needed so that we can enter into the major postmodern therapies individually and apply them to the qualitative researcher and their practice.

References

Avis, J. M., & Turner, J. (1996). Feminist lenses in family therapy research: Gender, politics and science. In D. H. Sprenkle & S. M. Moon (Eds.), *Research methods in family therapy* (pp. 145–169). New York: Guilford.

Bateson, G. (1972). *Steps to an ecology of mind: A revolutionary approach to man's understand of himself.* New York: Ballantine Books.

Bengston, V., Acock, A., Allen, K. R., Dilworth-Anderson, P., & Klein, D. (2005). Theory and theorizing in family research: Puzzle building and puzzling solving. In V. Bengston, A, Acock, K. Allen, P. Dilworth-Anderson, & D. Klein (Eds.), *Sourcebook of family theory and research* (pp. 3–33). Thousand Oaks: Sage.

Charmaz, K. (2014). *Constructing grounded theory.* Los Angeles: Sage.

Creswell, J. W., & Poth, C. N. (2018). *Qualitative inquiry and research design: Choosing among five approaches.* Thousand Oaks: Sage.

Daly, J. K. (2005). *Qualitative methods for family studies & human development.* Los Angeles: Sage.

Gergen, K. (1985). The social constructionist movement in modern psychology. *American Psychologist*, 40(3), 226–275.

Guba, E., & Lincoln, Y. S. (1994). Competing paradigms in qualitative research. In N. K. Denzin & Y. S. Lincoln (Eds.), *Handbook of qualitative research* (pp. 105–117). Thousand Oaks: Sage.

Klien, D. M., & Jurich, J. A. (2004). Metatheory in family studies. In P. Boss, W. J. Doherty, R. LaRossa, W. Schumm, & S. Steinmetz (Eds.), *Sourcebook of family theories and methods: A contextual approach* (pp. 31–67). New York: Springer.

Kuhn, T. S. (1962). *The structure of scientific revolutions.* Chicago: University of Chicago Press.

Lather, P. (1991). *Getting smart: Feminist research and pedagogy with/in the postmodern.* New York: Routledge.

Marcus, G., & Fischer, M. M. J. (1986). *Anthropology as cultural critique.* Chicago: University of Chicago Press.

Mertens, D. M. (2003). Mixed methods and the politics of human research: The transformative-emancipatory perspective. In A. Tashakkori & C. Teddlie (Eds.), *Handbook of mixed methods in social & behavioral research* (pp. 135–164).

Olesen, V. (2011). Feminist qualitative research in the Millennium's first decade: Developments, challenges, prospects. In N. K. Denzin & Y. S. Lincoln (Eds.), *The SAGE handbook of qualitative research* (4th ed., pp. 129–146). Thousand Oaks, CA: Sage.

Packer, M. J. (2018). *The science of qualitative research.* New York: Cambridge University Press.

Phillips, D. C., & Burbules, N. C. (2000). *Postpositivitm and educational research*. Lanham, MD: Rowman & Littlefield.

Plummer, K. (2011). Critical Humanism and queer theory: Living with the tensions. In N. K. Denzin & Y. S. Lincoln (Eds.), *The SAGE handbook of qualitative research* (4th ed., pp. 195–207). Thousand Oaks: Sage.

Prus, R. (1994). Approaching the study of human group life: Symbolic interaction and ethnographic inquiry. In M. L. Dietz, R. Prus, & W. Shaffir (Eds.), *Doing every-day life: Ethnography as human lived experience* (pp. 10–29). Toronto: Copp Clarke Longman.

Rosenau, P. M. (1992). *Post-modernism and the social sciences: Insights, inroads, and intrusions*. Princeton: Princeton University Press.

Schwandt, T. A. (2015). *The SAGE dictionary of qualitative research* (4th ed.). Thousand Oaks: Sage.

Wilber, K. (1998). *Marriage of sense and soul: Integrating science and religion*. New York: Broadway Books.

3
POSTMODERN THERAPIES AND APPROACHES

Introduction

Whereas the previous chapter addressed the major trends in the therapist, this chapter will quickly overview the evolution of therapy and the approach to treatment as it entered the postmodern era of practice. Even though this chapter is not meant to overview specific approaches, it is necessary to quickly visit them in order to see how the field arrived at postmodernism, where we will derive qualities of the postmodern practice of therapy from which the researcher can gain.

Starting with Freud and Jung, their approach to treatment was largely driven by analysis of one's subconscious, including dreams and subconscious drives. Even later therapists like Fritz Perls and Carl Rogers who approached treatment differently were also interested in interpreting and analyzing dreams of the unconscious. However, Freud and Jung were the ones to start the approach to treatment as the "analyzer," where they were the ones with the correct interpretations of one's psyche. With their focus on transference and countertransference, their approach to treatment was to allow that process to play out in treatment so they could accurately interpret hidden inner conflicts within their patients.

After Freud and Jung, the field of counseling did evolve in its approach to treatment. Like marriage and family therapy, the field of counseling largely focused on extreme diagnosing like schizophrenia, bipolar, and depression. These diagnoses, among others, became a large area of focus for treatment. Then came Rogers and Perls with Gestalt therapy that concentrated on the being of a person, how to care for clients, and how to be with clients. Still concerned with diagnoses, the Rogerian approach to treatment changed the field. It allowed treatment to be relational, personal, and for the therapist to be a genuine presence.

Then came the rise of treatments like behavioral therapy, cognitive behavioral therapy, and rational emotive therapy. This wave of the field was driven by proof. These approaches to treatment took on a form of assessing client's issues through standardized assessments and inventories. In treatment, the therapist brought in their tools for diagnosing and treating patients. Still to this day, cognitive behavioral therapy is well researched and validated in its efficacy.

Marriage and family therapy, as well as professional counseling, reached a point of many influences and many approaches to therapy. Therapists were faced with the dilemma of choosing which approach to therapy to use in their practices. Was one strictly a structural family therapist? Did one only practice cognitive behavioral therapy? Was there such a thing as a strategic–psychoanalytic–cognitive behavioral therapist?

Blow, Sprenkle, and Davis (2007) began to study change and advocated for theories of change. Therefore, within each model of therapy, there was a trend of studying the certain approach to change. What was it about Bowenian family therapy that influenced the family to change? How did cognitive behavioral therapy motivate change? As change was being researched within each model of therapy, so was its efficacy. Not only was there a plethora of models to choose from, which one was the best was also in the conversation.

Within this time of multiple approaches to therapy, there was also a rise in specific techniques suited to specific therapeutic issues. Was there one approach that was better than others in treating certain issues? What was the most effective approach to treat depression? Bipolar disorder? Infidelity? The question of a one-size-fits-all also became an area of concentration. Are there limits to what a model of therapy can do? Can it treat everything?

Modern workings

Marriage and family therapy and the field of counseling are commonly seen in two major waves: modern and postmodern. According to modernism, knowledge and truth are constructs placed within a hierarchy. Since the therapist was considered one that held a certain form of knowledge, they are hierarchically placed within the relationship of the therapist–client. This was especially true to traditional psychoanalysts like Freud and Jung; they held some answers to our internal psyche according to their ability to psychoanalyze. In other words, the therapist was seen as someone that *knew* something that the client did not.

In addition to the ability to psychoanalyze and diagnose mental disorders like Freud and Jung, in the modern approach to therapy the therapist had an expertise in cybernetics, or the study of feedback mechanisms and their communications. Bateson was largely influential in this era with his theory of communication and schizophrenia. His theory contributed to the field by providing therapists a theory of communication and how families interacted with each other. Families' interactions and behaviors were seen as a cybernetic process in which systems acquire information in order to regulate themselves (Nichols & Davis, 2017).

Family interactions were labeled as negative and positive feedback loops. If a system receives new information, it self-corrects in the form of a negative feedback loop, so that it stays on its course of maintenance. If the system takes a new direction because of the information that is received, it's known as positive feedback, introducing change into the system. Therefore, the system enters into a new state of homeostasis, or "normal" way of functioning.

These concepts were applied to families where therapists hypothesized that families themselves were behaving like a mechanical system, interacting in a way that maintained its status quo. If that status quo was problematic, then the therapist was charged with correcting the family's course; positive feedback.

These theoretical approaches to treating families gave way to general systems theory in family therapy and counseling. If a family's interactions were studied as efforts to maintain status quo, problems became an issue of maintenance rather than individual diagnosing. Interactions, the family's status quo, and the behaviors themselves were what was maintaining the problem, rather than the problem being the problem. Therapists began to view problems as circular instead of linear. The more one person did a certain thing, the more another responded in a certain way. It takes two to maintain a problem. At that time, this was a philosophical foundation in marriage and family therapy and some theories of counseling.

With this philosophical approach, the therapist was seen as a diagnostician, labeling behaviors, interactions, and changing the course of the family's status quo. Therapists were the "experts" of the therapy process. Jay Haley included directives in his practice and instructed families on which behaviors to change so that the problem itself dissolved. Salvador Minuchin changed the family's structure so that the family could function in a way that problematic behaviors were not maintained.

This modern wave of therapy was also known as first-order cybernetics, where the observer of the system remained intentionally separate. The modernist practice of therapy promoted the "dualistic and hierarchical notion of a client as the subject of inquiry and observation and placed a therapist in a superior expert position" (Anderson, 1997, p. 32). The effort of therapy, then, was a split one and the parties were considered separate entities: the client, the subject of therapy; and the therapist, the expert observer of the client's dysfunction. Therefore, therapy was conducted as such: the therapist observed, diagnosed interactions, labeled the system, and changed its course. And it worked.

However, others believed it was not possible to be a separate entity from that which the therapist treats. Spiegel (1957) early pointed out that the therapist was just as much a part of the family system as the family itself. The system, then, involved the therapist, not as an outside observer but as a transactional partner in the family, interacting, behaving, and influencing while being influenced by the family.

Carl Whitaker and Virginia Satir started to change the expert approach to treatment. They both became intentionally involved with the families they treated. Whitaker (1958) became so emotionally involved that he purposefully used a co-therapist to ensure he was not becoming too emotionally involved with the family. Satir was known for her display of physical affection, spending more of her hours in treatment hugging her clients. Heavily influenced by Carl Rogers, both Whitaker and Satir began a different era of treatment from their predecessors, one where the therapist was considered to be a part of the family system.

This second wave of therapy, where the therapist was a part of the family system, became to be known as second-order cybernetics. With roots in cybernetics, still believing in feedback loops, systems theory, and interactions, the therapist was philosophically placed with the network of interactions. The therapist's influence changed, and at the same time, the therapist was changing with clients. The therapist's interpretation of the family system became less a matter of expertise as it did a process of interpretation. Even though the therapist had knowledge of systems, their expertise was still influenced by the family, and the family by the therapist expertise, giving recognition to the systems theory of circular causality. Both were just as influenced as the other. Therapists were not capable of detached objectivity as they once were seen to be by first-order cybernetics (Freedman & Combs, 1996).

Second-order cybernetics was a philosophical shift in the field of therapy. The Palo Alto group first considered what it meant to treat a family as simply "observers," and therefore the objectivity of the therapist (Watzlawick, Beavin, & Jackson, 1967). Early on in their working, Bateson even cautioned therapists to be more aware of how they were involved in their studies with families, particularly in how closely they were driven by their own theories (Sulzki & Ransom, 1976).

With such an influence on the therapist, and with the therapist being a part of the system, the practice of therapy began to take the turn toward constructivism and postmodernism. What follows is my view of postmodernism within the field of professional counseling and marriage and family therapy. Even though not intended to be an exhaustive review of postmodernism, there will be some aspects of the philosophies as they pertain to how the field of therapy has evolved.

Constructivism

With the rise of second-order cybernetics, and the notion that the therapist was just as much involved in the therapy process as the clients, constructivism made its way into the practice of therapy. Like second-order cybernetics, constructivism was a philosophical theory of how one construes knowledge and originated in philosophers like Immanuel Kant, Jean Piaget, and Davie Hume. Constructivism posits that an external objective reality cannot be known, therefore knowledge represents what we construct within our own internal makeup (Maturana, 1978; Piaget, 1975). Therefore, objective truth is ultimately subjective to the individual experiences of a particular phenomenon.

According to constructivist thought, our reality is something that is constructed within and between individuals. In other words, we invent our world around us by way of others around us. This idea was also a major shift in the therapist in that it forced them to rethink the language of diagnoses and "problems" and what they knew to be dysfunction. If the reality of an individual is constructed within their own internal schemas, then the definition of dysfunction that therapists hold will inevitably be different than the experiences of the client. Therefore, the therapist cannot know the client's experience of dysfunction; that is left for the client to communicate and decipher.

The belief that the human experience is ultimately ambiguous and left to subjective interpretation was a major shift in therapy; we can only understand one's experiences, such as they are, from the interpretation of an individual rather than our level of expertise. The constructions therapists once held about therapy (diagnosing, abnormal, etc.) were beginning to be challenged and thereto, corrected (Anderson, 1997). Instead of believing in certain cognitive distortions (cognitive behavioral therapy), a specific structure and hierarchy of a family (structural family therapy), or one's overt conflict driven by their subconscious (psychoanalysis), the postmodern therapist believed in the client's perception and interpretation of their own experiences and lives. Within this correction, the stance of the therapist changed from being an expert, with expert knowledge and influence, to a co-author, one that learned from their clients as their experiences unraveled in therapy.

Hermeneutics

With the concept of constructivism came the tradition of hermeneutics. As a biblical studies approach, hermeneutics entered postmodern therapy as "interpretation," or the assurance of properly interpreting. Hermeneutics also largely concerns itself with understanding, where "understanding is always interpretive, there is no uniquely privileged standpoint for understanding" (Hoy, 1986, p. 399). Therefore, hermeneutics is not an attempt to gather truth, or correct knowledge. Instead, if hermeneutics is largely about understanding, and if gathering truth is not the end, then one cannot ever reach true understanding; one's meaning cannot be fully understood.

This became an important part of therapy by way of Harlene Anderson (collaborative language systems) and Michael White (narrative therapy), as they approached their practice from the stance of helping clients to interpret what was in front of them. From a hermeneutical perspective, it was the responsibility of the therapist to discover, not diagnose, through the process of construction and how clients organized their experiences and stories. The major shift in therapy came by doing this *collaboratively*. As a therapist gathered pieces of a client's experiences, they helped the client "make sense" of their lives. The therapist interpreted what the client's shared alongside them and with them.

I enjoy the example of how we see an apple. There may be a bright red apple sitting in front of us on a table. It appears to be upright, stem on top, large red belly, about the size of a baseball. However, even though we see an apple in front of us, it's not the way we perceive it. To simplify the biological process of our optic nerves, our vision is such that it sends messages to our brains so that whatever it is that we see in front of us, it is ultimately translated into our mental processes. That is how we "see" the apple: by way of our brains interpreting what we see in front of us. The apple, then, is in front of us, but we all see the apple differently, or we all interpret the apple differently. In reality, the apple is actually some distorted vision of a formation, but our brains make the apple into how we see it.

The idea of hermeneutics and interpretation became a specific philosophy espoused by therapists. One's "problems" became an issue of interpretation rather than a process needing to be "fixed." With the belief that we can never fully understand, specifically as it pertains to diagnosing and dysfunction, problems became something the needed to be interpreted and then communicated through the interpretation of the client. It was the therapist's job to understand the interpretation of a client's problems in order to conduct therapy. Even the act of inquiring about the interpretation of a client's problems became therapeutic; listening, understanding, and making sense of how a client perceives their problems became a central part of therapy.

There is something special that happens when we inquire from a constructivist philosophy. This requires the therapist to strip away their own perceptions of problems and to approach clients with a sense of naiveté (more on this in the following chapter). The hermeneutical approach requires a different sense of curiosity and listening. Rather than listening to "fix" or "solve problems," the therapist listened in a way that tried to help organize clients' lives. When this is genuinely done, clients can sense it. It's something that is felt by both the client and therapist. It is when both parties are engaged in this conversation that therapy happens. Change happens simply by way of inquiry. As will be discussed, the qualitative research can greatly benefit from adopting this form of understanding.

Postmodernism

The postmodern wave of therapy produced a generation of therapists that approached therapy with a healthy sense of skepticism. The postmodern therapist entered therapy with a different mindset, stance, belief, and practice than a modern therapist, or therapists that came before the postmodern wave: psychoanalytic, systemic, or modern therapies. The skepticism came from the belief of not having one right way to approach therapy and, therefore, approach clients. This gave birth to several postmodern therapies and beliefs.

Postmodern therapy, like postmodernism as viewed in science, was a reaction to a specific time and practice in therapy and counseling. At its most basic level, postmodernism is a critique. Ken Wilber (1998) views postmodernism as a broad phenomenon "occurring in the wake of modernism" (p. 43), and a continuation of the practices and beliefs of modernity, challenging the practices of scientific knowledge. Although there is no one author associated with postmodernism, philosophers like Derrida (1978), Foucault (1972), and Wittgenstein (1961) challenged overarching cultural narratives, privilege, universal truths, and the scientific method.

Not only did postmodernism question certain scientific, political, and religious truths, it also questioned the validity of certain therapeutic and counseling models. Postmodern therapy also expanded on the practices and beliefs of the modern approaches: psychoanalysis, cognitive behavioral therapy, and systemic therapy. Just like the scientific method was questioned as the ultimate way of knowing what we know, so were models of therapy questioned: is this the only way to treat a certain issue? Is there one "right" way to treat this case?

As it pertains to therapy and counseling, postmodernism is an attitude and a set of beliefs. The postmodernist believes that "there are limits on the ability of human beings to measure and describe the universe in any precise, absolute, and universally applicable way" (Freedman & Combs, 1996, p. 21). Another important belief the researcher can benefit from, as it is believed in therapy, is that there is no essential truth. Since we cannot objectively know reality, all we can do is interpret experiences of our clients and research participants and welcome the possibilities of different beliefs, attitudes, and conversations within therapy and research. "Where a modernist worldview would invite us to close down options and work methodically to identity a universally applicable interpretation, we invite ourselves to celebrate diversity. We want to think more like novelists and less like technocrats" (Freedman & Combs, 1996, p. 33). I appreciate the metaphor of a novelist, as presented by Freedman and Combs, because of the creativity is offers in the approach to therapy and research. Like a novelist creates a story as they go along their creative process and as the story unfolds as it is being formulated, the researcher and therapist also are unfolding their practices: data and therapy.

The metaphor of technocrat is also accurate with thinking about postmodernism as it stands in contrast to modernism. We see this happening when clinicians and researchers use the *Diagnostic and Statistical Manual of Mental Disorders* (DSM-5) to drive their practices. Specifically, for researchers, this happens when the researcher is aimed toward "proving," "validating," or even searching for efficacy. For those that do so, they run the risk of behaving as if the set of homogeneous disorders are true for all people that carry such labels, robbing them of the opportunity of unique experience. "When we treat people with this kind of 'objectivity,' we regard them as objects, thus inviting them into a relationship in which they are the passive, powerless recipients of our knowledge and expertise" (Freedman & Combs, 1996, p. 21). Where postmodernism differs from modernism is in the belief of people's experiences, and to be slow to believe and espouse labels of diagnosis and disorders placed on clients. Even though the DSM-5 has a healthy place in therapy, a postmodern therapist will be slow to adopt such a model of treatment because of the limits diagnoses places on clients' lives.

Social constructionism

Like postmodernism, the social-constructionist movement also has no one author in its origin. Instead, social constructionism was given rise to by the field of sociology. Berger and Luckmann (1966) wrote one of the first works, titled *The Social Construction of Reality*. Like postmodernism, they argued the possibility of multiple interpretations to knowledge and challenged the scientific method. However, what social constructionism added to the postmodern conversation was the social nature of knowledge and how we come to attain it.

In the more recent decades, social constructionism has grown to other social sciences, including therapy and qualitative research: Gergen (1985, 1994), Shotter (1993), Shotter, and Gergen (1994), and Harré (1983). Of the many definitions of social constructionism, I believe social psychologist Kenneth Gergen (1985) offers one of the most eloquent:

> Social constructionist inquiry is the process by with people come to describe, explain, or otherwise account for the world (including themselves) in which they live ... What we take to be experiences of the world does not itself dictate the terms by which the world is understood. What we take to be knowledge of the world is not a product of induction, or of the building and testing of general hypotheses ... The terms in which the world is understood are the social artifacts, products of historically situated *interchanges among people*. (pp. 226–227)

Given Gergen's definition, the relational aspect of knowledge is key to understanding the social nature of knowledge. For the therapist and the researcher, this social nature of knowledge is the foundation of their work. Truths, self-narratives, identity, therapy, and data are all the result of human relationships. The meaning of language and the special attention we give certain aspects of our lives, the way "problems" are described, the process of asking research participants question, and what we deem is important to each respective process and areas of our lives are all the result of relationships in which interactions and dialogue occur. The classic philosophical debate of "If a tree falls in the forest and no one is around to hear it, does it make a sound?" can be translated to our exchange of knowledge: "If there are no relationships, and information is given without interaction, is it truly considered knowledge?" My answer: no. Knowledge, in which ever form it may come, requires interaction in order for it to be knowledge.

Gergen (1985) challenged the notion of our amount of autonomy by saying our beliefs are fluid and constantly changing by the influence of our surroundings and contexts. This was very important to postmodern family therapists as individuals are largely rooted in their family contexts. Social constructionists believe that we are constantly sharing meaning-making interaction, constructing meaning through our interactions. Our meanings and reality, even problems, are made through the social availability and shared understandings (Daly, 2005). This became central to family therapists, as the family is one of the first relationships in which we construct our reality. The relationship exchanges that exist within a family became a key element for deconstruction for therapists.

The concept of a socially constructed reality invited therapists to help clients explore their beliefs and values, where they came from, and even to challenge them (Nichols & Davis, 2017). In this practice, it was the aim of therapists to uncover socially constructed problems and to discover their origins. More important, this was done collaboratively. The therapists were an important factor in helping clients uncover the origins of their problems and to create newly constructed truths. New realities emerged through conversation, in collaboration with client and therapist (Nichols & Davis, 2017). The social construction practice in therapy invited therapists to inquire about *how* clients experienced certain problems rather than asking about causal conditions.

Like the constructivist approach, the social construction philosophy also required the therapist to strip away their own understandings of problems. Instead, the therapist focused on how their client's problems were constructed and interpreted, specifically from the positioning of social interactions the supported and kept problematic situations alive.

There are several key ideas that most postmodern therapies have in common. I believe the major postmodern therapies to be collaborative language systems, narrative therapy, and solution-focused brief therapy. Each of these therapies will be expounded in the following chapters, specifically as they pertain to how the qualitative researcher can benefit from each approach. The therapist that espouses each practice embodies certain philosophies, characteristics, and positionings within the practice of therapy that can be utilized by qualitative researchers. It is my belief that when researchers take on these philosophies, they will produce richer data.

Postmodern common factors in therapy

Among the postmodern approaches to therapy, there are several common factors that each share. Even though each different approach has its own unique way of interacting with clients, conducting therapy, and approaching treatment overall, postmodern therapies share several qualities and philosophical stances that call for certain characteristics within the therapist. The following briefly outlines the common postmodern therapy philosophies as I know them to be. I argue that qualitative researchers can espouse these philosophies in approaching their research practices.

One-down

Postmodern therapists call the idea of collaboration, co-authoring, and interpreting a "one-down" position. The one-down philosophy is a specific mindset in which the therapist imagines themselves in a literal one-down positioning where the client becomes the leader of therapy. The one-down position creates a mental opening for the therapist so that their thoughts and minds can be free to openly listen and learn from their clients. Too often therapists and researchers are bombarded with their own thoughts and theoretical underpinnings; as a result, their mental space is crowded and muddied. In the one-down position, the therapist is the one that "leads from behind," becoming a curios learner rather than an expert leader.

The one-down position also allows the therapist to approach interpreting clients' lives from a more open place. As a constructivist, it is important to use the one-down position so that we can help clients and participants interpret their own lives. As a social constructionist, the one-down position is also important in that we understand the interactive process of learning and creating the shared space for knowledge. Specific to the researcher, the shared space of interviewing and research inquiry becomes a platform for one-down, entering the conversation with the mindset that the participant is in the lead and we are in a position where we ask questions based on the participant's offerings, not being driven by our own questions.

Language

To the postmodern therapist, language is a key element of therapy. Taken from constructivist and social constructionist thought, the language we use to construct and share our worlds is also foundational to the process of therapy. How clients described their problems, the word s they chose, and phrasing used to describe their reality is important to the process of therapy, namely, deconstructing. Rather than focusing on *what* their reality may be, the emphasis is on *how* they construe their reality. The process of languaging one's reality is also important to the process of change: just as one can construe their reality, they can also unconstrue it by way of language.

The power of language is also a philosophical stance in postmodern therapy. The therapist believes that language has the power to create realities, specifically realities of "problems" as language shared between individual, therefore the social aspect of constructing problems through language. The therapist believes that language is what makes experiences experiences, even negative ones. Given this power of language, the therapist is mindful of the language they use as well in their conversation. Together, both the therapist and client, and also the researcher and participant, hold the power of language to construct their realities, be them therapeutic or researcher data.

In regard to the power of language within therapy, the idea that the therapist is just as much of this process as the client is central to postmodern therapy. Although this practice had been discussed as early as by the MRI group in Palo Alto, postmodern therapy gave it intention within the practice. As the therapist inquires into how clients form their own realities, the therapist is also helping them form it. By way of inviting clients to share aloud their experiences, the therapist is helping them formulate how they experience their lives, and therefore become a part of that experience. The therapist is also a part of that process by helping clients explore origins, relationships, and meaning of their "problems," or deconstructing. In this positioning, the therapist becomes a tool in the co-construction of realities, creating new realities, which become a part of the therapy process.

Non-diagnosing

Solution-focused therapy was also a part of the postmodern wave of therapies. Solution-focused therapy follows in the philosophies of postmodernism. The practice itself is one of pragmatics, meaning the postmodern philosophies are translated into a useful, practical way of doing therapy. The solution-focused therapist believes in people, their resourcefulness, and their ability to create solutions within their own worlds.

With this belief in people also came the practice of non-diagnosing. Postmodern therapists believed in people so much, in their ability to overcome and be their own unique individual self, that diagnosing took away from that resourcefulness. With the power of language, so came the power of diagnosing language. The postmodern therapist believes that diagnoses have the potential to have power over one's life.

The solution-focused therapist believes that one person is not their diagnosis "all the time"; there are times when they are not their diagnosis or when their "problems" are not as severe. They believe that people have moments of not experiencing their problems, showing one's resourcefulness, or ability to ward off and fight away their own problems. People inherently have solutions in them; they only need to be explored. The narrative therapist believes that labels and diagnoses have power within their narratives, that diagnoses themselves have the power to influence the ways in which individuals live out their narratives, therefore indoctrinating them into the narrative of the diagnosis itself rather than the individual's unique experiences. Collaborative language systems is also non-diagnosing in that it approaches such labels without the assumption that therapists know what the label means for the individual and do not bring their pre-gathered knowledge into the conversation of diagnosing. Therefore, they discover the meaning of the diagnosis together with the client.

The researcher can benefit from this belief in that it drives the way we view people; the way we inquire is influenced by this belief. How we view the world influences the way we ask questions. When we believe in people, in their humanistic capacities, it drives us to ask different questions, as opposed to be driven by the belief in diagnosing.

Most postmodern therapeutic approaches, along with most modern therapy and counseling theories, will express that most of their "techniques" are in fact not techniques. For example, the narrative therapy approach in its "technique" of externalizing conversations (more on this in Chapter 5) will argue that the technique in ineffective if done as a technique. The same is true for solution-focused brief therapy and its miracle question (more on this in Chapter 6); it is not successful if it is used as a technique. Instead, in both examples, these "techniques" are something the therapist whole-heartedly believes in. If they are used as a therapy trick, taken from the therapist toolbox, they will more than likely be ineffective. Postmodern approaches to therapy call for a way of being, where the techniques within the therapy are something the therapist *is*. The way of being is foundational to postmodern therapy and so, too, qualitative research.

A way of being

According to my beliefs and practices of postmodern therapy, one of the most central aspects of all postmodern therapies is the therapist themselves. I believe that a postmodern therapist, and therefore researcher, obtain certain characteristics and personal qualities. The way I describe that is the therapist's *way of being*. Anderson (1997) expounds on this in her approach to therapy, where she describes that the personhood of the therapist is a major catalyst in therapy. This is similar to the beliefs of Carl Whitaker in his approach to therapy in what he calls the "existential encounter"; the personality of the therapist is a major factor in therapy. Recent research has given the therapist way of being special attention.

A common area of research in counseling and therapy is "common factors" among treatment approaches. This means that different treatment approaches to therapy and counseling have things in common that are used similarly in treatment. Fife, Whiting, Bradford, and Davis (2014) argue that a therapists' way of being in the common factors research is one of the most effective predictors of therapeutic success, more so than the approach to treatment. More than what therapeutic approaches have in common, they all share the therapist. The same can be applied to the researcher: even though there are many different approaches to inquiry, they all share the researcher.

A *way of being* refers to the "in-the-moment attitude that therapist have towards the client and provides a foundation for the therapeutic alliance" (Fife et al., 2014, p. 24). The researcher can benefit from this thinking in that the person of the researcher is one of most important tools they can use in their research, just like the therapist. There is a certain attitude that is shown and lived in by the researcher: an attitude of openness to the person of the participant.

An attitude of openness is not something that is *used* as if it is a means to an end, the end being data. When approached this way, we risk objectifying participants for the sake of research. Anderson (1997) refers to the way of being that shows how the researcher and therapist "conveys to the other that they are valued as a unique human and not as a category of people; that they have something worthy of saying and hearing; that you meet them without prior judgment" (p. 44). When this is genuinely done, it can be felt, in therapy and research.

A way of being speaks to the humanity of the researcher; their ability to be a "real" person with their participants, not only a professional asking a question. Like therapy, qualitative research takes place between two individuals; it is a person-to-person endeavor. Such engagements call for a sense of humanity from the researcher and therapist. Qualitative research, like therapy, calls for a genuine relationship.

This relationship is explained by philosopher Martin Buber. He describes our *selves* as being the truest in relationships (Buber, 1965). Who we really are is only seen in and through relationships. This applies to relationships in and out of therapy and research. When the researcher brings their truest self to the participant, it is also felt.

The way of being is at the heart of qualitative research, just as it is in therapy. When researchers bring their fullest, truest self to the research, it is responded to by participants who also bring their truest selves. When the researcher and participant are engaging in the process in their way of being, the result is true, rich data. Just like the researcher, "therapists who value the personhood of clients and put the clients' needs first are demonstrating a way of being that is conducive to a good therapeutic relationship" (Fife et al., 2014, p. 24).

The common factors research suggests that therapeutic efficacy is seen because of the therapeutic alliance. The equivalent therapeutic outcomes in qualitative research is richer data, both of which manifest themselves in a way of being.

What follows

In the proceeding chapters, the aforementioned postmodern approaches to therapy will be overviewed as they pertain to the qualitative researcher and their practices. Having outlined their common factors, the discussion will turn toward each model of therapy, its main tenets and philosophies, and how it can be utilized within qualitative research.

In Chapter 4, the collaborative language systems approach to therapy will be visited. Even though the chapter is not intended to exhaustively review the approach to therapy, some of the foundational ideas of the therapy will be overviewed. As a philosophical stance, and as an overall approach to conversation, the collaborative model will provide the qualitative researcher some insight into the process of researcher: formulating questions, approaching interviews, and data analysis (even though there are more facets and areas of the qualitative research process, I am condensing the overall process into these three sections in efforts to combine the therapy and the research process). The qualitative researcher, and what I call according to this model of therapy, the collaborative researcher, will be given insight into the therapy so that they can extrapolate and incorporate some of its practices into their research.

Chapter 5 will outline the narrative therapy approach. Practiced and researched widely, this approach offers significant insight into how individuals internalize and live within destructive cultural narratives. It also offers insight into what destructive narratives are. With such insight, the model approaches therapy from a position of advocacy, even political in its nature, where the narrative therapy is one that believes people are indoctrinated into narrow views of themselves because of destructive dominate narratives. Therefore, the approach has a plethora of philosophical underpinnings to offer qualitative researchers. The discussion will focus on some of the origins of the model of therapy, its major tenets, and its approach to therapy, namely, how it asks questions. This chapter will also outline a simplified research process according to the narrative approach to therapy: how to ask researchers questions, the interview process, and analyzing data from the narrative perspective. This chapter in particular will give special attention to the research agenda and the narratives within such a category.

Chapter 6 will outline the solution-focused brief therapy approach. Also considered among postmodern therapies, the solution-focused approach to therapy is unique in its practice. It is considered a more pragmatic approach, heavily influenced from the pragmatic days of the MRI group. However, what I believe to be commonly underrepresented, is its deep philosophical underpinnings of the power of language. Even though not intended to historically account its inception, the chapter will overview original philosophers that influenced its practice today, namely, philosophers of language like Wittgenstein and Nietzsche. The chapter will also overview some main techniques in its approach, which will be applied to researchers' approaches to their practices. The model overall will be used to overview the condensed process as outlined in Chapters 6 and 7: asking research questions, interviewing and data gathering, and data analysis.

Chapter 7 will visit a common discussion within postmodern therapy: hierarchy. With such an egalitarian approach, one that is centralized in collaboration and the one-down position, *where* the therapist and researcher place themselves within their respective relationships is important to each process. With an inherent hierarchy in therapy and research, such conversations are crucial for the researcher, specifically one that espouses the postmodern approach to therapy. The chapter will focus on schools of thought from foundational therapists and their insights into hierarchy and self-disclosure. Be forewarned: no conclusions on the matter are reached.

Chapter 8 will offer insight into the crucial task of writing. As a qualitative researcher, the task of writing is a constant throughout the entirety of one's career. The chapter argues that the qualitative researcher is, and ought to, consider themselves a writer. Through memos, interviews, institutional review board (IRB) applications, and the written results, the qualitative researcher is constantly writing. The chapter will give suggestions into writing practices, insight into the writing process itself, and overall encouragement I have found in other writers on writing.

References

Anderson, H. (1997). *Conversation, language, and possibilities: A postmodern approach to therapy*. New York, New York: Basic Books.
Berger, P. L., & Luckmann, T. (1966). *The social construction of reality: A treatise in the sociology of knowledge*. New York: Anchor Books.
Blow, A. J., Sprenkle, D. S., & Davis, S. D. (2007). Is who delivers the treatment more important that the treatment itself? The role of the therapist in common factors. *Journal of Marital and Family Therapy*, 33, 298–317.
Buber, M. (1965). *Between man and man*. New York: Macmillan.
Daly, J. K. (2005). *Qualitative methods for family studies & human development*. Los Angeles: Sage.
Derrida, J. (1978). *Writing and difference*. Chicago: University of Chicago Press.
Fife, S. T., Whiting, J. B., Bradford, K., & Davis, S. (2014). The therapeutic pyramid: A common factors synthesis of techniques, alliance, and way of being. *Journal of Marital and Family Therapy*, 40, 20–33.
Foucault, M. (1972). *The archeology of knowledge and the discourse on language*. New York: Pantheon Books.
Freedman, J., & Combs, G. (1996). *Narrative therapy: The social construction of preferred realities*. New York: Norton.
Gergen, K. J. (1985). The social constructionist movement in modern psychology. *American Psychologist*, 40, 255–275.
Gergen, K. J. (1994). *Realities and relationships: Soundings in social construction*. Cambridge, MA: Harvard University Press.
Harré, R. (1983). *Personal being: A theory for individual psychology*. Oxford: Basil Blackwell.
Hoy, D. C. (1986). Must we say what we mean? The grammatological critique of hermeneutics. In B. R. Wachterhauser (Ed.), *Hermeneutics and modern philosophy* (pp. 397–415). New York: State University of New York Press.
Maturana, H. R. (1978). Biology of language: The epistemology of reality. In G. Miller & E. Lenneberg (Eds.), *Psychology and biology of language and thought* (pp. 28–62). New York: Academic Press.

Nichols, M. P., & Davis, S. D. (2017). *Family therapy: Concepts and methods*. Boston: Pearson.
Piaget, J. (1975). *The development of thought: Equilibration of cognitive structures*. New York: Viking Press.
Shotter, J. (1993). *Conversational realities: Constructing life through language*. London: Sage.
Shotter, J., & Gergen, K. J. (1994). Social construction: Knowledge, self, others, and continuing the conversation. *Annals of the International Communication Association*, 17, 3–33.
Spiegel, J. P. (1957). The resolution of role conflict within the family. *Psychiatry*, 20, 1–6.
Sulzki, C. E., & Ransom, D. C. (1976). *Double bind: The foundation of the communicational approach to the family*. New York: Grune & Stratton.
Watzlawick, P. A., Beavin, J. H., & Jackson, D. D. (1967). *Pragmatics of human communication*. New York: Norton.
Whitaker, C. A. (1958). Psychotherapy with couples. *American Journal of Psychotherapy*, 12, 18–23.
Wilber, K. (1998). *The marriage of sense and soul: Integrating science and religion*. New York: Broadway Books.
Wittgenstein, L. (1961). *Tractus logico-philosophicus*. London: Routledge.

4
THE COLLABORATIVE RESEARCHER

Introduction

Collaborative language systems is known as one of the founding models of therapy in the postmodern wave of marriage and family therapy. The model of therapy itself is rooted in the postmodern philosophy of social constructionism, where meaning is created and interpreted by one's own experiences through and within social situations and collective knowledges. One's experiences, languaging, and life are key focuses of the collaborative approach.

There are several key philosophical stances and characteristics found within the collaborative therapist that can be utilized by the qualitative researcher. This chapter will outline the philosophical stances taken by the collaborative approach and visit some of the characteristics of the practice of therapy. Each of these will be applied to the qualitative researcher.

Philosophical stance

Where once the approach to therapy was named collaborative language systems, Harlene Anderson, founder and creator of the approach, now thinks of it as collaborative practices. Anderson explains this shift in names by way of the philosophical stance. To label the approach as "therapy," or even the word "systems," offers a presumption of what the approach assumes (therapy) and the theoretical knowledge behind it (systems). "Collaborative practices," then, remains open to the possibilities of conversation beyond therapy and systems. This same philosophical stance one takes in collaborative practices becomes central to the entire process of the qualitative researcher.

The collaborative approach to therapy and research requires a certain positioning of the researcher. It is a position in which we are mindful of how we relate to clients and research participants. Anderson (1997) describes her philosophical stance as follows:

> This position ... I refer to as a *philosophical stance* – a *way of being* in relationship with our fellow human beings, including how we think about, talk with, act with, and respond to them. It reflects an attitude and tone that serve as the backdrop for my relationships with clients and the therapy process, how I locate myself in a conversation. It is an authentic, natural, spontaneous, and sustained position that is unique to each relationship and each discourse. It brings the *person* of both client and therapist back into the therapy room. And it shits away from thinking in terms of our roles and functions as therapists to considering our relationship with the people we work with. (p. 94)

This philosophical stance, specifically in terms of Anderson's mention of functioning, is unique in the sense that the researcher is mindful of the shift from their functioning role as a researcher to their *relationship* with the participant. In the collaborative practices approach, the researcher puts aside the research process (function) and focuses on the relationship present in the *context* of the research, not the research itself. Present in the research process is a shift of thought that exudes as a way of being; the relationship takes precedence over the research and its agenda. When the collaborative researcher places the relationship in the forefront, the entire experience of *data* shifts. Data, then, is seen an outcome of the relationship between the researcher and the participants; data is the means, not the end.

This positioning encourages the researcher to call onto themselves and to examine the way they view the world (one's epistemology) and *who* they are as a person. The tension between the professional and personal is the point of reference for the relationship of the researcher and participant. Within the context of research, then, where does the researcher stop being the researcher and start being a relational being? What does the researcher believe himself or herself to be? What values do they hold toward people in general? "The values and biases that we hold – our philosophy of life – influence the way we position ourselves with, or the stance we assume with, other people" (Anderson, 1997, p. 94). If the researcher views themselves as a "research professional," then the outcomes of their research process, data, and the relationship to their participants will follow suit. However, if the researcher holds a humanistic philosophy, and views himself or herself as a relational being who is *with* their participants, then their data will also follow suit. This philosophy of positioning is not something that is "done," as if guided by a particular theory. It is an *approach* to research, not so much a theory or a model of research itself (Anderson, 2007).

In collaborative practices, theory is something put aside for the purpose of the process and relational component of research. Shotter (2005) believes theory serves as an instructional map that guides practice. To lean too heavily on theory, however, also runs the risk of preunderstanding, undermining the uniqueness of research participants and the relationship within the process (Anderson, 2007). To emphasize a philosophy requires an ongoing analysis, inquiry, and reflection with the self and the research process (Anderson, 2007). This ongoing reflection on a philosophical stance is a constant experience in the researcher. Before starting the research process, during interviewing and data collection, and data analysis, the researcher is continuously analyzing themselves and the research. The research starts, then, with the researcher and their capacity to practice this philosophical stance.

Where to start

The collaborative therapist, like the qualitative researcher, starts the process with questions. If a therapist asks "Where do I start?" the answer is with questions. The same is true for researchers. Starting with questions is a specific position in which researchers use their natural curiosity and the conversation itself to guide their questions. From this positioning, questions are informed by the conversation, rather than *pre*formed (formed before the conversation starts). When researchers position themselves in such a way, they allow themselves to be led by the conversation, trusting the participant and the conversation to guide their questioning. From this place of being led, researchers are constantly moving with the participant's/client's language, ideas, phrases, demeanor, or affect.

Beginning the process with the mindset of questions is not an exercise or a strategy. Instead, similar to a Rogerian approach to therapy (Anderson, 2001), it is a position in which we are *with* the participants throughout the entire interaction. The entire phenomena of therapy, like research, becomes an experience where the conversation and data collection become a live organism that is constantly evolving, moving, changing, and rearranging in the moment. The researcher, then, is also changing, moving, and evolving with the conversation and participant. In the collaborative practices approach, the therapist, and therefore researcher, obtains a skill as a philosopher would—to continue conversation within the conversation itself (Goolishian & Anderson, 1987). We start, then, with questions as a part of the fluidity of the evolving conversation.

Conversation

Within the collaborative practices approach, conversation is more than merely talking. Once again, this approach poses philosophical questions about conversation: What makes a conversation successful, specifically to therapy?

What makes a research interview successful? What is the difference between talking to your best friend and talking to a therapist or a researcher? What is it about a good conversation where you lose track of time? What makes it a "good" conversation? To the focus of this chapter, can such qualities and practices be replicated? I argue, at the very least, they can be articulated.

In this approach to therapy, and there too research, the researcher deeply believes in the transformational power of conversation: dialogue, creating opportunity for self-agency, possibilities to inquire about your conversational partner, and the opportunity to be transformed themselves as researcher within the partnership. To be a relational being is to be in conversation (Shotter, 2004; Gergen, 2009). The collaborative researcher believes that conversation is the very essence of our being. "The primary human reality is person in conversation" (Harré, 1983, p. 58). Shotter (1993) also believes that

> Life by its very nature is dialogic. To live means to participate in dialogue: to ask questions, to heed, to respond, to agree, and so forth ... Those denied this possibility can, to say the least, be expected to feel humiliated and angered. (p. 62)

The researcher and participant both enter into conversation bringing elements of themselves: their humanity, beliefs, everyday life, and, importantly, self-identity (Anderson, 1997; Gergen, 1994). It is in conversation where the wholes of two people are entered and met. Conversation, then, becomes a joining of two people, rather than a superfluous exchange of mere words.

When two people join in conversation, they both risk becoming involved with one another, being influenced by the other, and will continue to carry the conversation with them when they leave it. No conversation is a single event, it is continuous in that it keeps living within each individual (Anderson, 1997). Each conversation has the power to impact both the researcher and participant.

The researcher is aware of the impact of conversation, and therefore enters it with purpose. The conversation, within this context, is intentional, purposeful, and has its own expectations (Anderson, 1997). Therefore, the collaborative researcher approaches the conversation with the intent of being *with* participants and the conversation itself.

Withness

There is a way of being with participants and clients where we are with them. The act and positioning of being with is described in the term *withness*. Shotter (Shotter, 1994, 2004, 2005) highlights the contrast between withness and aboutness thinking. Withness thinking calls for true dialogue, a genuine sense of being with our conversational partner, entering into their rapport, and even embodying the flow of thought. This is in direct opposition to thinking *about* someone, in which thinking about someone forces the person into an object, arguably with no consciousness, only the means to justify or support our own ends.

As we enter into conversation, questioning, data analysis, and gathering artifacts, we are constantly with our participants. This communicates the opposite of *having* participants, interviewing or analyzing data *about* the participants, or conducting therapy *for* the participants. Each conjunction other than *with* communicates action done to, for, about, or toward the participants. The collaborative philosophy instead emphasizes the positioning of with; we are conducting research with our participants, we are having therapy with our clients. "Withness conversation allows for voices to emerge that have often been stifled or withheld" (Hoffman, 2007, p. 70). Therefore, withness allows data to emerge from participant's voices because of the positioning of the researcher.

Anderson had the following to say about withness in the context of the researcher and their relationship with participants:

> I think it begins with your first contact with your participants, how you introduce yourself, how you meet and greet them, as someone whose experience and opinions you are interested in learning about, not as someone that you're trying to sell something to. You really want to think about the relationship from the very beginning. You want to be doing something with each other. You want them to have a sense of ownership – if you can imagine that. That this is also mine and I am helping him by answering his questions and giving him information. Taking the time to get to know your participants a little bit is important in building a good relationship, even if the relationship may be brief and temporary. Some researcher just gathers their participants, have them sign the form, and then start with their questions.
>
> You are inviting your partner/participant and asking them to be in a relationship with you, in conversation with you.
>
> If you think about it, like in therapy, you want someone to be your conversational partner. For me, it is the same in research as well. Therefore, you can see that I am much more interested in face to face in terms of talking to people rather than sending someone a questionnaire. (Personal conversation, September 9, 2019)

Not-knowing

Along the question of where to start, one of the primary assumptions of collaborative practices is the "not-knowing" stance (Anderson, 1997). Charmaz (2014) also suggests a similar approach to qualitative interviewing, where the researcher enters an interview with a mind that is open, curious, and willing to let the participant inform the process. Anderson presents not-knowing with more emphasis on the characteristics of the therapist, which can translate to the research process that the researcher can adopt.

The first is that the researcher is not in a position of the expert – the participant is. Clients in therapy and participants in research are the experts of their own stories. How they have constructed, lived, and experienced their lives is something we literally do not know. We come to know the lives of our participants only through conversation and by being *with* them. In the not-knowing stance, the process of being in conversation with research participants inherently places a challenged on what we think we know (Shotter & Gergen, 1984). Therefore, the researcher becomes an avid learner of the participant's life and assumes that he/she does not know as much as the participant knows about their own reality. If the researcher enters the conversation assuming they know something, anything, about their participant's experiences (or their potential to offer us data), the uniqueness of the participant's life lessens. As the researcher collects data, it is important to keep the not-knowing mindset, and not be driven by data preknowledge. "If we always see and hear things as we are accustomed to, then we will miss, neither see nor hear, that which is different and unique" (Anderson, 1997, p. 143). Therefore, with the not-knowing stance and learning from participants, the researcher enters the conversation with a large amount of uncertainty.

Uncertainty

Not knowing requires uncertainty. With the not-knowing stance, the researcher must be willing to doubt. Anderson (1997) promotes the following regarding the willingness to doubt:

> To be uncertain requires that we leave our dominant professional and personal discourses – what we know or think we know – suspended, hanging in front of us; that we be continually aware of, reflect on, and be open to examination by ourselves and others. This requires being able not to understand too quickly, to let go of early assumptions and stereotyping thoughts, to avoid premature understanding, to doubt what we think we know, and to prevent valuation our knowledge over a client's. Instead, we must be able to have an open mind, open to challenge and change, open to the unexpected. This is part for what allows us to have the room in our head for the other, the space for possibilities that is a critical aspect of dialogue. (pp. 134–135)

It is quite difficult for researchers to enter the process of their research without a set of already-acquired knowledge. For researchers that have piles of data, or who have collected extensive interviews, or who have ongoing projects that last for years, their professional discourses are that much more solidified. However, it is a philosophical practice to continually enter researcher with not-knowing, opening up ourselves to be led by the process rather than leading it. It is a risk to do so.

Risk

The researcher must also be willing to risk in the collaborative practices approach. The collaborative researcher must be willing to risk himself or herself, letting go of the comfort of his or her own knowledge, expertise, and conceptualizations of research itself. This risk makes one vulnerable, open to influence, and open to change. The researcher, then, risks being open to influence with their participants. Just like the therapist sets aside their own expertise in therapy, the researcher must set aside their research agenda and allow themselves be influenced and led by the participant—their lives, their experiences, and their own expertise.

When an agenda drives the researcher, they run the danger of early-arrived-at diagnostic impressions, interpretations, and treatment strategies (Gergen, Hoffman, & Anderson, 1995). Agendas mistakenly lead researchers. The research itself ought to drive the entire conversation of research from start to finish. The difference lies in the ability to trust the conversation within the context of research and risk following its direction. If researchers force an agenda onto their participants, or if they try too hard to advocate for their own outcomes, the process has lost its richness. The researcher must have the context of the research in mind, and at the same time let participants lead the conversation with the context of the research, which requires a strong sense of humility.

Humility

Suspending the researcher's knowledge, risking one's self in the process, and allowing participants to guide all require humility. The researcher is humble about what they know: research, methods, the process, or the topic being researchers. Suspending our expertise, or putting it on pause for the moments of research, is something intentionally done. The process of research, interviewing, or analyzing data, is not driven by our expertise, rather it is humbly put aside in order to allow participants own lives and experiences lead that process. The not-knowing stance, along with the humility it asks for, "prevents the artificial and premature closure that often results from a preplanned outcome. Operating from a position of *knowing* independently predetermines the possibilists and destroys the co-development of new meaning through stories and narratives…" (Anderson, 1997, p. 136).

What not-knowing is not

Not knowing does not mean a sense of dumbness or deceitful ignorance, being neutral, or not having opinions. The Collaborative researcher still maintains their sense of self, beliefs, stances, and overall epistemologies, even though they may differ from that of the participant. Not knowing does not mean we literally know nothing, but that we are *beyond* what we know; therefore new knowledge is to be determined based on our relationship with our participants (Derrida, 1978).

As relational beings, the researcher cannot be a blank screen, idealess, without opinion or biases, or completely neutral. Instead, the researcher is aware of these and brings them into the research process – personal and professional experiences and knowledges. The researcher must be able to collaborate with all they bring to the research; challenged and be challenged in their beliefs and biases. Collaborating and approaching research within this philosophical stance means committing to true dialogue; sharing and exchanging our biases and beliefs with that of the participants in an egalitarian posture, where our knowledge does not supersede that of the participants.

The not-knowing stance asks for a specific posture, rather than an approach to conversation (Bruner, 1990). Derived from the practice of therapy, this posture considers the therapist and researcher's expertise. Instead of focusing on diagnosing, treatment, or the researcher's agenda, the focus is on the understanding of the client and participants. There is a shift in the efforts to structure, formulate, or be "experts," to allowing ourselves to be driven by the need to understand.

Change through conversation

Another primary philosophy of the collaborative practices model is that change happens in conversation (Anderson, 1997). Therefore, in therapy, conversation becomes the primary "technique." As Anderson states, conversation is more than just talking, it is our very essence; how we construct our language and how our language is constructed is seen through conversation. Conversation becomes very important to the process of research because it is a means of expressing the entire being of the individual. The researcher ought to approach data collection, or the idea of data itself, through the philosophy of conversation. When we enter into conversation, we are witnessing our participants change in front of us. In turn, by being in the conversation, the researcher also changes. The researcher is invested, emotionally connected, and willing to be a part of their participant's story; they too become a part of the data. Within this philosophy, data is more than an accumulation of statements that support our agenda; data is the outcomes of two people in conversation, changing with each other.

Dialogical space

The opportunity for conversation involves a dialogical space (Anderson, 1997). Dialogical space refers to the metaphorical space within the conversation itself (Anderson, 1997; Anderson & Goolishian, 1992; Goolishian & Anderson, 1987). Both the researcher and participant become partners in dialogical space, in which they both create room within themselves and the conversation to entertain multiple ideas, beliefs, and opinions. In order to begin the process of dialogical space, the researcher must set aside their own thoughts, or at the very least allow room for other thoughts to be entertained. The abstract concept of the conversation itself also needs to be present, where we imagine the conversation as a present party that holds both research and participant, along with their ideas and thoughts.

True conversation, however, holds dialogues, not monologues. A monologue, or an exchange of monologues, is a static, linear process that excludes other ideas outside the monologue being shared. When agendas drive research, we tend to receive monologues from participants, rather than hosting a dialogue. Dialogical space requires mutual exploration and development of conversation.

Mutual exploration and development

Within the collaborative practices approach, the process of therapy is as a mutual search to understand clients and their struggles (Anderson, 1997). In this process, both the researcher and participant join in *shared inquiry*. Both the researcher and participant explore, together, the meanings and realities the participant brings to the research conversation. Through mutual exploration, the researcher takes the role of a genuine learner. As the researcher expresses their genuine curiosity through questions, the participant is invited to join the researcher in the process of inquiring about the research at hand. As this process unravels, the researcher and participant form a *conversational partnership*, or a mutual relationship in which monological processes turn into dialogical processes.

Mutual exploration is necessary to develop understandings that reflect and inform the personal, first-person narrative of clients. Mutual exploration is also necessary to gather rich data. The researcher must also present themselves from a position of equality, nonhierarchical (see Chapter 8 for further discussion on hierarchy). As the researcher approaches the participant from a position of a genuine learner, the participant is invited into the data collection process, or the conversation. The process of collecting data, then, becomes a *conversational partnership*, where both researcher and participant equally engage in data collection and formation.

Conversational background

When two people are engaged in conversation, mutually explore each other's dialogue, and are genuinely curious about the dialogue at hand, it creates a present third party. Two people are engaged in the conversation with the presence of the conversation itself. Anderson (1997) refers to this as conversational background. There is an invisible, abstract presence in which two people are engaged: conversation itself. According to the therapeutic approach, this is where change happens. According to research practices, this is where *rich* data is gathered.

For the researcher, approaching interviewing with conversational background can produce a richer interview process and, therefore, richer data. A common question is how does one do this. This is the wrong question. Conversational background is not something ones *does*, as if it is a fancy trick to be called upon. Rather, it is something that *happens* by way of our own selves. The researcher is the kind of person that naturally engages, is curious, and genuinely wants to be in conversation.

Conversational background requires a sense of belonging to the conversation and dialogue, making a distinction from an exchange of monologues (Anderson, 1997). When we belong to the conversation, we trust the generative process in being genuinely curious about our conversation partners, inviting them to express and share their experiences, stories, and internal dialogues. By belonging, we also place trust in participants, believing in their ability to join in dialogue. True possibilities arise within conversational background. When conversation is fluid, shifting, and generative itself, the conversation has the *possibility* to go anywhere. Therefore, the possibility of data is exponentiated when the researcher and participant engage in conversational background, true dialogue.

The qualitative interview becomes a conversational reality, a space for conversation. According to Shotter (1993), conversation is a space where different lives, different ideas, and different experiences can become a single unit, where the other tries to understand and live with the other for the moment, one turbulent flow on conscious activity. Conversation, then, is also a metaphorical space where the different backgrounds within each conversational partner come together to become one. Consider Anderson's (personal communication, September 9, 2019) reflections:

> The background is the conversation. It is important to keep in mind that the background of the conversation includes broader and local cultural discourses, people's everyday life experiences, and professional discourses. Each person, the professional and the person you are interviewing or having a conversation with, are having conversation with so many other people that influence their ideas and what they think. In terms of the conversational background, basically, I talk these days in terms of space, the type of space you want to create. I mention the notion of metaphorical space and what kind of space you want to create; that is part of the background in which the conversation happens.
>
> Maybe we can think of it as the atmosphere, or environment, that you are hoping to create with and for yourself and another person, that is more rather than less inviting of them to join you in. This connects with

the notion of withness, being and engaging with another person. There's a very interesting Japanese concept call Ba. Ba refers to an environment in which is similar to the notion of withness. It is the kind of environment and space we want to create and invite others into.

It starts with the person; it begins with the first contact, early on. When you think about the conversational background, what would someone think about their preconceptions about a person who is a therapist, or who is a researcher? Not that you will ask them that, but we need to consider it before we enter into therapy and research.

It is about how a researcher can avoid being intrusive. I think you want to be careful about the questions you ask, how you pose them; the relationship is part of the background to those questions.

Other conversational philosophies

Host and guest

The collaborative practices approach views the therapy process as one of a host–guest (Anderson, 2012). The therapist enters therapy as a guest, where we are the guest in the client's story and experiences. The researcher can also enter the research process as a guest. Where the therapist is limited to one hour at a time as a guest, the researcher has the privilege of interviewing, transcribing, and analyzing data. Therefore, the entire process of research is practiced as a guest, as a privilege to be a part of someone's story and experiences. The participant, then, is the host. They are hosting us in their lives. This is a different mindset and way of being with clients and participants. When the researcher enters with a mindset of a guest, we treat the entire process differently, as if we were respecting someone's home in which we are guests. When participants are seen and treated as hosts, the respect used encourages them into richer conversation.

> As the researcher, you are the host of your guest, the participant. In addition, at the same time, I find it helpful to think they are hosting me. In other words, they are hosting me in their life. I do not want to be an intrusive guest, in their life. Therefore, it is important to think about what kind of host and guest you want to be. What will enhance the potential for the kind of relationship and conversation you hope for. (H. Anderson, personal communication, January 9, 2019)

Maintain questioning attitude

By keeping an attitude of continuous questioning, the researcher acts as a continuous consumer. It is not an attitude of cynicism, critique, or more importantly, judgment. It is an attitude in which the therapist is a constant consumer. When in conversation with a person, we are in the position where we *want* something they have and can offer us: their story. When a conversation is approached with this attitude, the positioning of inquiry also changes.

The collaborative researcher can benefit from this attitude in that as a consumer, we are in the market for data: a person's story. Data, then, should be approached with the attitude of constant questioning. Whether it is an interview, documents, artifacts, pictures, or paintings, the researcher approaches all with the attitude of questioning, consuming the data presented.

Avoid generalizing

A way to maintain a questioning attitude is to avoid generalizing, or not knowing before meeting research participants. Avoiding generalizing requires a large amount of awareness, introspection, and depth of mind in the researcher. How we view the world influences the way we ask questions. A part of our worldview includes generalizations. Therapists commonly enter therapy with generalizations such as diagnoses, definitions of dysfunction, attachment, or relationship systems. Even though these concepts are important to therapy, when taken into the therapy process, they guide inquiry.

When we enter the research process, it is a common practice to begin with an established theory, epistemology, or ontological assumption. Even though this practice is common and sometimes needed in the research process, it can be a danger to inquiry. Our own epistemologies and ontological assumptions have the power to potentially guide the research process in the wrong direction, meaning the direction not led by the participant but our own line of questioning. When we avoid generalizing and maintain a constant attitude of questioning, the possibility for organic, rich inquiry presents itself.

Privilege local knowledge

Approaching therapy and research without generalizing communicates privileging our participant's knowledge. As therapists and researchers, when we enter with an already-set group of knowledge, assumptions, epistemologies, and diagnoses, we run the risk of devaluing our conversational partners' stories. We assume privilege when we carry generalizations into each respective process: we give privilege to our own knowledge rather than upholding that of our participants. In turn, data is compromised. Data ought to influence the researcher, rather than the researcher influence the data.

Knowledge and language as interactive and social processes

Language is an interactive process in that the knowledge gained from conversation influences both the researcher and participant; both are transformed. As a collaborative researcher, our knowledge, assumptions, and inquiry, in general, are all guided by our participants. Conversation itself drives our inquiry. Therefore, our positioning is flexible and open to what we are presented with. As participants share their stories, and as we consume their stories, our questioning becomes driven, redirected, or spontaneously led. Our inquiry follows where our participants lead, as well as the flow of the conversation.

Asking not to interrupt the flow of conversation

Research inquiry, when conceptualized collaboratively, means to maintain a certain flow: the process of asking questions, being led by participants, and further inquiry are all based on participants' stories, holding an organic flow to process itself. The conversation is not interrupted by our own agenda, preconceived knowledges, or generalizations. Instead it flows from our participants' stories, our own curiosities and continuous consumption of their stories, and our participants' engagement in our curiosity of their stories.

Relational expertise

Harlene Anderson refers to the collaborative practices approach as relational expertise. The researcher and therapist are both experts in relationships, meaning they both invite conversation. Anderson explains this as never having met a person that is not a "talker." Rather than viewing participants as people who are withdrawn, not having a lot to say, or shy in general, the approach focuses on how we engage them. It is about asking the right questions and remaining curious about the right things: their stories. When we engage participants from our own agenda, when our curiosity is driven by our own assumptions, we are inviting the wrong relationship. On the research agenda, Anderson (personal communication, January 9, 2019) has the following to say:

> Some students I have advised start out with a specific question, but then they begin to modify their question or questions, or sometimes they find that their question has no relevance to the participant as they begin to engage in collaboration and their relationship with their participants. It is being able to hold your overall research question, aim, or agenda, tentatively. The agenda is the map you start out with, but as you get off on your journey, you take some detours. If you are influenced at all by a collaborative perspective, as you begin asking your questions, the responses that come begin to lead the researcher and the participant in a different direction.
>
> You also have to take into consideration the context in which you are doing your research inquiry. If that is that context of the university,

then what are the university's expectations and requirements of you, particularly if you are doing it as a degree requirement? Therefore, that begins with the conversation you have with your advisor, and I think it is important, if possible, to have an advisor that fits with your own preference, your conceptual framework from which you ant to approach your research. How to navigate having one foot in one world and another foot in different world. The relationships expand into the contexts of research you are practicing in as well as the relationship with the participant.

Being public

As a part of relational expertise, the researcher also makes themselves public. When we engage with participants, and when our curiosity is driven by their stories, we add to the process with our own stories as well. There is a sense of mutual engagement when we make ourselves public, which also contributes to efforts in minimizing hierarchy and power. Both can be easily dangerous to the collaborative process. Listening and speaking are equally important. Therefore, the inner thought and dialogue of the research are an important aspect of the conversation (Anderson, 2005).

Feminist critique

A common feminist critique of therapy, and most therapeutic approaches, is the power difference present in the therapy relationship. There is inherent hierarchy in therapy and research, between therapist and client and researcher and participant. The therapist, with their expertise, knowledge, and clinical insight, naturally holds a sense of power over their clients. The researcher, with their driving agenda for scholarly activity, also holds a sense of power over their participants. The collaborative therapist tries to minimize hierarchy as much as possible. A way to try to minimize that hierarchy is to be public, disclosing information from the side of the researcher and therapist.

Approach to research

This section offers a brief overview of a research process using the collaborative approach as offered by collaborative language systems in postmodern therapies. The approach intentionally removes the wording of "method," as method implies a grouping of procedures in which the researcher *must* follow to subscribe to that chosen method. Instead, I am choosing to call this an approach so that the truest sense of collaboration, originally intended by Goolishian and Anderson (1987), can be practiced in a research process.

Asking questions

The collaborative researcher is one of particular interest to me in that the approach to therapy is unique and challenging to the therapist. The therapist is charged with a responsibility to conversation, curiosity, and willingness to genuinely engage in dialogue. With the preceding outlined tenets of collaborative language systems, conversation is more simply done in the context of therapy; the conversation can naturally and organically generate dialogue within such a space. Clients can present their issues, and the therapist can engage with curiosity, spontaneity, and openness to the possibilities of directions of the therapeutic conversation. As mentioned before, the context of research is somewhat different than that of therapy.

The challenge for the researcher comes in the ability to engage in fluid, spontaneous conversation. This particular challenge comes by way of a research agenda and asking "research questions." True to the model of therapy, the therapist does not enter the therapy conversation with an agenda, or a set of preplanned questions that drive the therapy session. Therefore, they let the clients guide the conversation. However, both the client and therapist start from somewhere.

Like the model of therapy, formulating research questions starts with curiosity. Like the therapist, the researcher is genuinely curious, entering the research questioning by way of not-knowing. Not only do collaborative researchers ask questions from a deep sense of curiosity, they ask questions about the questions they are asking to ensure the questions are formulated from curiosity rather than an agenda. For example, Gehart, Tarragona, and Bava (2007) argue that asking research questions is an aspect of the researcher's "learner" position: "What should be studied? Which questions are important? How best do we answer these? How do we make sense of the answers?" (p. 375). I add: How can I ask these questions so that the participant's voice will be leading the answers rather than my own curiosity overpowering their contribution?

A research question, or a set of overarching research questions, ought to be examined by the researcher, or if they are working for a university or institution, by their advisors or governing body. The researcher has the responsibility to examine their sense of curiosity in their questions, more so than their loyalty to their research agenda. The research question starts with a desire to learn, curiosity, and, more importantly, the openness to be led. The not-knowing stance and the learner position are a great place for the researcher to start asking research questions. Like therapy, the positioning easily translates to formulating a research question.

A warning the collaborative researcher must heed: Be mindful of your relationship to your subject matter (Gehart et al., 2007). The collaborative researcher strives for the learner position and a deep understanding of their research subject. This requires a specific relationship with their subject matter, one that is intentionally detached as a researcher, opposite of the scientific method that strives for objectivity.

To ask a research question is the ultimate sense of curiosity, where the collaborative researcher is best suited for given their positionings. When I train beginning therapists who don't know what to ask in therapy, I offer them this advice: Be curious and care. You cannot go wrong with that both in therapy and research.

Interviewing and data gathering

The qualitative interview is one of the most common efforts in gathering data. The special part of the research process, in my opinion, is the interaction with human subjects in order to gather data. The collaborative researcher approaches the interview differently than most other interview processes.

One unique stance the collaborative researcher takes in interviewing is the idea of *who* the researcher is. True to the spirit of collaboration, the label "researcher" and "participant" offer an amount of hierarchy that can potentially communicate some sort of expertise on the part of the researcher. Therefore, the collaborative researcher ought to examine this notion of researcher–participant. Instead, the interviewing process and conversation ought to take place not between a researcher and a participant, but between two researchers (Gehart et al., 2007). Gehart et al. (2007) further describe such a relationship as follows:

> Both the designated researcher and the invited researcher jointly participate in the dialogical process. They are in conversation about the topics of inquiry and each can contribute to its focus, which is usually informed by the conversation itself as it unfolds. (p. 377)

Like the therapy process, the researcher practices *being public*, emphasizing the stance of co-construction and the generative process of data. As the researcher listens to answers, they must be public about their interpretations, understandings, and own thoughts, also being mindful of their own preunderstandings. Even though having preunderstanding is somewhat unavoidable, the researcher can make efforts to minimize this during the interview process. The researcher can lessen their preunderstanding by *maintaining coherence* (Anderson, 1997). By maintaining coherence, the researcher uses the participant's words, language, tone, speed, and volume, all in effort to stay in sync with their stories and at the same time allowing their story to lead the research interview.

What about a set of interview questions? Specifically, for students of a university or for faculty members that need to answer to an institutional review board (IRB), a set of interview questions are needed. However, the collaborative researcher has many options in formulating the research interview. They can start with one question: What do you think my research team needs to know about this topic? (See Appendix A and B for examples.) With such an approach, the researcher only needs one, vague, loose sense of curiosity about a research topic, trusting the process of conversation to generate data. The "interview questions," then, emerge from what is being shared between the researchers rather than a scripted set of questions systematically asked to each participant.

Another option with slightly more structure is where the researcher can enter the interview with "starter questions," and ask the participant on input of the accuracy or helpfulness of the questions in answering the original research question (see Appendix C for example) (Fiensilver, Murphy, & Anderson, 2007).

I see the possibilities of interviews along a continuum of conversation. At one end, there is a structured interview, that asks the same questions to each participant. On the other end, you have a set of two questions, for example in phenomenology research studies (what did participants experience and how did they experience it), with more room for conversation and ad lib questions. I view all of these options as conversational possibilities, where the research is either shaping conversation or is generating conversation. Like therapy, the collaborative approach to interviewing has the same goal: to generate conversation and knowledge and understanding.

Data analysis

According to the collaborative approach to therapy, conversation is continuously happening. Therefore, meaning-making is continuously happening. When thinking about data analysis, or "making sense of the data," that process is also continuously happening. All meaning-making is a social activity (Lemke, 1995), which also pertains to the process of data analysis: the collaborative researcher is making sense of the data or the conversation.

The process of analysis starts when the researcher decides to formulate a research question, when the researcher is gathering literature, and when the writing starts early in the process. Therefore, the "making sense" of the research question, and therefore analysis, starts before the actual interview and postinterview data. In fact, the analysis process begins internally, when the researcher is *thinking* about a research question.

Like therapy, Anderson (1997) believes in the internal dialogue being a form of conversation; we are putting our thoughts into words through the process of conversation. There is a thought-into-words process (Vygotsky, 1986) important to the collaborative researcher, which Anderson calls *expanding and saying the unsaid*. The process of analyzing unravels throughout the entire research process: "forming, saying, and expanding the unsaid and the yet-to-be-said – the development, through dialogue, of new meanings, themes, narratives and histories – from which new self-descriptions may arise" (Anderson, 1997, p. 118).

With this in mind, data analysis cannot be separated from the overall research process. New knowledge is continuously happening throughout, not only in analyzing data. The emphasis is on the co-construction of data, the meaning generated between the researchers, the literature, their advisors, and their own thoughts. As researchers organize and gather information, they take their gathered knowledge into the interview process. Another warning to the collaborative researcher: knowledge gathered through literature, advising, or IRB direction is not *pre*knowledge taken into the interview process, instead, it is cumulative curiosity, mounting from the previous conversations taken into the conversation during the interview.

Postinterview, then, is a continuation of the gathered knowledge, and therefore cumulative curiosity. Data gathered and generated from the interviews is a continuation of curiosity the researcher has gathered throughout the entire process. Analyzing their data is also a continuation of the meaning created from such conversations. From thinking about research, to asking research questions, to collaborating with their advisors, to interviewing, the researcher is entertaining multiple conversations, therefore, multiple possibilities for meaning to emerge. The interview, also co-constructed, also becomes a source of meaning-making, which in turn results in data. To analyze such data, the researcher continues the process of conversation: data analysis is one more conversation the researcher entertains in the process.

Conclusion

I believe the collaborative language systems approach to therapy to be one of the most foundational postmodern approaches to therapy. Anderson paved the way for postmodern therapists and thinkers. The approach to therapy offers many philosophical stances and underpinnings for the therapist that the researcher can also utilize in their practices. The philosophy of conversation itself is a stance the researcher can be mindful of: the *way of being*, the possibilities of conversational space, and the suspending of our knowledge in order to engage in conversation – turning monologue into dialogue within the metaphorical space of conversation.

The specific approaches to therapy are also beneficial to the research process. Central to postmodern therapy overall is the not-knowing stance, where the researcher enters into the process with the practice of suspending their expertise, knowledge, researcher agenda, and overall assumptions of the very topic they are researching. Although not completely new to the postmodern conversation of knowledge, this chapter specifically offered characteristics of the not-knowing stance and articulated the personhood of the researcher that espouses such a stance: humility, risk, and uncertainty of the possibilities of the conversation.

Like other postmodern therapy approaches, the collaborative approach calls for a way of being. Being in conversation, espousing the not-knowing stance, and engaging in conversation, these are all qualities of the researcher; it is who they are. Instead of tricks that are used to enhance our research or our data, this approach calls for a certain type of researcher. A similar argument will be made when considering the following approach of narrative therapy, of which I am labeling the narrative interviewer.

References

Anderson, H. (1997). *Conversation, language, and possibilities: A postmodern approach to therapy*. New York, New York: Basic Books.
Anderson, H. (2001). Postmodern collaborative and person-centered therapies: What would Carl Rogers say? *Journal of Family Therapy*, 23, 339–360.
Anderson, H. (2005). Myths about "not-knowing." *Family Process*, 44(4), 497–504.
Anderson, H. (2007). The heart and spirit of collaborative therapy: The philosophical stance—"A way of being" in relationship and conversation. In H. Anderson & D. Gehart (Eds.), *Collaborative therapy: Relationships and conversations that make a difference* (pp. 43–61). New York: Routledge.
Anderson, H. (2012). Collaborative relationships and dialogic conversation: Ideas for relationally responsive practice. *Family Process*, 51, 8–24.
Anderson, H., & Goolishian, H. (1992). The client is the expert: A not-knowing approach to therapy. In S. McNamee & K.J. Gergen (Eds.), *Therapy as social construction*. Newbury Park, CA: Sage.
Bruner, J. (1990). *Acts of meaning*. Cambridge, MA: Harvard University Press.
Charmaz, K. (2014). *Constructing grounded theory*. Los Angeles: Sage.
Derrida, J. (1978). *Writing and difference*. Chicago: University of Chicago Press.
Fiensilver, D., Murphy, E., & Anderson, H. (2007). Women at a turning point: A transformational feast. In H. Anderson & D. Gehart (Eds.), *Collaborative therapy: Relationships and conversations that make a difference* (pp. 269–290). Routledge/Taylor & Francis Group.
Gehart, D., Tarragona, M., & Bava, S. (2007). A collaborative approach to research and inquiry. In H. Anderson & D. Gehart (Eds.), *Collaborative therapy: Relationships and conversations that make a difference* (pp. 367–387). New York: Routledge.
Gergen, K. J. (1994). *Realities and relationships: Soundings in social construction*. Cambridge, MA: Harvard University Press.
Gergen, K. J. (2009). *Relational being: Beyond self and community*. New York: Oxford University Press.
Gergen, K. J., Hoffman, L., & Anderson, H. (1995). Is diagnosis a disaster: A constructionist trialogue. In F. Kaslow (Ed.), *Handbook of relational diagnosis* (pp. 102–118). New York: John Wiley & Sons.
Goolishian, H. A., & Anderson, H. (1987). Language systems and therapy: An evolving idea. *Psychotherapy: Theory, Research, Practice, Training*, 24, 529–538.
Harré, R. (1983). *Personal being: A theory for individual psychology*. Oxford: Basil Blackwell.
Hoffman, L. (2007). The art of "withness": A new bright edge. In H. Anderson & D. Gehart (Eds.), *Collaborative therapy: Relationships and conversations that make a difference* (pp. 63–80). New York: Routledge.

Lemke, J. L. (1995). *Textual politics: Discourse and social dynamics.* Bristol, PA: Taylor & Francis.
Shotter, J. (1993). *Conversational realities: Constructing life through language.* London: Sage.
Shotter, J. (1994). *On the edge of social constructionism: "Withness-thinking" versus "aboutness-thinking."* London: KCC Foundation.
Shotter, J. (2004). Acknowledging unique others: Ethics, "expressive realism," and social constructionism. *Journal of Constructive Psychology,* 18, 103–130.
Shotter, J. (2005). *Wittgenstein in practice: His philosophy of beginnings, and beginnings, and beginnings.* London: KCC Foundation.
Shotter, J., & Gergen, K. (Eds.) (1984). *Texts of identity.* London: Sage.
Vygotky, L. S. (1986). *Thought and language* (rev. ed.) (A. Kozuli, Trans). Cambridge, MA: MIT Press. (Originial work published 1934).

5

THE NARRATIVE INTERVIEWER

Introduction

This discussion will center on narrative therapy, its philosophical underpinnings, and its practices. Narrative therapy and the narrative therapist will be analyzed in order for the qualitative researcher to benefit from its practices and ideals. This chapter does not intend to propose a methodological approach to qualitative research; the narrative philosophies can be applied to all approaches of qualitative research. As such, this chapter will apply the philosophies of the narrative therapy approach to the qualitative researcher.

Narrative therapy was founded by Michael White, who was interested in the way people formed stores of their lives, but especially how society formed stories for people. Rooted deep in the philosophies of French philosopher Michel Foucault, narrative therapy studies people within the context of power, knowledge, politics, and privilege.

Foucault studied the different ways Western society categorized and "labeled" people: sick, madness, sexuality, and criminality. Foucault believed that people have power in society as it relates to different dominant discourses in society. Discourses, according to Hare-Mustin (1994), are ideas, statements, practices, and institutional systems that all share common values. Discourses have the power to sustain worldviews, or the way society views certain areas humanity. According to Freedman and Combs (1996), "discourses powerfully shape a person's choices about what life events can be storied and how they should be storied. This is as true for therapists [and researchers] as it is for the people who consult with them" (p. 43). Therefore, the people that have enough power in society also have the power to formulate discourses that shape society, discourses of what it means to be "sick," therefore separating them from the people that have the power to shape such discourse. As a result, the ones in power also had the ability to influence how "sick" people lived, that is, in mad houses, institutionalized, or exiled from society (Foucault, 1975).

Foucault also believed that knowledge and power were inseparable. Discourses in society deem what is true and right. Dominant discourses hold the popular truths that society lives by and accept as right. Discourses, then, have the *power* to hold knowledge, or what we *know* to be right, true, and acceptable in society. Those that have the power to control discourses also control knowledge (Freedman & Combs, 1996).

White, along with Foucault, believed that people begin to internalize these dominant discourses set by society. Most of these discourses can be problematic and destructive to individuals. When individuals internalize these discourses, the discourses themselves begin to story one's experiences, making the discourses truths of our identities. According to White (1991), people are "actively participating in their performance of stories that she finds unhelpful, unsatisfying, and dead-ended … these stories do not sufficiently encapsulate the person's lived experience or are very significantly contradicted by important aspects of the person's lived experience" (p. 14).

This is a central belief to the narrative therapist: there is *always* a live experience outside of the dominant discourses we tend to espouse and internalize, the discourses that have marginalized individuals outside the boundaries of the dominant story. To this end, the narrative therapist also believes that "problems" happen when we are indoctrinated into narrow and self-defeating views of ourselves (Nichols & Davis, 2017), which is the result of internalizing destructive, dominant discourses.

The qualitative researcher, like the narrative therapist, would do well to also espouse these beliefs, entering research and interviews believing that participants do have experiences outside their discourses. For example, in a recent study I have been a part of, my research team and I interviewed men who had extramarital affairs. It would be a hinderance to the participant, and to the data collection process, to believe that the participant had an affair based on traditional thoughts that research and media have portrayed: chauvinism, self-centeredness, a failing relationship, and so on.

Even the research agenda has the possibility of hindering this process if researchers do not allow room for participants' experience to determine the process. Researchers run the risk of overly influencing the data as a result of relying too heavily on the research process: not deviating from their research question, not adjusting interview questions to participants' experiences, or not allowing the process to be organic.

It is a different approach to data collection and the research process itself when the researcher believes that their participant has experiences outside of their extramarital affair, or experiences that are driven by the dominant discourse of a "dysfunctional relationship." When we approach participants with the beliefs and practices outlined in the following, the result is a different, richer data.

Politics of power

In narrative therapy, the therapist is primarily concerned with asking questions. White and Epston (1990) argue that questions are the primary vehicle for conversation in therapy. Questions, then, are the means by which the therapist gathers elements of the clients' lives, stories, and experiences. Gathering information leads the therapists to separate clients' "problems" from the clients' themselves.

The narrative therapist, then, is an expert in inquiry. They know what questions to ask that help clients to see the influence destructive stories have had in their lives. The narrative therapist's expertise also lies in knowing how to ask questions in which they themselves believe that the person they are working with is resilient, can create different and preferred storylines, and is not their own problem. The philosophical stance of believing that people are overall and inherently "good" is a position the narrative therapist takes. It is communicated in their means of inquiry.

A way of approaching therapy is the belief that throughout the process of discovering stories and experiences of the client, the therapist becomes a part of the client's story, hence the co-construction or co-authoring. The therapist is a part of the client's story by way of being the one who asks and learns from the client. By being an active learner of the client, and by way of the client deconstructing their problematic stories, both the therapist and the client are changed. The same holds true for qualitative research, specifically narrative research. When both parties are engaged in the storyline and the process of inquiry, both will learn and change in the encounter (Pinnegar & Daynes, 2007).

The narrative therapist, and the qualitative researcher, uses and believes in a set of ideals and techniques used in therapy. I will outline the specific techniques and describe them in a way that pertains to the qualitative researcher.

Narrative therapy is rooted in listening. The following techniques are all a form of listening that the narrative therapist believes in. More than merely hearing words being spoken, the narrative therapist, and therefore the qualitative researcher, listens in specific ways.

Interpretation

Therapists and counselors have the proclivity to listen for clinical things, areas of the clients' lives that stick out that can be addressed in the process of therapy. Be it diagnoses, relationship dysfunction, erosion of boundaries, self-defeating thoughts, or among a plethora of other therapeutic contextual issues, these are things we can "do" something about, process through, or try to change. The therapist can be victim of the discourse of therapy, and so the researcher the discourse of research (White & Denborough, 2011).

When a therapist listens with an ear for diagnoses, they will find them. When a researcher asks questions driven by their research agenda, they will also find them. Both run the risk of limiting the unique experience of the client and participant. Freedman and Combs (1996) believe the following regarding the narrative therapist:

> When we meet people for the first time, we want to understand the meaning of their stories for them. This means turning our backs on "expert" filters: not listening for complaints; not "gathering" the pertinent-to-us-as-experts bits of diagnostic information interspersed in their stories; not hearing their anecdotes as matrices within which resources are embedded; not listening for surface hints about what the core problem "really" is; and not comparing the selves they portray in their stories to normative standards. ...
>
> If our listening is guided by a theory that say people must "feel their pain" in order to be whole, we will bring forth painful stories. If we have a special interest in disempowerment as an issue, we will invite people to tell us stories of how they have been deprived of power. We can end up making the very thing that people came to therapy to escape more real, more vivid, and more oppressive. (pp. 44–46)

Just like in therapy, the researcher also runs the risk of further oppression when their listening and interpretation are guided by their own "theory" or agendas.

This is a difficult line for the researcher to follow: How does a researcher not follow their research agenda in order to allow participants their own unique experience? The answer lies in the researcher's beliefs. These techniques, the interpretation of an individual's experience in a way that understands their experience for its uniqueness and oppression by dominant discourses, are more than techniques, they are *who* the researcher is.

If the researcher listens for and interprets things according only to their research agenda, they will inevitably leave other aspects out. Which is why *not-knowing* is so important to the narrative therapist and the qualitative researcher.

Not-knowing

As mentioned before, the not-knowing stance was largely introduced to therapy by Harlene Anderson and Harold Goolishian in collaborative language systems. The not-knowing stance, as adopted by narrative therapy, is similar in that the therapist is not the "expert" bringing their expertise, their already-knowing position to therapy. Instead, they approach the process of therapy with a preunderstanding, being informed by their clients. This approach does not communicate "I don't know anything." The therapist and researcher are experts in the process of therapy and of inquiry itself.

The qualitative researcher that espouses narrative therapy beliefs is the expert on stories, discourses, and the way people are oppressed by such dominant, problematic stories society has constructed. The researcher is also an expert in social constructionism, as believed by narrative therapists. They know how interactions and relationships form individual knowledge, and how society promotes dominant stories and that they are collectively internalized by individuals.

By not-knowing, we listen for discourses in our participants lives, but also for discourses in our own lives. As we listen and ask questions, we are also questioning the assumptions we are making, therefore trying to not know what the experiences of our participants are. We ask ourselves:

> Am I understanding what it feels like to be this person in this situation, or am I beginning to fill in the gaps in her story with unwarranted assumptions? What more do I need to know in order to step into this person's shoes? (Freedman & Combs, 1996, p. 45)

Not-knowing generates a curiosity that *feels* different when in conversation. When we are genuinely curious and want to know more about the stories and discourses and experiences of our participants' lives, they feel it. And the result is seen in the rich data that is collected.

Deconstructive listening

Deconstructive listening is a logical next step to not-knowing in narrative therapy. By *deconstructing*, we as therapists and researchers are interested in exploring meaning: symbols, words, texts, contexts (Derrida, 1988). With the postmodern bias, it is impossible to find "one true meaning" of any word, symbol, text, or context. Each individual will inevitably experience something differently than the next. Therefore, trying to understand what one individual experiences, what something means to them, is an attempt to fill in gaps of understanding. In other words, "my experience is as such, but yours may be different, so let me ask about it."

When we listen deconstructively, we *believe* that one story has many meanings, and that one person's experiences is not the next person's. Even as people speak, the words they choose to describe their stories may mean something different to us as the researcher or therapist. Asking for clarification, meaning to such words, or, more importantly, not assuming we know what they mean by their choice of words, is crucial to deconstructing. This process also helps participants generate deeper meaning to their stories. When we ask deconstructing questions, the storytelling process slows down, participants focus on meanings of their experiences, and their narrative becomes more enriched and their story has more meaning.

Co-construction of knowledge is an important part of deconstructive listening. Gergen (1985) believed that the co-construction of knowledge was a social interaction form of inquiry "by which people come to describe, explain, or otherwise account for the world (including themselves) in which they live" (p. 266). As the researcher listens deconstructively and asks clarifying questions, meanings in the participants story become co-constructed through such interaction. Inquiry itself is a social process of data collection. The deconstruction process, together with the researcher and participant, provides a richer story, description, and data.

People are separate from their problems/externalization

The idea that a client is separate from their problem was foundational to narrative and postmodern therapies. Michael White (1987, 1988, 1989, 2007) introduced the idea by believing that his clients were not the problems they brought into therapy; they were instead being impacted, influenced, or struggling with that problem. There is a clear separation from the client as a person and their reported problem: depression, bipolar, codependency, alcoholism, dysfunction ... I could go on.

Like most postmodern therapies, there is something that is important to this "technique": it is not a therapeutic technique and it is only limited to therapists. Therefore, this applies especially to the qualitative researcher. Externalization, believing that people are separate from their problems, is something that is personified by the therapist and also researcher. This is who the person is rather than a fancy trick.

The qualitative researcher would do well to espouse this belief. When we believe that people are separate from their problems, we naturally ask different questions and listen for different aspects of their lives. Instead of listening for relapses from an "alcoholic," we listen for areas of their lives that are not influenced by alcohol. Instead of listening about an affair committed by someone that has been unfaithful in their marriage, we listen for their struggle against infidelity. Listening in an externalizing way presents more possibilities for our participants to produce different data, not the sort that is carried by labels.

Freedman and Combs (1996) offer a list of externalizing questions: What is problematic here? What is the nature of this problem? How does it show itself? What does it feel like for this person to have this problem in his or her life? What is influencing this person from having experiences he or she would prefer?

By asking these questions, overtly and internally, we begin to perceive our participants as separate from their problem. As a researcher, externalization is applied in viewing the participant separate from the phenomenon we are studying. To continue with the infidelity study, the narrative interviewer (different from narrative research methods) would do well to view their participants as separate from the acts they have committed, for example, separate from the discourses and narratives that maintain a problematic view of infidelity.

According to Nichols and Davis (2017), "externalizing helps clinicians [and researchers] develop a more sympathetic view of clients who engage in 'inappropriate behavior'" (p. 276). When the researcher practices this belief and views their participants separate from the phenomenon being studied, participants will follow and view themselves as separate from the thing they are being studied for. With such separation, when the participant believes they are not what they are being studied, it creates a different sort of curiosity and conversation, one in which possibilities for other meaning, personhood, and data reveal themselves. There is a difference in data: one in which a participant feels they are the means to information because of what they have experience and another in which participants do not feel they are what they are being studied. The latter, externalized conversation in data collection results from a client not internalizing the discourses they are being studied for.

Internalized discourse

Epston (1993), along with Adams-Westcott, Dafforn, and Sterne (1993), expounded on the idea of individuals internalizing dominant discourses promoted by society. They argue that when individuals experience trauma, dysfunction, or cultural phenomena deemed as "bad" or "wrong," they internalize such events to the extent of influencing identity. Foucault also argued that when we internalize powerful discourses laid out by society, we treat ourselves as problematic objects, inherently flawed and corrupted. Therefore, one's sense of being becomes distorted because of the internalized problematic narrative: divorce, infidelity, codependency, needy, narcissism, just to name a few. Foucault even went as far as to say that internalization also causes us to treat our bodies as if they were problemed, diseased, or faulty.

The problem with internalized discourses is that the researcher is also at risk of promoting such discourses. Given the aforementioned beliefs, it is important to the researcher to believe in externalization and that participants are separate from their problems or the phenomenon they are being studied for. Researchers, even qualitative researchers, have the potential to objectify individuals for the sake of research itself. Externalization is a counter to such objectivity (Freedman & Combs, 1996). Just like it is important for the narrative therapist to adopt an externalizing worldview, so too must the researcher retain their perceptions so that problems, research questions, and topics are objectified, not participants.

Subjugated discourses

We have thus far mentioned dominant discourses and narratives. However, it becomes problematic when individuals live outside of those dominant discourses, when their experiences are different or "not normal." These experiences, and therefore the discourses that surround them, are considered subjugated discourses. Paré (1995) describes different ways by how individuals come to know their reality, which are paraphrased by Freedman and Combs (1996):

> We are prisoners of our perceptions – attempts to describe reality tell us a lot about the person doing the describing, but not much about the external reality; and [what particularly pertains to subjugated discourses] knowledge arises within communities of knowers – the realities we inhabit are those we negotiate with one another. (p. 20)

When individuals negotiate their experiences based on the discourses, they are in negotiation with the discourses that come from dominant, problematic narratives. If their experiences live outside margins of the dominant, societally accepted norm, their experiences tend to be exiled into subjugation. Therefore, it is critical for the researcher to be mindful of participants' subjugated experiences.

Deconstructive questioning

The researcher must always be mindful of the discourses shaping society, dominant and subjugated. It is equally important to be aware of the discourses that shape our perceptions, clinically or research. As mentioned before, the externalizing belief is critical to the researcher and therapist.

The narrative therapist believes that people are not their problems; they are separate from their problems. Instead of someone's identity and characteristics obtaining an internal flaw, narrative therapists believe that problems exist externally, separate from the person. Once narrative therapists can establish the participants as separate from the phenomena being studied, they can enter into a place of asking deconstructing questions.

Just like deconstructive listening calls for clarification, focus on words being used, and not assuming we understand the meaning being conveyed by the participant, this form of questioning works towards objectifying the thing being studied, not the participant.

I believe the interview space is appropriate for asking questions that work to understand the influence of the phenomena being studied on the participant. If the research topic if infidelity, it is good to ask the participant questions about how "infidelity" has influenced their life, discovering how the narrative of infidelity (or codependency, alcoholism, and pornography) has subjugated their experience. Deconstructing questioning also helps to remove the influence of the internalized discourse.

Relative influencing questioning

Michael White (1988, 1989) began the practice of relative influencing questioning as a way of helping the externalizing process. He structured conversations in a way that helped his clients see that the problem they were coming into therapy for was external to them, and that especially had some sort of influence on their lives. For clients, it was therapeutic to believe and feel that they themselves had a relationship with the problem instead of being the problem. For a therapist, it also helped get clients to see how they can turn the influence of the problem around.

Rather than being the problem, the person has a relationship with the problem; this belief can aid researchers in their process. As you approach participants, ask questions and engage them in conversation; the belief of separating and externalizing is helpful in furthering the conversation. If the researcher believes that the topic the participant is being researched for is *not* the participant themselves, the conversation and data take a different form. Relative influence questioning as a belief (not a technique as practiced in therapy) helps keep the participant's/client's identity separate from the research topic/problem at hand (Freedman & Combs, 1996). This separation, or the belief that the participant has struggled with alcoholism (as opposed to being an alcoholic), also helps create a space in which different questions are asked. It is a different question and belief to ask "What has your experience been with alcoholism?" (assuming the participant is an alcoholic) as opposed to "How has your struggle been against alcoholism?" (assuming they are not an alcoholic, but that they have had a struggle against/with it).

The qualitative researcher, with the belief found in relative influencing questioning, believes they are researching a topic at hand, not the individual. The participants are separate from the topic being researched; the researcher, along with the participant, is researching alcoholism.

What the narrative therapist believes

It is difficult to not have a theory of normality, or to suspend all ideas of what is normal, dysfunctional, and even healthy. However, the narrative therapist does believe in certain things that the researcher can also use in their practice.

The narrative therapist believes that people *want* to live in their preferred stories. People want better lives and have the means to live in them. Whereas dominant discourses tend to oppress an individual's lived experience, the narrative therapist believes that people are capable of deconstructing and living in their preferred stories.

The narrative therapist also believes that people are hindered by dominant discourses, limiting their lived experience. This belief is especially important to the researcher in that the researcher can assume that the thing their participant is being researched about is not their preferred story: depression, infidelity, dysfunction, or anything else participants offer us as data. This belief directly deobjectifies participants since we are approaching the data collection process with the belief that participants are not what they are being researched about.

Instead, their lived experiences are seen as on the outside of the dominant societal discourse. This approach can be very empowering for participants and clients of therapy.

Approach to research

Inquiry from the perspective of narrative therapy is unique in that the therapist is mindful of *how* they ask questions and, therefore, the purpose behind asking questions. Narrative therapy is a conversation and seeks to expand narratives, open experiences to new moments, and focus on the power within the individual to harness such stories. The philosophies behind such questionings are perfect for the qualitative researcher.

Research questions

Qualitative research is not far different from narrative therapy. As mentioned before, both the therapist and the researcher are experts in inquiry. Particular to narrative therapy, the therapist is an expert in asking questions that generate experiences (Freedman & Combs, 1996). The therapist is not interested in gathering information, solving a "problem," or learning and uncovering dysfunction. Instead, they are asking questions so that their clients can begin to experience their lives in their untold stories, lives that center on their own experiences rather than within the dominant, problematic cultural narratives.

Asking a research question, then, from the philosophy of narrative therapy is similar. Not to be confused with narrative methods to inquiry, the narrative researcher asks questions that seek to uncover and generate experiences. Where narrative methods seek to ask questions of storied experiences, life stories, and timelines or sequencing of events in one's life (Creswell & Poth, 2018), the narrative researcher's aim is to formulate a research question that generates new thought and, therefore, new experiences.

To do so, the researcher must be aware of their own values and how these values shape their questioning. As mentioned before, how we view the world influences the way we ask questions; this is epistemologically true for the narrative researcher. The way we as researchers hold our values easily translates to our research agenda. Before we formulate research questions, and during the process of asking research questions, researchers must be mindful of their own narratives they bring to the process, their epistemological beliefs, and their curiosities are shaped as such.

Karl Tomm warns against the dangers of asking questions with the wrong positionings. Tomm (1998) suggests therapists, and I argue more strongly researchers, are to examine the emotional posture from which questions are asked. Tomm (1988) also believes that questions ought to *call forth* issues, positions, or views, which ultimately call for answers. More important, Tomm

(1987) argues when a question is asked, it is not the person asking the question who determines the direction of the conversation, but the one answering determines where the answer will lead the asker.

Therefore, when proposing a research question, the research must be aware of the positioning from which they are asking: As suggested by Tomm, which is the emotional state from which they are asking the question, how can the research question provide the participant an experience, and what is the narrative carried by the researcher. Even the term *researcher* has political and cultural implications that may not be well suited for the collaboration a narrative therapist aims for. To alleviate the power and positioning of a researcher, Epston (2001) offers the term *co-researchers*, which means both the researcher and the participants are entering into the research process together, inquiring and discovering together. He describes it as follows:

> I have always thought of myself as doing research, but on problems and the relationships that people have with problems, rather than on the people themselves. The structuring of narrative questions and interviews allow me and others to co-research problems and the alternative knowledges that are developed to address them. (p. 178)

Narrative interviewing

The narrative therapist enters therapy with the intention of creating a space for conversation, exploring narratives, and opening up conversation for new narratives to unfold. Similar to the solution-focused brief therapist (which will be discussed in the next chapter), the narrative therapist listens for areas of their clients' lives in which stories have not been discovered, allowing the answer to questions to lead the conversation. Freedman and Combs (1996) refer to this as *opening space*.

The narrative researcher also enters the interview process with such a space. This particular type of approach to interviewing is less structured than most interviews. The semistructured interview format offers guidance and "structure" to the conversation while allowing some flexibility for the researcher to ask other questions of clarification or further curiosity. This format is well suited for the narrative researcher. However, when asking questions, it is important to allow the conversation to be guided by the participant, our co-researcher, rather than our set of questions.

The narrative therapist also does this through the not-knowing stance, as offered by Anderson and Goolishian (1992), where the therapist enters the therapy conversation without preknowledge or preunderstanding. They allow their process of questioning to be informed (not *preformed*) by what the client offers. The narrative researcher approaches interviews with a similar intent.

The not-knowing stance, even though valued and encouraged, is done with intention. Freedman and Combs (1996) offer the suggestion to enter therapy with the purpose of not-knowing while keeping the narrative metaphor, that is, to engage clients in deconstructing questioning, identifying preferred stories, and developing those stories with them. Therefore, the narrative researcher enters an interview with not-knowing and intention.

The intent is to approach questioning with the narrative metaphor. Even though the research interview is not therapy, a similar belief in questioning is used: the belief in the power of narratives.

Analyzing stories

Analyzing data is a continuation of such a belief. Stories of people's lives are powerful and are influenced by different societal and contextual factors. The same is true for the researcher analyzing data: the way in which they analyze is also influenced by different contextual factors, of which they are to be paid special attention.

Like therapy, the practice of analyzing data is derived from the tradition of hermeneutics. As narrative researchers, we understand that it is impossible to not interpret, or to not listen with the intent of understanding. Hermeneutically speaking, listening *is* interpreting. Whether the therapist is understanding individual narratives, their contextual placings, or the impact on an individual's life, the therapist is listening with such understandings.

When analyzing data, the same efforts of understandings are continued. The narrative researcher is one who uses the philosophies of Foucault and Derrida and are mindful of the power they hold in analyzation and research overall. The philosophy of "let the data speak for itself" does not apply with this philosophy. The researcher must be forthright in their analyzations. Whether their methodological approach be ground theory, ethnography, or even a statistical analysis, *where* the researcher analyzes from, that this, their positioning of the "researcher," ought to be transparent; *how* the researcher analyzes, their strategies, reasons for such strategies, and their willingness to interpret in the way they choose, all must be transparent. This includes how researchers arrived at themes, why they chose themes, which details they chose to focus on in the participant's story, and the reasons such details were important to them. There is an amount of reflection required in such a process.

The researcher must pay careful attention to themselves in this process and how they are analyzing data. I call this deconstructing analyzing. In therapy, the therapist listens deconstructively to stories, their origins, influences on the individual, and ways their problematic narratives have saturated their lives. The researcher does something similar with themselves as they analyze, mindful of their positioning as they analyze and how and why they are analyzing in such a way. Questions to ask are: What influences are being placed onto these themes/codes/details? What is behind the thought of reaching these conclusions?

Where do these interpretations come from within me? How is it that I arrived at such ideas and schemas about the data? Where do these ideas live inside me? What is driving such interpretations?

The researcher, as a co-researcher, ought to be mindful of their power and influence over the interview and analysis. As a means of minimizing their position (more on this in Chapter 7), their efforts in deconstructing their analysis helps their hierarchical influence.

Conclusion

To be a narrative therapist requires an awareness like no other approach to therapy; an awareness of political narratives, dominant stories, and problematic ways individuals internalize such. To be a narrative researcher (not be confused with narrative research methods) requires the same. The narrative researcher is one that is mindful of the narratives at work when researching.

When we approach research from the narratives of agendas, scientific methods, and to gain information, we are doing the process and our co-researchers (participants) a disservice. Researching from a narrative approach means we ask questions mindfully, listen deconstructively, and analyze with the same intent of furthering preferred storylines. As we will also see in the next chapter, where we look determines how we will ask questions. If the narrative researcher is not mindful of dominant narratives at work, they are looking and researching in the wrong places.

References

Adams-Westcott, J., Dafforn, T. A., & Sterne, P. (1993). Escaping victim life stories and co-constructing personal agency. In S. Gilligan & R. Price (Eds.), *Therapeutic conversations* (pp. 258–271). New York: Norton.

Anderson, H., & Goolishian, H. (1992). The client is the expert: A not-knowing approach to therapy. In S. McNamee and K. J. Gergen (Eds.), *Therapy as social construction*. Newbury Park, CA: Sage.

Creswell, J. W., & Poth, C. N. (2018). *Qualitative inquiry & research design: Choosing among the five approaches*. Los Angeles: Sage.

Derrida, J. (1988). *Limited Inc*. Evanston, IL: Northwestern University Press.

Epston, D. (1993). Internalized other questioning with couples: The New Zealand version. In S. G. Gilligan & R. Price (Eds.), *Therapeutic conversations* (p. 183–196). New York: W. W. Norton.

Epston, D. (2001). Anthropology, archives, co-research and narrative therapy. In D. Denborough (Ed.), *Family therapy: Exploring the field's past, present and possible futures*. Adelaide: Dulwich Centre Publications.

Freedman, J., & Combs, G. (1996). *Narrative therapy: The social construction of preferred realities*. New York: Norton.

Foucault, M. (1975). *Discipline and punish: The birth of the prison*. New York: Vintage Books.

Gergen, K. J. (1985). The social constructionist movement in modern psychology. *American Psychologist*, 40, 255–275.

Hare-Mustin, R. T. (1994). Discourses in the mirrored room: A postmodern analysis of therapy. *Family Process*, 33, 19–35.

Nichols, M. P., & Davis, S. D. (2017). *Family therapy: Concepts and methods*. Boston: Pearson.

Paré, D. A. (1995). Of families and other cultures: The shifting paradigm of family therapy. *Family Process*, 34, 1–19.

Pinnegar, S., & Daynes, J. G. (2007). Locating narrative inquiry historically: Thematics in the turn to narrative. In D. J. Clandinin (Ed.), *Handbook of narrative inquiry: Mapping a methodology* (pp. 3–34).

Tomm, K. (1987). Interventive interviewing: Part II. Reflexive questioning as a means to enable self-healing. *Family Process*, 26, 153–183.

Tomm, K. (1988). Interventive interviewing: Part III. Intending to ask lineal, circular, reflexive and strategic questions? *Family Process*, 27, 1–15.

Tomm, K. (1998). A question of perspective. *Journal of Marital and Family Therapy*, 24, 409–413.

White, M. (1991). Deconstruction and therapy. *Dulwich Centre Newsletter*, No. 2.

White, M. (2007). *Maps of narrative practice*. New York, NY: W. W. Norton.

White, M., & Denborough, D. (Ed.) (2011). *Narrative practice: Continuing the conversation*. New York: W. W. Norton & Company.

White, M., & Epston, D. (1990). *Narrative means to therapeutic ends*. New York: W. W. Norton.

6
THE SOLUTION-FOCUSED RESEARCHER

Introduction

Solution-focused brief therapy was a major force in the postmodern wave of therapy and counseling. Along with narrative therapy and collaborative language systems (now collaborative practices), solution-focused brief therapy believes and espouses the same postmodern approach to therapy. The practice of therapy, however, does differ slightly from other postmodern approaches, so does the positioning of the therapist. This chapter will overview certain philosophies of the solution-focused therapist and how the researcher can use them to drive their inquiry.

Philosophy of language

Solution-focused brief therapy (SFBT) is rooted in Wittgensteinian philosophy and Buddhist thought (de Shazer & Dolan, 2007). Where some approaches to therapy include "techniques" or "interventions," SFBT promotes tenets derived from philosophical thought, or, as I like to define it, things to think about. The qualitative researcher can benefit from the following things to think about taken from the SFBT model of therapy.

Solution-focused brief therapy is designed to be brief, future oriented, hopeful, optimistic, and solely oriented toward solutions. These therapeutic designs are rooted in postmodern thought, where language and one's experiences are central in driving the therapy process. The positioning of the therapist and how they *are* in therapy, however, is centered on solutions by means of languaging.

Like most postmodern thought and approaches to therapy, language is central to conversation. According to SFBT, language is a means toward solutions: the language of solutions is quite different than the language of problems (Nichols & Davis, 2017). As Wittgenstein puts it (1958), "The world of the happy is quite another than that of the unhappy." Therefore, the power of language is a means to maintain problems and, at the same time, to maintain solutions. Like the therapist, the qualitative researcher ought to believe in the power of language and its ability to form one's world.

Therapists that espouse this model of therapy are trained in and believe in the power of language, using it to conduct therapy; focusing on words, phrases, or thoughts that describe either solutions or problems. The researcher would do well to also have this quality of training. Looking for words that describe phenomena (problems or solutions or the research at hand) is a skill that both the therapist and researcher need to obtain. Both are experts in language.

The solution-focused therapist/researcher

The SFBT therapist has a certain positioning in the therapeutic setting from which the researcher can also gain. The therapist first accepts that there is a hierarchy in the therapeutic relationship. However, the hierarchy is not one of power or privilege; it is considered egalitarian and democratic. This is a common philosophical underpinning of this model of therapy and of postmodern therapy in general. The SFBT therapist believes in taking a position *with* their clients, where the therapist asks questions about solutions from the belief that clients have the ability to create their own solutions. This is a positioning that presents a natural collaboration, from where the therapist asks questions so that their clients can work toward their own solutions. The mindset of asking to help versus asking to "fix" is present in this positioning. This will be expounded on in the following chapter.

With an egalitarian hierarchy, the SFBT therapist never passes judgement. They also avoid making any judgement or interpretation of their client's behaviors or wants (de Shazer & Dolan, 2007). When a therapist or researcher brings their own agenda, set of diagnosis, ideas of normality or dysfunction, or set of questions to the conversation, it creates a limiting effect on the conversation where the conversation is guided by "solutions" found within diagnoses. The SBFT therapist seeks to expand rather than limit the client's repertoire of solutions with an egalitarian approach. Even though the term *egalitarian hierarchy* may be an oxymoron, in the context of SFBT it fits the positioning and idea of "leading from behind." With the belief that clients have the ability to create their own solutions, and with the practice of not passing judgement or interpretation, the SFBT therapist asks questions in a way that nudges clients in the direction of their own solutions.

In the therapy process, the researcher places an amount of trust in the client by leading from behind (Backhaus, 2011). When the therapist trusts the client, they believe that the client knows best about their own lives, they are the "expert" of their own experiences, and that they know what solutions fit into the context of their lives. Therefore, like other postmodern therapies, the therapist is not the expert. With this model of therapy, the therapist is the expert in finding solutions as presented by the clients; where you look is where you will find solutions (Nichols & Davis, 2017). Therefore, the therapist brings their expertise of asking the right questions into the therapy room, following the lead of the client and being guided by their stories.

The same philosophical stance can be used by the qualitative researcher. There is a large amount of trust we place into participants and their stories. Their lives they bring into our research process must be a process of trust. I think it's common for researches to use participants for their own research agendas, only using aspects of participants stories as data that pertains to their research at hand. However, when we trust the participant, we believe that their experience is true and that they know their lives better than the researcher.

Just like the solution-focused therapist brings expertise in asking the right solution questions, the researcher brings their expertise in the research process, asking the right questions that pertain to the participant, not the research agenda. Even though certain questions need to be asked, the qualitative researcher, similar to the SFBT therapist, is one who can be flexible and curious about participants stories. Data derived from the stories is secondary, a result of asking the right questions.

Regarding the SFBT therapist and the qualitative researcher, Dr. Sara Smock Jordan (personal communication, August 8, 2019), the editor of the *Journal of Solution-Focused Brief Therapy*, has the following to say:

> SFBT is a model that is inductively developed. When we think about the qualitative researcher and SFBT, it's a great pair because … depending on their various methodologies, a qualitative researcher is wanting to gain an experience, wanting to hear about a phenomenon, do ground theory, whatever it might be, they are starting from gathering information and more inductively than a quantitative researcher. A lot of models in the field of marriage and family therapy/couple family therapy, social work, any field that uses systemic models, is that those approaches start with a theory. We believe a certain behavior starts "this way," whether it's attachment theory or dysfunction. SFBT is different because Steve de Shazer of his approach to theory, it's a theoretical. That's true in the sense that Steve did not find a grand theory regarding behavior. He wanted to, but he could not come up with one explanation for change in human behavior. That was his original goal. He was fascinated with Erikson's account of change. He started searching and couldn't find anything but was interested in Wittgenstein in the idea that one should renounce all theory. This became clear in his writing: we don't have a theory to explain

behavior change. It became known to Steve and those who studied him that SFBT is not rooting in theory. However, we believe, and from his writings, that Steve has a little t theory. The difference is big T points to one reason on why things happen. Little t talks about reasons for behavior and change being contextual. That being conversation, language, and context. Even though Steve did not subscribe to a Big T theory, he did to a little t theory. And how that applies to qualitative research is that it's the same for qualitative work. Qualitative work is about the little t. And we believe that. I think qualitative comes from that point.

(For more of the interview, see Appendix B.)

The miracle question

A common question asked by the SFBT therapist is the miracle question. The way the question is used and approached in the therapy session also offers the qualitative researcher some guidance in their approach to asking questions. During the question, the therapist asks the client to think about their "problem," and if they were to fall asleep one night and their problems miraculously went away, all their problems were solved, what would their world look like. The goal of the miracle question is tied deep in the Wittgenstein's philosophy and the postmodern thought of language. Since language has the power to shape our reality, so does asking questions that are geared toward solutions. Therefore, the question aims to steer client's toward solution-oriented language, in hopes that their language of solutions will in turn materialize in their lives.

A challenge with the miracle question is the responses clients give. Some clients say, "I don't know." Others say, "All my problems would go away, and I'd be happier." Others still might say, "I'd win the lottery." These common responses call upon the skill of the SFBT therapist. During these conversations and answers in therapy, the therapist must be savvy enough to understand what their client is trying to say given their vague answers toward solutions. For example, with the "I'd win the lottery" response, the therapist must be able to see within the world of the client and be curious about what the client's life would look like if they did in fact win the lottery. What would they be doing differently, how would they behave differently, how would someone on the outside be able to know they were "happier" having won the lottery?

The therapist must be able to take their own conceptualizations of the client's miracle world and be able to ask more questions about it so that the client can produce more specific language about that world. The qualitative researcher can benefit from the same skill: to take answers participants offer and be able to conceptualize the participants' depiction of their experiences and ask more questions regarding their stories. As an SFBT researcher, the researcher approaches interviews, data analysis, and even forming research questions with this practice in mind. From the skill of the miracle question, the researcher keeps in mind the world potentially offered by their participants, of which its conceptualization starts with the research question, being mindful of the way questions are formed and the language used to ask questions. During the interview process, the same skill is needed to dive into participants' lives and experiences. The researcher must be able to take the practice of conceptualizing their participants world and inductively forming questions from the offerings of their participants. The same holds true for data analysis, keeping in mind the process during which participants offer their stories, our conceptualizations of their stories, how we translate that in order to ask further questions, and how the process organically unfolds.

Problem talk versus solution talk

The use of language and its ability to create one's reality is crucial to the therapist and so too the researcher. "The world of problems is different than that of solutions" (Nichols & Davis, 2017). The researcher can benefit from this positioning by believing in the power of language; how stories, problems, and people's lives are language. According to constructivist thought, we create our realities through language. Language is the vehicle for experiences; language is what makes experiences experiences. When much focus, attention, and language is put on problems, that world is in turn created. The opposite is also true: when much focus, attention, and language is put on solutions, that world is also created. As researchers, we follow participants' language, experiences, and worlds, following where they lead us.

If it ain't broke, don't fix it

People know what is wrong with their lives, and people know what they need. The therapist does not pour into the process their own ideas of what is wrong, what needs to be fixed, or what clients need. It is a skill to enter into a therapy session and not try to "fix" what we think is dysfunctional, wrong, or something that needs to change. In order to effectively embody this belief, the therapist must set aside their own agendas, biases, and preconceptions.

The researcher must also do this; to enter into the research process with no expectations of any sort of data that might be exposed or brought to light. The tension lies in our own research agendas and the possibility of outcomes. Where does our own agenda take over that of our participants' experiences, expertise, and stories? In this belief, the researcher also must be able to be flexible with their agenda, allowing it to be led by the participants. Researchers must not be married to their research agendas when espousing this position. The researcher ought to be prepared in letting their agenda change, shift, and be guided not by their own knowledge and expertise, but that of the participant.

Normal

The solution-focused therapist does not believe in a normal way of functioning. Nor do they believe in diagnosis. Normalcy and diagnoses assume a binary reality, that a person is that way all the time or not. Normal alone assumes the need for one to behave, think, or live in a way that is that way, and if one does not, they are not considered normal. Normalcy also assumes permanence, and when one is not permanently normal, they are then not considered normal.

In the world of solution-focused therapy, there is no such thing as normal. Clients are experts of their own lives, and therefore, they know what they need. That matter is not up for questioning by the therapist or the researcher. There is also no such thing as a disorder; the model of therapy is completely asymptomatic. The SFBT therapist does not believe in one "right" way to live one's life, according to and not according to a diagnosis.

It would benefit the researcher to also believe in people, normalcy, or problems in this way. Approaching interviewing and data collection can be driven by this belief. Our research agenda already assumes something about people, specifically when we create research criteria, such as participants need to be X, Y, Z in order for inclusion in a study. The difficulty with this approach lies in where our agenda ends and where participants' lives begin.

It is impossible to not have a research agenda; the actual practice of researching already assumes an agenda. However, taking on this belief presents a different way of being with people. When we assume "people are not their problems all the time," our approach to interviewing and data collection and even data analysis changes. We naturally let data become generative from participants' experiences rather than our agenda-driven guide to gathering the "right" data.

> I would say that as a SFBT therapist and researcher, my "agenda" is to find out what works for that person in that context through a dialogue. That is my agenda for a conversation. If I was a qualitative SFBT researcher, I think I would have the same type of agenda. I think my method might be different, I think assumptions would be the same, though, if I'm coming from the idea that everybody has all the resources they need, some of the major tenets of the model, I think that would show through in my research as well as my practice as a therapist. So, agenda is not a word that, again, we are very careful about language, I wouldn't say I would use the word agenda. I think as a researcher you do [have an agenda], I think the word I would use is assumptions. What assumptions does the researcher hold? And how is their interaction with their participant conveyed? I would say usually through an interview. That's going to be the main way in which your assumptions are going to be conveyed to the participants. Do your assumptions affect your results? Of course, they do. I think that qualitative research does a good job talking about the bias

of the researcher. They don't do a good job talking about the process of gathering the information and the biases that are there in terms of asking the questions, the words that they use, how they phrase certain things. That is what's needed.

How do they put aside, or set aside, or suspend their ideas about the things they are researching themselves?

It opens up possibilities for people to be more transparent and less judged. It also opens up the richness of the study because you're going to get more of a variety of experience versus those that only participate because they ascribe to that term infidelity.

I would say curiosity. And that fits with SFBT. We are curious. And that is such a great word. It shows the assumption of "I don't know but I want to learn more." In a sense, all science is curiosity. It's in a very neutral way, because it takes away the assumption of language. The word curiosity, to me, is a much more respectful word to use and it still captures exactly what we are doing. So why wouldn't a qualitative researcher's questions reflect that nature of curiosity versus a very blatant question —again, all questions have assumptions — but assumptions that are detrimental or harmful or not useful to gather the process of information in the spirit of curiosity.

The process is just as important as the content, especially in SFBT. I've had conversations in life in general, and it's so off-putting to me that I don't want to answer. I get defensive about it because of the way it's asked. I think it shuts people down. You can also say that it's not ethical. They feel coerced because they already started the interview. (S. Smock Jordan, personal communication, August 8, 2019)

Not problems all the time

The solution-focused therapist believes the same toward "problems." People are not their problems all the time; there are times when the problem is not as severe or when it should have been worse, but it was not. This assumes and believes the best in people: people have the ability and natural resources to not let problems become something worse, therefore, they are already doing something right.

Problems *always* display exceptions (de Shazer & Dolan, 2007), therefore, problems are transient. Consider the verb *to be*. For example, when therapists enter therapy with a diagnosing mind, when clients *are* bipolar, the languaging of the diagnosis, specifically the verb *is,* is powerful. In order for a client to obtain a diagnosis from a therapist, they must externally qualify for such a label. According to the DSM-5, we have such qualifiers for diagnoses. These diagnoses – bipolar, depression, schizophrenia – "encourages us to assume that the words refer to an entity about which we can generalize" (de Shazer

& Dolan, 2007, p. 135), one that projects and places an external reality on the client. When someone *is* something, it also assumes they *are* that all the time, with finiteness. Regarding the verb *to be*, Smock shares the following:

> Going back to the evolution of the SFBT model, I believe that there were these key interventions developed inductively from the client. For example, the miracle question was inductively created from a client. The client said a miracle would have to happen in order for something to change. So again, it evolved and it was all about the client, and it wasn't about a big T. We think this is how change occurs and we are going to create this intervention based off this philosophy of change. All this came from the client. All the solution-focused videos, for example, are all titled with language used by the client. Therefore, it's all about the client and always has been.
>
> In terms of the qualitative researcher, and the idea of Wittgenstein's idea of to be, we have really changed from focusing on interventions to asking pre-session change questions to asking about overall what's changed, which gives the birth of exceptions and people aren't their problem all the time. The entire model and process has evolved all based on the clients.
>
> The development of the model is so focused on language and conversation, and works for the clients and doing what works, they developed these interventions as a philosophy, as a process, to get back to qualitative research.

Perhaps this is why Alcoholics Anonymous is so powerful for people who have not had a drop alcohol for 20 years. They present themselves as, "Hello, I'm ___, and I'm an alcoholic. I've been sober for 20 years now." The verb here, "I *am* an alcoholic," leads us to believe that alcoholism is a steady state, consistent, and permanent. Which also leads us to believe, if such a state is indefinite, that a cure is not possible (de Shazer & Dolan, 2007). Wittgenstein (1961) goes as far to say that the verb *to be* also offers an expression of existence. To be something implies that something is continually in a state of existence. Therefore, an individual is an alcoholic, despite their best efforts of 20 years of sobriety; they are still constrained by the existence of their alcoholism by the simple use of their grammar (de Shazer, 1997).

The therapist and researcher believe that people are constrained by their narrow views of their problems (Nichols & Davis, 2017). People assign meaning to their behavior, which in turn limits their range of solutions. When the researcher brings this view of people into the research process, the experience is different for both the participant and the researcher. The researcher can enter into the research process believing in this condition of finiteness or believing that their participants are not what they are researching. For example, in a recent study I conducted, a man or woman who has committed an extramarital affair, it would be a mistake for the researcher to enter into the interview believing that their participants *are* unfaithful partners, as if the act of infidelity was still in progress, and always in progress (let's hope not). When the researcher believes in their participants, it opens up the possibilities for other experiences, conversations, and languaging to emerge.

Compliments

An important "technique" to the solution-focused therapist is to offer compliments. Compliments are usually used in the form of validation, recognition of competencies within the client, recognition of how the person has coped, or how well they are doing in the mist of their "problems" (Backhaus, 2011). However, compliments are given sparingly and discerningly, as it is a common critique of SFBT. If the therapist offers too many compliments, they run the risk of seeming disingenuous, fake, or dismissing of the issues presented by the clients.

With the risk of being insincere, it is important for the researcher to be mindful of how much they believe in their own compliments being offered. When I teach this technique, I explain to my students that compliments are not used as a fancy therapy trick that pushes people to solutions. The same is said for the researcher: compliments are not a fancy trick that produce richer data. Compliments, or being complimentative, is something the researcher *is*; it is not something merely done. As the case with most postmodern therapies and techniques, it is what the therapist is that is more effective than something pulled out of a therapy tool box.

The researcher, then, is also someone who genuinely looks for areas of the participant's life to compliment. When the researcher embodies this, exudes compliments, the experience is different; the entire research process is different, from interview, to data analysis, to the written results. Being a person that looks to compliment is seen in everything the researcher does, as opposed to something that is an attempt to produce something from the aim of the researcher.

What would be the most helpful for us to talk about today?

A solution-focused brief therapist normally starts off each session with a variation of the follow question: "What would be the most helpful for us to talk about today so that you feel like this hour is productive?" There are several therapeutic ideas that are taken from this question. By asking, the therapist is giving the client the power to lead the session, which is grounded in the "follow from behind" stance. The therapist is also giving the client space to formulate their own solutions, which is rooted in the idea of the clients being the experts of their own lives, therefore they know what they need for the hour more than the therapist does. This question also assumes that the therapist's ideas of solutions are suspended for the time of the session so that the client's solutions can be made central. This also has several research applications.

According to Backhaus (2011), this question encourages the client to get the heart of the matter of which they are seeking therapy. The researcher can also approach the interview and data collection process in the same way. Getting to the heart of the research, then, is something the participant leads us in. Therefore, we begin the process of collecting data, the heart of the data, from the lead of the participant. For example, suppose I am researching university professors and their experience of the tenure process. To begin the interview, a solution-focused question (a question derived from the philosophy of the therapy, not so much oriented toward solutions themselves) would be worded in a variation of the following: "I/we are conducting a research project about university professors' experience with the tenure process. What do you think would be most helpful for us to know regarding your experience with tenure?" Or, "What is the best information you can provide our research team regarding your experience with the university's tenure process?" By asking these questions in therapy, the client is immediately placed in charge (Backhaus, 2011). As the researcher asking these questions, the participant is placed in charge as well. The participant is also seen as the expert of their experience.

This is a philosophical shift in approach to research, just like it was in therapy. The therapist is not the leader, expert, or conductor of the therapy session in postmodern therapy; neither is the researcher. The researcher, then, allows the participant to lead. In other words, the participants conduct the research interview, and the questions we ask are followed by their stories. This raises the question of interview questions: How does the researcher ask their set of questions if the participant is leading? The research process is usually driven by agendas, sampling, and participants that have some expertise in the topic being researched. When believing in the power of language, we allow participants to lead the process, despite our own agendas.

To my knowledge, this practice is not done; entering the research interview with no agenda, only the question of "What would be the best information for my research team regarding ___?" However, this is how therapy is conducted: not entering the session with a preset list of questions (maybe some beginning therapists practice this, but it is not true to form with postmodern therapy). What if the research interview was also conducted this way?

The solution-focused therapist knows how to ask questions by way of listening for solutions in client's stories, highlighting them, and keeping the conversation set on them. This is a different skill than other problem-solving therapies (de Shazer & Dolan, 2007), a skill that requires putting the therapist's own ideas of solutions in the background and focusing on the material the clients offer. The same can be true for the qualitative interview. By beginning the interview with "What would be the most important for us to know about your experience with the tenure process?" we are placing their experience in the forefront, and listening to areas of their story that could be expounded on, highlighted, or that will keep the conversation ongoing. This too is a different skill, different from most traditional, structured, and semistructured interviews.

Semistructured interviews do allow such flexibility for the researcher to ad lib, create their own conversation within the questions, or to allow for the participant to follow their own ideas. However, I am arguing for less structure to the interview; to enter the interview or data collection process with a central research question and to allow participants to guide the interview process. The term *inter*view can arguably imply a narrow, limited, or confined (inter) sense of vision or sight (view). Perhaps a more accurate term would be *open*view, or *outer*view. Rather than being directed, led, or even structured into the questions asked by an interview guide, the participant is placed in the expert role by allowing them (to be *open*) to formulate their own data with the help of the researcher, asking questions organically generated by the conversation at hand. According to the SFBT therapist, solutions are truly the clients' solutions, the therapist only helps them get there. To the qualitative researcher, data belongs to the participant. The researcher only helps ask questions to expound on the participants' experiences.

Following the philosophy of Wittgenstein, de Shazer and Dolan (2007) argue the same approach as a therapist, to remain in a place where we suspend our presuppositions entering therapy and, in this conversation, research:

> Of course, eliminating anything hypothetical and all explanation means that therapists must work hard to simply *stay on the surface of the conversation*. All that is left is the conversation itself – listening and talking – and the description of the conversation looking into the working of our language. (p. 106; emphasis added)

This is beautifully said. I believe research to be, in its truest form, a conversation. The SFBT model of therapy gives us insight and applications for approaching data collection and interviews. The researcher, like the therapist, is in the practice of staying on the surface of conversation, not entering into the interview with a list of questions or trying to have participants answer a certain way to support a research agenda. The research must obtain the skill of staying on the surface of conversation, being able to follow it with enough curiosity and interest that the conversation itself generates questions.

This also requires the researcher to be skilled in *looking* as opposed to *thinking*. Wittgenstein (1958) describes this in his example of games:

> Consider for example the proceedings that we call "games." I mean board-games, card games, ball-games, Olympic games, and so on. What

is common to them all? – Don't say: "There *must* be something common, or they would not be called 'games'" – but *look and see* whether there is anything common to all. For if you look at them, you will not see something that is common to *all,* but similarities, relationship, and a whole series of them at that. To repeat: don't think, but look! (p. 27)

The SFBT qualitative researcher must also be trained in looking, staying on the surface of the conversation, and putting aside their "thinking." To ask, "What would be the most important for us to talk about today?" or "What is most important for my research team to know about ____?" is to practice looking. The design of the research itself should be secondary; it follows and is formed after the initial question is set (Shavelson & Towne, 2004). After the researcher asks the initial research question, just like the SFBT therapist asks, then the process can organically flow.

> Peter and Insoo both wrote *Interviewing for Solutions*, and they are asking the question what it is to interview and the process of asking questions. Not so much therapy but interviewing someone in a solution-focused way. And so their process of teaching that was called "Listen, Select, Build" [more on this later]. You listen to what the client says, expectations, goals, resources. And then you would select those nuggets and pieces of possibilities. Possible solutions, possible places to go. And then you would build off of those. Maybe you would restate what the client says or ask a follow-up question. Maybe you would alter [which words they chose]; we've talked about language formulation. That's a restatement of what the other person says, it could be in an altered form, you can delete certain words, you preserve certain words, and you give a summary of what they've said. In this Listen, Select, Build process, it's actually what we do as SFBT therapists. I would debate that all therapists do this, all therapists listen for certain things, have a framework of where they want to go, and they build off of that. And that's how they do therapy. I don't know if other approaches would identify it that way, but that's what they do.
>
> I would even argue that the qualitative researcher also does this. So I think there is a parallel between Peters and Insoo's Listen, Select, and Build and the qualitative researcher. We are describing the process in quantitative terms, in qualitative processes. We are able to operationalize what's going on moment by moment. If we know what's going on moment by moment, we can train qualitative researchers, using the same analysis of language; both therapists and researchers. But the qualitative researcher can especially benefit from the analysis of language.
>
> Specifically, our topic choice. What words do we use that match our model or theory or wherever we want to go? Things from linguistic

literature, how do you phrase a question? What does a formal question even mean? Specifically, with therapists, they are trained in one specific model and they adhere to it and are told what not to do, and that always doesn't translate well into the therapy room. The same is true for the qualitative researcher, studying moment-by-moment analysis, studying language and questioning. (S. Smock Jordan, personal communication, August 8, 2019)

Approach to research

What follows is my interpretation of a researcher that espouses the stances and philosophies of the solution-focused brief therapist. With similar beliefs in inquiry, the following is a general overview of a simplified research process; not intended to propose a set methodological approach but rather a belief in the overall research process.

Asking questions

The solution-focused researcher, like the therapist, is one that is skilled in asking questions. The solution-focused therapist knows how to ask questions by way of finding solutions. Deep in Wittgenstein's philosophy, the therapist plays the "language game" (1958), basing their therapeutic conversation about the language of problems and solutions, where the language used to describe each has the potential to create each respective reality.

To the researcher asking research questions, the language used to ask questions is crucial. Of course, every sentence we use, every thought we internally compose comes with some sort of implicit bias, presupposition, or schema formed within our thought organizations. The solution-focused researcher is one that practices self-reflection in their inherit bias, which also influences the way they ask research questions.

Like other postmodern approaches, this also requires a suspension of knowledge. Asking questions, specifically from the stance of the solution-focused researcher, is also a practice of letting the participant lead the conversation, while the researcher knows how to take what the participant offers and ask more pointed questions about the overall research question. Therefore, to ask a research question is to be mindful of *how* we as researchers approach asking questions overall and more carefully to one end of research.

Interviewing and data gathering

True to the model of therapy, the researcher asks one research question in the same way the therapist enters into the therapy session with one question: "What would be the most helpful to talk about today?" The design of the research itself should be secondary; it follows and is formed after the initial question is set (Shavelson & Towne, 2004). After the researcher asks the initial research question, just like the SFBT therapist asks, then the process can organically flow from there.

With this question comes deep Wittgensteinian philosophy in that the researcher uses the answers from that question, in such form as its offered, and builds upon that. Therefore, in the interview, the only question the researcher need is the one central research question. The interview is not as structured in that it allows the participant to lead and for the researcher to inquire as the conversation unfolds. To the therapist, this process is knowns as Listen, Select, Build (De Jong & Berg, 2013; de Shazer, 1991, 1994).

In Listen, Select, Build, the therapist begins with listening. The solution-focused therapist is skilled in paying careful attention the language clients use to describe problems. But noticing specific problem description language, they are also noticing language for solutions. One unique skill that pertains specifically to the solution-focused therapist is that they know where to look for solutions; they pay mindful, detailed attention to language of problems that they instinctively notice language of solutions. This is a necessary skill for the researcher: to begin with their initial research question, and to listen closely in order to select certain words and language the participant uses.

In the "Select" portion, the therapist intentionally holds onto words the client uses to describe solutions. Looking for solutions, the therapist uses the words the client shares to describe exceptions (times when the problem was not as strong or did not take over), or things that are important to the client The same skill is called for in the research interview. When asking an initial research question, the researcher pays careful attention to the words the participant uses to describe and answer the research question. From their answer, the researcher selects phrases or thoughts or words used to answer the question. The phrases or words the researcher chooses to hold onto are the words used to build and formulate the next question.

In the "Build" process, the therapist invites the client to further elaborate on their constructs of solutions in their lives. From the language selected by the therapist, they use the client's descriptions to further engage in the conversation of solutions. The same skill can be applied to the interview. The researcher, after asking the initial research question and after selecting the phrases and language the participant uses to answer, the researcher builds the next question and invites the participant to further elaborate on the description of the question/topic at hand.

The solution-focused researcher is looking for ways to ask their participants about the central question at hand. Just like the therapist is primed to look for solutions, the researcher is primed to ask questions about the central curiosity. From what the participant offer, the therapist then asks more questions, all centered in their original research question. How they ask questions and the language they use are important to finding the "right" data for their research.

Analysis

Solution-focused brief therapy has evolved in its time in practice. In the most recent years, the model's mechanism of change has been of great interest. What is it that exactly accounts for change in therapy? What is at the root of the therapeutic relationship that causes and promotes change? These questions are still being answered. However, the researcher in their data analysis can benefit from the process by which these questions are being answered.

A group of researchers – Janet Bavelas, Peter de Jong, Adam Froerer, Harry Korman, Sara Smock-Jordan, Christie Tomori, and Sara Healing – have been using psycholinguistic theory and microanalysis to study communication between therapists and clients as mechanisms of change. Of their extensive research, one of the facets they engage in is the laboratory experiments that provide evidence for co-construction as a basis for an approach to treatment (Bavelas, Coates, & Johnson, 2000, 2002). The researchers are in the process of studying moment-by-moment interactions between the therapist and client, and both quantitatively and qualitatively studying each interaction. This type of analysis is important to the researcher as well.

Even though the interview and analysis are not quantified, the process of analyzing the researcher's interviews can benefit from the moment-by-moment attention of co-construction. Specifically, how the process of Listen, Select, Build is in the interview. I advocate for the researcher to be public in their process of hearing what participants say, why they chose to focus on such words or phrases, and how those phrases formulated the following interview question. I chose this as part of the analysis process because it is rare (from my knowledge) for the researcher to analyze themselves when analyzing data.

When analyzing data, the researcher is also highlighting their Listen and Select portions of the interview. The phrases participants used, the words that furthered the research question, and thoughts that provoked more curiosity about the research question are all analyzed for further categorization, coding, or thematic schemes the researcher chooses.

Conclusion

Like the model of therapy, the solution-focused research approach requires a certain skill: knowing how to ask questions. The therapist is a philosopher, a postmodern linguist, and a constructivist conversationalist; one that knows how to find solutions within the language used in therapy. The researcher is similar in that they know how to utilize their participants' stories in order to answer research questions.

The researcher is also artful in conversation and interviewing. Using Listen, Select, Build, they enter the interview with one central research question and can use the conversation itself to build upon and formulate the interview. Like the therapist, the solution-focused researcher is also skilled in linguistics, or

TABLE 6.1 The postmodern researcher

	Research question	Postmodern philosophy	Interview/data gathering	Analysis
Collaborative practices/the collaborative researcher	Asking from not-knowing, mutual learner, participant's voice leads, mindful of relationship to subject matter, ultimate curiosity	Not-knowing, mutual dialogue, metaphorical space, being public, host/guest, social-construction	Takes place between two researchers, public about interpretations and understandings, questions emerge from the conversation, Not-knowing	Socially constructed, "make sense" of the data and conversation, not separate from the research process, continuation of curiosity
Narrative inquiry	Generate experiences, how values shape questions, examine postures from where questions are asked	Externalizing conversations, deconstructive listening, deconstructive questioning, internalized, relative influencing, unique outcomes	Co-researchers, creating open space for conversation, flexibility in asking questions, not-knowing, belief in the power of narratives	Hermeneutics, analyzing stories, deconstructive analyzing, mindful of researcher's analysis, minimizing hierarchy
The solution-focused researcher	Where to look to find answers, language used to ask questions	Not their problems all the time, a diagnostic, non-normal, world of problems/solutions by language	Listen, Select, Build; participant leads, asking questions derived from answers that pertain to central question	Moment by moment, public in their analysis, language used in Select

paying careful attention to language used to formulate solutions, or, for the researcher, language used to formulate data. With such skills, the researcher will enhance their quality of data.

What follows is a brief conversation in other postmodern thought that has been alluded to in these approaches chapters: hierarchy and self-disclosure. The writing process is also discussed in Chapter 8 from my perspective and practices of writing for the qualitative researcher (Table 6.1).

References

Backhaus, K. (2011). Solution focused brief therapy with families. In L. Metcalf (Ed.), *Marriage and family therapy* (pp. 287–312). New York: Springer Publishing Company.

Bavelas, J. B., Coates, L., & Johnson, T. (2000). Listeners as co-narrators. *Journal of Personality and Social Psychology, 79,* 941–952.

Bavelas, J. B., Coates, L., & Johnson, T. (2002). Listener response as a collaborative process: The role of gaze. *Journal of Communication*, 52, 566–580.

De Jong, P., & Berg, I. K. (2013). *Interviewing for solutions* (4th ed.). Belmont, CA: Brooks/Cole.

de Shazer, S. (1991). *Putting difference to work*. New York: W. W. Norton & Company.

de Shazer, S. (1994). *Words were originally magic*. New York: W. W. Norton & Company.

de Shazer, S. (1997). Commentary: Radical acceptance. *Families, Systems, & Health*, 15, 375–378.

de Shazer, S., & Dolan, Y. (2007). *More than miracles: The state of the art of solution-focused brief therapy*. London: Routledge, Taylor & Francis Group.

Nichols, M. P., & Davis, S. D. (2017). *Family therapy: Concepts and methods*. Boston, MA: Pearson.

Shavelson, R. J., & Towne, L. (2004). What drives scientific research in education? Questions, not methods, should drive the enterprise. *American Psychological Society Observer*, 17, 27–30.

Wittgenstein, L. (1958). *Philosophical investigations*. Oxford: Basil Blackwell.

Wittgenstein, L. (1961). *Tractus logico-philosophicus*. London: Routledge.

7
HIERARCHY AND SELF-DISCLOSURE

Introduction

Among postmodern thought, and specifically within the practice of therapy, hierarchy has been a positioning of particular interest. With the evolution of therapy, the positioning of the therapist has changed from the days of Palo Alto, the Mental Research Institute (MRI), and the systemic therapist where the therapist was considered the "expert," with knowledge, interventions, and the ability to point out dysfunction where it lived in the system. The shift to postmodern therapy presented a different sort of therapist in that the approach to therapy was intentionally egalitarian as co-conversationalist (Anderson, 1997), co-authors (White, 2007), and both working together to find solutions (de Shazer & Dolan, 2007). With this specific positioning of the therapist came the conversation of hierarchy and where the therapist fits within the power dynamic and relationship.

The contexts of both therapy and research are somewhat different in terms of hierarchy and how self-disclosure is used. In distinguishing between the two, the differences are subtle. However, the consistent argument of this book is that both the researcher and therapist share characteristics and qualities. Therefore, this chapter will delve into the slight differences between therapy and research contexts. and highlight the similarities between the two endeavors regarding hierarchy and self-disclosure.

Endless debate

Even though the debate of hierarchy will not be settled within this chapter, the philosophies of this book will be applied to the relationships between the researcher and participant as the therapist and client. The direct qualities of the therapist are slightly different in this particular discussion in that we will focus on only the therapist's relationship with their clients and their position of "power." However, the same approaches to people are the common thread: be it researcher or therapy, we are both experts in inquiry. We are also, people.

Hierarchy in therapy is difficult to overcome and deny. The counselor and therapist are in position of expertise in which they are sought after for counsel. The fact that therapists are in demand inherently puts them in a position of hierarchy. The same is especially true for therapists in training who are supervised; they are in a position of hierarchy with their clients and their supervisor is in a position of hierarchy over them. Even postmodern therapists that assume the one down-position will adhere to the hierarchy within the therapist–client relationship and try their best to minimize that hierarchy. Hierarchy is inevitable. It will always be a part of a relationship. However, within who the hierarchy lies is a thought to be explored in what follows.

Feminist critique

The feminist critique of therapy is vast. For our conversation, the feminist critique of therapy will include ideas about hierarchy and self-disclosure. Kitzinger (1987) argues that when therapists, or anyone in the social sciences and helping professions, enter into therapy, their hierarchy already puts them in a position of power by placing the client in an objective place, meaning they are the object of study, help, or case conceptualization. She also argues that the observer – the therapist, psychologist, or social scientist – has no direct access to the individual being "studied." Therefore, any "objective" help may be unwarranted in terms of the individual experiences that are not being accounted for within such a position of power. As a postmodern therapist, it is an endeavor and responsibility to be mindful of their sense of power.

Similarly, White (2007), within the philosophies of Michel Foucault, also believes in the responsibility of the therapist to be mindful of power within several contexts: therapy, the therapist's place of privilege, client's lives, and society's political conversation at large. Therefore, the narrative therapist also tries to minimize hierarchy by combating the narratives of power, including the narrative of the therapist, and what they might be preconceived as.

Harlene Anderson speaks to the idea of hierarchy in therapy as it relates to the feminist critique by treading the subject carefully. Her positioning is one of caution, distinguishing between *being public* and *transparent*. She argues that being public allows the therapist to share their inner dialogues and monologues, prejudices, wonderings, speculations, opinions, and fears (Anderson, 1997). Such a belief allows room for self-disclosure if it is initiated by clients. This is different from being transparent since, as Anderson states it, "I do not think that another person can see through us or we through them" (p. 103). In this regard, "expertise" is quite limited. The therapist, like the researcher, does not need to have all the answers from which they are being asked.

The therapist

The term *self-disclosure* itself can create some discomfort in therapists. Specifically for therapists in training who are steeped in ethical conversations, self-disclosure may be an idea completely off limits. One of my favorite writers on therapy, Yalom (2002), shares advice with therapists on the subject. He argues that self-disclosure can be a useful tool in therapy in that it produces rich here-and-now experiences for the therapy process, of which the therapist is very much a part of.

> It is counterproductive for the therapist to remain opaque and hidden from the patient. There is every reason to reveal oneself to the patient and no good reason for concealment ... Therapist self-disclosure is not a single entity but a cluster of behaviors, some of which invariably facilitate therapy and some of which are problematic and potentially counterproductive. (p. 83)

However, he goes on to warn:

> To engage in a genuine relationship with one's patient, it is essential to disclose your feelings toward the patient in the immediate present. But here-and-now disclosure should not be indiscriminate; transparency should not be pursued for its own sake. All comments must pass one test: is this disclosure in the best interest of the patient? (p. 87)

When the therapist discloses, there ought to be some form of intent behind it, not merely for the sake of self-disclosure. The therapist shares for the sake of the client and for the sake of the therapy process overall.

Sometimes, I argue, it is appropriate for the therapist to initiate the process of self-disclosure. If the therapist begins and opens up to clients first, in theory, it will also engage the client and enhance the therapy process. In this case, it is useful for the therapist to lead by example. After the process has become a safe space for self-disclosure, the therapy becomes a richer experience.

Self-disclosure can be a means of minimizing hierarchy, if done well. The feminist critique of therapy believes that the therapist asks questions about clients' lives and expecting them to share the most intimate details of their struggles, which in turn is not reciprocated. This creates an imbalance, a power difference, or an unequal relationship within therapy. With this dynamic, the power seemingly lies only within the therapist, with all the questions and expectations of clients sharing while the therapist does not.

116 Hierarchy and self-disclosure

Therapist self-disclosure, I argue, is a feminist practice to therapy, where the therapist shares their own struggles, ideas, opinions, and biases. This is a careful balance and a great skill most therapists do not have. A therapist ought to know the proper amount of disclosure according to each conversation and client. They ought to know when self-disclosure is too much and too little, beneficial or not to the therapy process. When done well, true conversation is had and the therapeutic process is enriched. Both therapist and client are a part of the process and both benefit from the endeavor.

Consider the following conversation between myself and Dr. Sara Smock-Jordan (held August 8, 2019) regarding self-disclosure within the practices of therapy and research:

Me: How do you feel about disclosure as a therapist and researcher?

Smock: It's more about the conversation in therapy. The conversation becomes the relationship. However, I think, this is my personal view, if a client is saying that they are having a specific situation, and it would be helpful for them to normalize, and again, it's more of a gut thing, but I do it with clients who are asking for it. For me, that is very solution focused. The same thing with education. Our model doesn't necessarily talk about educating the client, but if the client asks for education, if we didn't give them or provide them that information, that would not be serving our client, that would not be benefiting our client. So, I do the same thing with self-disclosure. The way I [practice self-disclosure], if a client asks me point-blank, something that I thought would be helpful to them about myself, that did not compromise the personal/ethical relationship. For example, the question if you have children. If they are asking me that, and it's not of that boundary violation, then sure, I have kids. If that helps them be able to carry on the conversation or co-construct, that's fine. As a therapist you have a boundary and limit. Like anything else, I don't think anything is off limits within ethics and legality. It's about what evolves and what the client is asking for. As long as you keep all of that in perspective, I think you follow the client's lead.

Me: I completely agree. What I've been thinking about is that line: where is it that one crosses that line from following their lead to inserting ourselves. I think, with disclosure, that's a very fine line. But, if the conversation calls for it, and they ask you questions …

Smock: Again, it's about the client. When I train supervisees I say, "If sharing something about myself is of my own benefit, or for me to, or if it's about me, I don't do it. If it's about the client, then I do it. I don't talk about myself because I want to talk about myself. I mean, we're human beings. I think as a researcher it's more challenging because your role as a researcher is very different, it's a one-time shot, or a few. You're

Hierarchy and self-disclosure

curious, like a therapist, but I think there'd be more of a boundary, perhaps, with self-disclosure as a researcher than as a therapist.

Me: That's totally fair. I'm having a hard time translating the therapist's practice of self-disclosure to a researcher's practice of self-disclosure because I feel like, for the benefit of the client, yes. But as a researcher, if they disclose, are they doing it for the data? For the agenda?

Smock: If it's chitchat, then OK. I think in an interview, some initial chitchat is OK. But if then, the participant turns to the researcher and asks, I think that would be much more boundaried. If you want to use the agenda or curiosity ... Here's the difference, this might be helpful: as a qualitative researcher and interviewer, if I am interested in interviewing a participant, I am interested in getting their information. I am not concerned about the co-construction of our story. In the therapy session, I am interested in the co-construction of their solutions. It's collaborative. I don't see that the same as a qualitative researcher. I don't think it's as a collaborative process. I think that it's more informational curiosity gathering. But it is not collaborative. For the most part. I know you have questions as a researcher that builds from their answers, but you're not co-constructing a reality, you're gathering information. And that's the difference between therapy and research.

(For more on this conversation, see Appendix B.)

The researcher

Similar to the therapist, the researcher is in a position of seeming power and hierarchy. The researcher may be in a position of the "expert," as an academic, a scientist, or a worker in any helping profession. Like therapy, there is a balance of sharing and sharing too much, appropriate and inappropriate self-disclosure.

A main difference between therapy and research, when it comes to hierarchy and the place for self-disclosure, is the context of each relationship. The time and context of therapy tends to be longer and more sustained than research. Where the therapist and client can have a relationship that lasts anywhere from 2 months to 5 years; however, the researcher is limited in their time with their participants to one or two meetings. Therefore, self-disclosure has more opportunity within the context of therapy, which also means the inherent hierarchy within the relationship has the opportunity to mend itself, and efforts to minimize it are longer held.

Host and guest

However, despite the short time frame of research, the qualitative researcher does have the opportunity to initiate a relationship with participants. Harlene

Anderson's concept of host and guest strongly applies to the hierarchy, and self-disclosure, in research. According to Anderson (personal conversation, September 9, 2019), the researcher is at the mercy of the participant, whereas in therapy, the therapist is sought out:

> The hierarchy is always there. Again, keep in mind the context. But with the research participant, you are at their mercy, the researcher is. You are basically asking participants for a "favor." So really the researcher is asking a favor. So, if you ask someone a favor, how do you approach it? How do you set the tone for what you're doing and why you're talking to them and inviting them in.

This difference in the context of the relationship between therapist and researcher also means the difference in hierarchy and opportunity for self-disclosure. Since the researcher is at the mercy of the participant, the principle of least interest applies (Eslinger, Clarke, & Dynes, 1972), which states that the person within any relationship with the least interest in the relationship holds the most "power." Although originally applied to family and dating relationships, it is at the mercy of the one least interested that the one with interest approaches and functions within the relationships.

The same is true for the researcher and participant. It is safe to say that the researcher is the one in the relationship with more interest, and the participant is the one there as a "favor" to the researcher. Granted, this may not be the case in every research scenario. At the same time, in my experience, researchers seek out participants that agree to take part in studies. Hence, the researcher, more often than not, is the one with far more interest in the relationship than the participant.

With researchers seeking out participants, the personhood of the researcher is very important. The relationship of guest and host begins from the very first contact with participants. The responsibility lies on the researcher to create a welcoming environment in which the participants feel adequately hosted. The environment of hospitality, welcome, and warmth are central to the atmosphere of the relationships. Since the relationship is limited, these characteristics of the researcher are much more crucial to the relationship. If done poorly, the researcher runs the risk of misestablishing the hierarchy, setting themselves in a position of overt power and authority.

At the same time, the researcher is also a guest in the life of the participant. Therefore, as a guest, as one would be in someone's home, it is the responsibility of the researcher to enter into the participant's metaphorical home with manners, composure, respectful of the metaphorical space, and at the same time not be intrusive. There are specific aims toward the researcher being a guest. As a guest, we want the participant to feel empowered, as if their metaphorical home is admired and appreciated. This is also in attempt to minimize the hierarchy.

Expertise?

In the context of research, I argue that the hierarchy is as such: At the top of the hierarchy lies the participant; we are at their mercy. This takes a shift in mind, approach, and demeanor in the researcher. With the participant at the top of the hierarchy, we as researchers are humbled being in their goodwill. After all, it is their experiences we are curious about, not so much the other way around. Therefore, the researcher ought to approach the participant humbly, with curiosity, and with the mindset of having the luxury to speak to them.

Isn't the researcher the expert, though? Yes and no. First, no. Like most postmodern therapies, the therapist approaches and treats the client as experts of their own lives; our clients know more about their experiences than we as therapists do. The same holds true for the research participant. They know their experiences (of which we want to research) better than the researcher does. Expertise, then, lies in our ability to position ourselves in the hierarchy and ask questions.

Second, yes, as researchers we are experts, but not as we think it to be. Being able to position ourselves in a place where the participant is the expert at the top of the hierarchy requires expertise. *I am an expert in being second in the hierarchy; I am an expert at letting my participants lead me. I am an expert at being curious and asking questions from the conversation itself.* The expertise of the researcher means knowing about the process of research and being able to conjure the exact means of asking questions: curiosity, humility, willingness to let the conversation flow, and the postmodern philosophies we have already mentioned. The researcher is also an expert is knowing when and how to self-disclose.

Self-disclosure expertise

Self-disclosure is not a tool one uses for a specific end goal. It's not a fancy trick that leads us to a magical ending or secret result. Like most therapeutic techniques, they are not tools in a therapy toolbox that we bring out as a secret weapon. The postmodern therapist believes in their "techniques." They believe in the philosophies in which they are using in the therapy room. The same holds true for self-disclosure: it is not a fancy trick to get our participants to open up and give us amazing data. Instead, it is an outcome of the process of a relationship, not so much used, but organically created within the flow of conversation.

This is especially true for the researcher and their participant. True to the constructivist school of thought, the researcher is just as much a part of the process of data as the participant. Therefore, as the participant is asked to share details about their life, the researcher also ought to have similar expectations placed on them. Just like the therapist, this is a careful balance, even more so given the timeline of the researcher and their limited time frame of relationship between them and their participant. This balance of self-disclosure becomes much more meticulous within the research context.

Just like therapy, knowing when to self-disclose as a researcher, and how much, is a skill. The skill lies in knowing people. I believe both the therapist and researcher to be people people. They love being a part of relationships; their way of being is reflected in their presence with people. Both know how to ask questions and to allow conversation to be guided by curiosity rather than agenda. Where with some people self-disclosing may go well and produce a richer experience for both the researcher and participant, others may not take to that level of openness very well, hence the skill of people.

When the researcher shares anything about themselves, when they are opening up themselves to the participant, they are doing so believing in the benefit that will come of it; they are doing so believing in the power of relationships. They also believe that data is an outcome of such a relationship. Therefore, they are equally a part of that relationship as well.

There is no straightforward answer to self-disclosure. There is, though, a skill it requires. It is a skill that is refined and developed with years of experience. Yalom (2002) believes that the therapist uses self-disclosure to create a sense of here and now. The researcher can also use the here-and-now experience in their data collection and interviews.

Expertise in hierarchy

The same can be said about positioning in the hierarchy. When the researcher places themselves in a position that is less than, second to, or even from behind the participants, it's done as a genuine act, it is who the researcher is. It is not a trick, strategy, or a means by which we are trying to produce an experience or data. It is a genuine effort that is a part of the researcher and what they believe to be true about the relationship they are hosting and being a guest to.

The same sense of hierarchy is practiced throughout the entire research process. Once the researcher gets to the place of transcribing and analyzing, their positioning does not change. The same mindset of host–guest is constant throughout the process. When the researcher places themselves in the position of being at the mercy of the participant, even when writing, it creates a different mental space of analyzing, as opposed to the thought process of being the one that is in charge or responsible for the data analysis.

Ironically, this is the case with the researcher. In fact, the entire purpose of their project is to *not* be an expert. The researcher, like the postmodern therapist, is in a position of needing information from the participant, which places the participant as having expertise. The researcher, in their research, literally does not know what they are trying to understand.

The researcher also ought to believe in their philosophy of hierarchy – where they fit in the positioning of the relationship. If a researcher believes they are in the position of being at the mercy of participants, then that hierarchy will organically be established. Relationships can never be completely equal and egalitarian. They will always waver. However, the researcher can be mindful of where and how they are positioning themselves. The researcher is in the position of being led by putting themselves in the metaphorically lower position.

Postmodern hierarchy

A lack of hierarchy is inherent in most postmodern therapy philosophies. The not-knowing stance is a clear example of the researcher minimizing their "authority" and expertise in the entire process, humbling themselves by putting their preknowledges aside. By letting conversation and data collection be generative, the researcher is placing themselves in a position where the end product is minimally about them. The researcher is merely a vehicle in which the process is made into a coherent form.

Within the postmodern framework of therapy, and of conversation, hierarchy is not linear. When the postmodern therapist espouses philosophies of curiosity, leading from behind, and not-knowing, their positioning is already a hierarchical shift. This is in sharp contrast to the modern approaches to therapy.

The modern therapist, for example, Jay Haley with his approach to strategic family therapy, considered his idea of a family structure and hierarchy within the family the one to work from. Therefore, he would lead the therapy process from his own belief of what a family ought to look like. His "directives," or interventions, all centered on his belief of proper family function. In such an approach, the therapist was clearly considered the "expert," placing them in an authoritative position, which created a clear hierarchical separation from the therapist and the client.

The same is true for the traditional, psychoanalytic approach to counseling. Freud's approach to psychoanalysis was similar in the regard of "knowing" or discovering unconscious conflict within his patients. Therefore, it was ultimately his interpretation and diagnosing, based off his belief of the patient's unconscious conflict, that was the drive for healing and the process of therapy itself. Even his theory of psychosexual development was ultimately a result of his years of studying patients' inner conflict, conflict he believed to stem from unconscious drives of aggression and libido. With his knowledge and theories, he arguably placed himself in the expert position, above that of his patients.

The postmodern approach to therapy is the opposite of such traditional, modern approaches. Hierarchy is a big difference in that the therapist specifically places themselves in a one-down stance. Instead of patients learning from the expert, the therapist places themselves in the learner position, learning from their clients' experiences and stories.

The qualitative researcher, I believe, naturally places themselves in a learning position, similar to that of the postmodern therapist. Instead of having a theoretical base of knowledge, an idea of family functioning in which the whole approach to therapy is based on, or the belief of inner conflict at the root of all problems, the researcher is naturally curious about their area of study. With this sense of natural curiosity comes the natural diminishing of hierarchy.

The key is for the researcher to belief in this approach, to personally espouse this philosophy of the learner. What we believe will inevitably exude itself through our demeanor. If we, as researchers, believe ourselves to be experts or people that have some set of knowledge, then we do our participants a disservice.

One-down

The postmodern therapist also does not believe in diagnoses, which also requires a philosophical stance where the therapist is "one-down" by being curious about the client's experiences rather than obtaining the preknowledge of diagnosis. The researcher, by adopting the philosophy of no diagnosis – or whatever other preknowledge comes with the researcher agenda – also places themselves in a position of openness and vulnerability to be led, which also minimizes hierarchy.

When the therapist believes in the power of diagnosis, they also believe in the power of the story a diagnosis can have on the client. The danger is for clients to internalize the stories diagnoses tell them. When a therapist goes into therapy with the preknowledge of a diagnosis, they run the risk of taking away from the unique experience and story of the client, giving too much trust in the story of the diagnosis to tell the story of the client rather than the client telling their own story.

The same is true for the researcher. When we approach the entire process with an idea, or even a hope of the data will find, we endanger the participant's experiences, and therefore limit the richness of our data.

When asked about the one-down positioning of the researcher, Anderson (personal conversation, September 9, 2019) had the following to say:

> I think of it more as walking alongside. I'm thinking about going on a walk, here to there. And I would like to tell you about my walk and have you join me on my walk. But you have to keep in mind the context, hierarchies, and power differentials, including the relationship of the researcher in terms of whoever they are beholden to; an advisor, an editor, a publisher, or colleague. There are so many people in that. It goes back to conversations, and who should be speaking to whom, when, where, why, and about what. The first conversation starts with the advisor, starts with your publisher, starts with talking with colleagues about your idea, what do they think, what questions come to mind. It's not layers, it's multiple conversations, and each one helps inform the next one and the steps that you will take.
>
> Hierarchy and power may not be appropriate for what the context of research is. But, maybe it's the notion of influence. It gets complicated

unless you think about it from a particular context. If you're working within an organization, and they have a grant to do a particular kind of research, you are beholden to the tradition, the agency, and the funder.

(For more of this conversation, see Appendix A.)

When asked about the issue of hierarchy and one-down with different conversations with an institutional review board (IRB) and academic advisors, Anderson had the following to say:

> I don't think it takes away from the hierarchy. Some people do questionnaires, or they have them do question by question. That's just not the way you get the most important kind of information that comes from talking with people. You have to be able to let them digress. This is difficult, even for people that say, "I'm really a social constructivist practitioner." When you really get down to it, and I think what they should be doing in terms of gathering information, they just can't do it. For example, one of the things I think is important, once you talk to your participants, gather your data, and process your analysis, is to go back to your participants after you've looked at everything. Maybe there is something you didn't think about or cover, and you ask that, so you have a second conversation with them. I am also interested in asking what kind of thoughts they might have had after our conversation. Or, since then, because if you're doing research from the perspective that I propose, relationships and conversation with people, it changes along the way.

Conclusion

The conversation of hierarchy will remain a difficult one. This conversation has highlighted the differences between the therapist and the researcher while also focusing on their similarities. When done well, and carefully, the practice of self-disclosure can be effective for each respective relationship and to minimize hierarchy.

Even though each relationship will inevitably obtain some amount of hierarchy, the key is for the therapist and researcher to know how to manage such hierarchy, be aware of their positionings of influence and power, and work to minimize such differences. From the postmodern philosophies, the efforts to minimize such hierarchy are to approach each relationship from the "one-down" position, placing the therapist or researcher in the learner position. With such philosophies like *being public*, the therapist and researcher do not hesitate to be open about themselves within the context of each relationship. As a caution, such practices do require a skill in knowing how and when to offer such information Although a difficult conversation, one that will always be a topic of interest, it is important for the researcher and therapist to consider such thoughts.

References

Anderson, H. (1997). *Conversation, language, and possibilities: A postmodern approach to therapy.* New York, New York: Basic Books.

de Shazer, S., & Dolan, Y. (2007). *More than miracles: The state of the art of solution-focused brief therapy.* London: Routledge, Taylor & Francis Group.

Eslinger, K. N., Clarke, A. C., & Dynes, R. R. (1972). The principle of least interest, dating behavior, and family integration settings. *Journal of Marriage and Family*, 39, 269–273.

Kitzinger, C. (1987). *Inquiries in social construction series. The social construction of lesbianism.* Los Angeles: Sage Publications.

White, M. (2007). *Maps of narrative practice.* New York, NY: W. W. Norton.

Yalom, I. D. (2002). *The gift of therapy: An open letter to a new generation of therapists and their patients.* New York: Harper Perennial.

8
ON WRITING

Introduction

Writing is difficult. Do not let anyone tell you otherwise. There are some people to whom writing comes more naturally to than others. There are some people who require a large amount of hard work and effort to accomplish something well in writing. Whichever category you fall under, this chapter is for you. The researcher, the therapist, and the writer can all benefit from this chapter, which will cover the process of writing, the written results, and the social construction of writing. As a small preface, most of the upcoming advice comes from my experiences in writing; my feelings, practices, and applications to the research process. I believe the writing experience to be an intimate one. How I proceed to write about writing is equally as intimate.

Starting the process of writing

According to the famous words of William Wordsworth, "To begin, begin." There is no simpler advice to the writer, especially the qualitative researcher. It is important for the researcher to practice a habit of writing and to consider themselves a writer. Qualitative research, and its practice of memoing and transcribing, is largely a writing endeavor. How to start the process looks different to most people. Following are thoughts and tips that are helpful to me, which I hope you will also find helpful.

First thoughts

There is a tremendous amount of energy behind first thoughts. Natalie Goldberg (2005) believes that as a writer you should not hinder yourself by thinking about writing. There is a flow, an unhindered stream of consciousness that is alive in your first thoughts. This is my advice to all writers: Let your thoughts flow, vulnerable, exposed, and unencumbered. You can go back and edit your words later, but to capture your raw, alive thoughts is crucial to the writing process. When you go back to edit your words, you must ask yourself, "What was I thinking when I wrote this?" More important, "What was I feeling when I thought this?"

The feelings and energy behind the first thoughts are who the author really is. There is a sense of the actual person behind first thoughts. If they are too edited, you lose who is writing. Therefore, it takes a certain amount of concentration, focus, and intent to gather thought. Of my favorite books on writing, William Zinsser's *On Writing Well* is one I frequently reread. Zinsser (2006) believes that clear thinking is essential to good writing. When we think clearly, we communicate and write clearly. Therefore, our product is that much better. To expound on that thought, I believe that clear thinking is also clear feeling. The passion in the writing, behind the subject matter, and within the author, are all found in the first thoughts.

It is a good practice for writers is to get in touch with their thoughts and feelings (yes, I'm a therapist and I believe in feelings). Writers ought to know what they are thinking, feeling, and processing during the writing process. As they learn to be in touch with themselves, they are being engaged with the subject matter and the writing process in general. Just like Zinsser (2006) believes that clear thinking is clear writing, I also believe that clear thinking is clear feeling and, therefore, clear writing. If the researcher can use the avenue of writing to explore their thoughts, and their feelings, the outcome will naturally be good writing. Writing comes first, though. Write first, then think and feel your way through it as the writing and project unfold.

Along with the idea of first thoughts, Natalie Goldberg (2005) also gives herself permission to write the worst work possible, in which she approaches writing anew and fresh every single time she sits down to write. The qualitative researcher can take good advice from such permission. When the researcher writes, analyzes, or collects data, they ought to give themselves permission to put out in writing things that are not good. Ann Lamott (1994) calls this the "shitty first draft." She even goes as far to say that all writers have them, even the good ones. Bad first drafts make for better second drafts and even better third drafts. "A clear sentence is no accident" (Zinsser, 2006, p. 8), therefore, the researcher would do well to allow themselves the space to err and also to improve on that.

Similar advice is offered by Roy Peter Clark (2006). The writer would do well to limit self-criticism early in the writing process. Allow yourself space to think and write through muddy thoughts. There is also a need to be mindful to the voices in your head that communicate that self-criticism. Hear what they are saying but limit them until you finish thinking through your muddy stages of writing.

Writing, then, ought to be where the researcher begins. The researcher, after all, is a writer. Creswell and Poth (2016, 2018) urge researchers to begin writing their research ideas before they discuss them; rather than talking about them, write them. Be it abstract, vague, rough, or somewhat a concrete idea of research, it is good practice for it to be written. This is not for the sake of the research, but for the researcher in their practice of writing. It is important for the researcher to be in the habit of writing, hence starting early in the process and throughout. When the researcher begins to write from the early stages of their project, they have the chance to see their ideas on paper (or the word document). Writing provides the space for loose ideas to be tangible through visualization – you can literally see your thoughts written out on the page; "seeing is a key to writing" (Zinsser, 1983, p. 12). More than that, beginning the project with writing provides the researcher space to explore themselves, to be introspective, and to try to understand their own inner workings and thoughts and the way they unravel.

The practice

I personally believe it to be good practice to write every day. Stephen King (2000) suggests the same. He argues that his profession is to be a writer; that is his job. Therefore, when you have a job, you do it. Even when you take days off, you're still working because you love the craft. Which is why the everyday practice is so important: because we love to write and research.

Zinsser has similar advice. He sees writing similarly in that it is a job that is to be done. When we are feeling tired or lacking energy, we still go to work. The same is true for the writer and researcher. We still write, even on days we don't feel like it. He compares this to an artist: that artist that lacks inspiration is either starving or going broke. They do their art, inspired or not. Therefore, write, write, write.

I have a daily goal of 500 words a day. The goal may or may not be met, but the daily practice is the hope. There is a pace, a cadence, even a rhythm of the daily practice. The mental work and the physical act of putting things on a page or a word document are all a part of the writing process. It happens daily. A painter cannot say, "I only paint on the weekends." Nor can a professional bodybuilder say, "I only workout twice a week." Writing is such a task that requires continuous thought and practice. I personally also like to read about writing.

When the writer approaches the practice every day, they keep their thoughts in shape and, just as important, their ability to write. Natalie Goldman believes that the only way to learn how to write is to write. Do it every day. It is not by taking writing classes or reading about writing and how to write (or by reading this chapter). It is only by writing that writing happens.

The research writing process

The difficult part about writing in qualitative research is the space between the researcher, the one being researched, the data itself, and the writing process.

There are too many different factors at play to completely capture the entirety of the experience. The writing process, when reflecting about data and analyzing, ought to be energized by first thoughts, the emotion of the engagement, and the personality of the author/researcher.

There is a process and space in which truth exists within the research project. True to a postmodern, constructivist epistemology, truth exists only by way in which we communicate and use language and share within interactions. As the researcher interviews, collects data, analyzes, and refines the data, they are working with *truth*. They are gathering and deciphering through an amalgamation of people's truths. At the same time, as a co-constructivist, the researcher is also carrying their truth to the data collection and analyzation process. The interaction in which things are shared and where data is gathered is where truth lives. Just like the social constructionist believes that languaging and interactions are what make our knowledge knowable, the interaction between the researcher and participant is also where knowledge is known, where truth is made.

Writing is such an interaction. Steven Pinker (2014) believes that writing is not a natural process. He argues that writing is different than speaking in that we are extra mindful of how we write, with the words we choose to communicate certain ideas and complex issues. Therefore, there is a disconnect between what we think and what comes out on the paper or word document.

It can be argued that there is something lost between the writer and what is being written. This does not have to be necessarily true. My hope is that what comes across on paper is the essence of what the writer is communicating. It is the process in which the interaction between the researcher, the participant, and the refinement of truth is displayed. The written result, then, is the most truthful expression of the construction of data.

In terms of social constructionism, the written result continues the construction of knowledge. We communicate through our written result. Therefore, what is shown on paper is the result of several different interactions and processes between lots of people. There is something sacred about the space in which writing happens. It is a transcendence of ourselves in that we further people's stories, lives, and experiences in such a way that can be comprehensible. It is a space in which we as researchers help people make sense of their lives and in the process come to know people on a different, more personal level.

Where to start?

There is also a need for the process of how we come to ask questions. The researcher already practices reflexivity, memoing, or presenting their bias in efforts to maintain an ethical, trustworthy product. However, it is less so with the process of knowing the researcher's questions and the process of how the research questions came to be. This is also a part of the writing process: the communication of the mental dialogue in which the researcher reached their questions, the choice of using certain words that aim to gather data according to their agenda, and specifically the process by which those thoughts came to be questions.

Memoing is an important process to the qualitative researcher. The act of memoing ought to be in all researchers' repertoires. When the researcher practices writing in the context of memoing, they are also practicing the flow of thoughts. As mentioned before, the first thoughts have tremendous energy; memoing is a good place to practice first thoughts. Not only first thoughts but also a refinement of thoughts. It is a mistake to wait to begin writing until you have good thoughts to put on paper. Even before thoughts are formulated, the researcher ought to write in order to think, not being intimidated by the dreaded blank page.

It is surprising to me how little memoing is shared and promoted in qualitative research as a form of academic writing. There is a generative process in memoing that results in formulation of greater ideas; therefore, it is a form of practicing writing itself. We give no qualms to football teams that practice their drills for hours on end, for musicians who play their instruments seemingly all day. Memoing is the same for the qualitative researcher. It's the practice of writing and of thinking. When the writer and thinker put their thoughts on paper or a document, their process of thinking becomes more refined, tangible, and therefore workable. Writing, after all, is thinking. Whether thoughts are concrete or fussy, memoing is a way to work on them. Zinsser (2006) promotes writers to write, rewrite, and rewrite what they've written. The same is true for memoing: a clear thought is no accident. Sometimes, thoughts need to be refined, rethought, and thought about what's been rethought.

The researcher also does not need to worry about writing in sequential order. Saldaña and Omasta (2018) offer the advice of writing what comes to the researcher and to not get stuck on one area of the project. If the researcher is having a hard time thinking and writing through the literature section, jump to another area of the study and writing process so that the flow and practice of writing can continue. The goal of nonsequential writing is for the researcher to keep their writing muscles in shape rather than becoming paralyzed by writer's block.

Saldaña and Omasta (2018) also suggest that writing is prewriting. All written efforts or documents, be it memos, transcriptions, transcribing itself, or field notes all contribute to the final product. The researcher, then, is strongly encouraged to keep with the writing process no matter where they are writing. Just like all roads lead to Rome, all writing leads to the final product.

When it comes to academic writing, the process of rewriting is crucial. Stephen King (2000) believes that in order to be a good writer, no matter what discipline, above all, the writer must read and write, a lot. If our craft and job depend on our ability to write in academic journals and circles, thenthat mustbe our practice: read academic things and write academically, alot. According to King, there is no way around this. Ann Dillard offers similar advice: practice a habit of writing and studying the craft as much as possible.

Written results

The philosophy and practice of writing relate to the written results. A clear analyzation of data is no accident. It requires hours on end, just like the professional musician, to clearly and carefully refine our thoughts and analyzation of data.

The previous positioning of host and guest apply to the written results. When we sit down to write results, we are still guests to our clients, and we host them in our writing. In an interview with Harlene Anderson, she mentions how within the relationship of the researcher and participant, the researcher is at the mercy of the participant. From the initial contact, and even throughout the writing process, we have the luxury of someone else's story. When we write, we invite others to the experiences we have had with our participants. Our data, displayed through writing, ought to symbolize our positioning with our participants: we are a guest in their lives and their experiences are hosted in our writing. As we interact with the data, as we formulate and analyze, we are still treating the participant as a guest that we have invited to our home of research. At the same time, we are still being a guest in their experiences. Therefore, as a researcher, we live as a guest in the experiences of our participants that is itself data.

It is important for the qualitative researcher to consider themselves a writer. The practice of writing is important to the process of therapy and research, specifically the written results. The better the researcher is at the practice of writing, the easier time they will have with their written results. This is not to say that they will be great writers or even expert analyzers, but that the practice of writing will strengthen their efforts in analysis.

Just like Stephen King (2000) writes in his memoir that a writer must write and read a lot, I think good analysis cannot happen without constant reading of data. For the researcher, I think is it important to not only read about research, but to also continuously read their data. The qualitative researcher must make a practice of reading their data, daily, not only when they are "working." This is also a part of the experience of researching: reading.

Edit, edit, edit. That's all I have to say about that.

Good writing is good editing. It is a mistake for the writer and the researcher to consider these two as separate entities; they are not. Editing is the essence of writing (Zinsser, 2006). Editing is where writing happens, not putting words on the page. The editing process is crucial to the writer and the researcher in that is forces the researcher to look at themselves. To be vulnerable, editing takes a tremendous amount of courage; to go back and read what you have written, to see how potentially shitty the first draft is, and to tackle the task of making coherence of your first thoughts, it all takes courage. My advice to you: Have courage in writing.

The experience of writing throughout

During the editing process, the researcher must be mindful about the experiential part of research and writing. During the writing, the researcher has the opportunity to experience their participants anew, as well as themselves. There are multiple times in the research process when the researcher can to do this: the interview, the analyzing, and written results, and, if they choose to, the presentation of the results. The relationship established with the participants does not end at the interview; it is continued through each endeavor and step of the project.

The researcher would do well to be mindful of the relationships during the entire process, including their contribution to the relationships. During the interview, the researcher is mindful of their contribution to the data, how they are co-constructing the data and contributing to the conversation. This requires a sense of self, an awareness of their being and who they are in the relationships. This continues beyond into transcribing as well.

Transcription

I believe the best practice for the researcher to frequent is to interview and transcribe themselves their transcription. I believe there is something lost when the researcher interviews and chooses to have someone else transcribe. When the researcher transcribes, they are taking one more opportunity to reexperience their participants and the relationship in which they established. Through transcribing, the researcher also can practice presence again, as if they were conducting the interview again.

During the transcription, the researcher can continue to be mindful of what was said, how they contributed to the conversation, and how they influenced the relationship; how they co-constructed the data. In the space of transcribing, the researcher can also practice reflexivity in the specific context of how they influenced the process. There is little attention paid to memoing and reflexivity in the way that researchers influence data. Therefore, the researcher is mindful of how they dialogued as they transcribe.

Analysis

During the analysis, the same practice is continued. The researcher, when coding and creating themes or categories, is mindful of their own presence transitioned from the interview to the analyzation. This is a careful process. There is the potential and opportunity for the researcher to practice presence during these phases; how they analyze, where they insert their own selves into the analyzation, and where they let the data speak for itself.

The philosophies and concepts discussed in previous chapters apply to the written results as the researcher continues to reexperience their participants. For example, the not-knowing stance; during the transcribing and the analysis, the researcher must also practice not-knowing. Once in the stance during the interview, the researcher has the time to slow the interactions during transcribing, therefore adding another level of not-knowing to the process. Analysis offers another opportunity for the researcher to slow down and to be mindful of their presence of not-knowing.

When coding, creating themes, or developing categories, the not-knowing stance is still practiced. The not-knowing stance is something that the researcher embodies throughout the entire process. This is a difficult balance during the analyzation of data. How does the researcher practice not-knowing while creating philosophical and analytical codes in the data? When does the expertise of the researcher begin and one is able to be analytical and critical of data with a researcher's mind?

There is a philosophical space in which the researcher enters when they are mindful of reexperiencing participants and the research process. When interviewing, it is easier to practice the aforementioned philosophies and stances. However, when transcribing and analyzing, it is a bit more difficult since the presence of the participants is lacking; it is only ambiguously there by way of listening to interviews and then analyzing data. However, the practice of approaching the first minute of contact remains throughout.

The Japanese concept of *Ba* applies to the entire process, similar to conversational background presented by Anderson (1997): the space, Ba, that creates an environment, a place where the person *feels* the conversation, is engulfed in it, and is equally a part of themselves and the conversation and environment in which it is happening. The metaphorical space in which conversations happens does not leave the researcher or the researcher does not leave that space throughout the process. Toward that same end, the researcher continues the dialogue throughout the transcription and analysis.

The metaphorical space continues into analysis. This is especially true for researchers that collaborate. When a team analyzes data together, the same philosophical stances apply: not-knowing, conversational background, metaphorical space, and mutual engagement. The process of analyzing together is dialogue at its truest form. Not only are the researchers mindful of the data at hand, and how the is derived, but they are also mindful of their contributions to the analysis process. The metaphorical space of conversation and dialogue extends from the researcher and participant into the conversation among the research team.

Research team

The experience during the process of analyzing is important to the quality of data produced. True to the solution-focused brief therapy model of therapy, and most postmodern approaches to therapy, there is no agenda when entering a conversation with clients. Even though researchers have a primary research question or idea and curiosity, that curiosity ought to be the conversational background in the analysis process. To that end, researchers as part of a team also have to be mindful of the agendas they bring to the research process, specifically the process of analyzing and writing data.

The generative flow of conversation, driven by the overarching research question, in combination with the data at hand, all produce the perfect storm of what is referred to as a trialogue: dialogue between the researcher and the participants, which is where data lives, and then the dialogue between the researchers themselves (see Figure 8.1). Both analysis and data, then, happen within such a multilayered conversation. Data happens in conversation with the participant, which is brought back to the team, which in turn is where analysis happens. The analysis process also goes back and forth between analyzing and the data. Therefore, among the team and the data, there is a larger conversation happening or a multilayered conversation where the dialogue between data

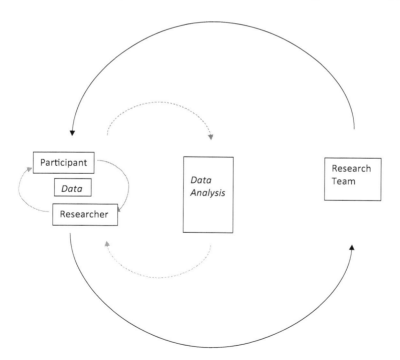

FIGURE 8.1 Analysis trialogue.

and analysis is one that is already embedded in the trialogue of participant, researcher, and team.

When analyzing results with a research team, the conversation is between three different entities, where the research team is one entity on its own, where dialogue happens between them, and the conversation between them and the participants. The experience of the multilayeredness of these conversations is important to the data process. As mentioned earlier, the positioning of the researcher does not stop, even within the research team and analyzing.

The writing process is still considered a continuation of the conversation process between the researcher, the team, and participant. The difficulty within the writing process, and the challenge for the researcher, lies in keeping the attitude, presence, and stance during the writing process and communicating that to the audience.

In order for the researcher to communicate their approach to their process, memoing becomes a very important means. I believe too few researchers publish their memos. At the same time, too few researchers memo about their experiences during the research process; from formulating research and interview questions, to their experience in their interviews and data collection, to analysis with their team, and writing.

In order for the audience to better understand the process behind the researcher, it is the responsibility of the researcher to be forthcoming with such experiences.

Philosophies of reexperiencing

The experience of the researcher during all phases of the research process is very important: asking a research question, data gathering, analysis, and writing. Carl Whitaker refers to a similar idea in therapy; he calls it the "existential encounter." He believes that the person of the therapist is the catalyst of change throughout the entire therapy process. The character, personality, presence, and *way of being* of the therapist, he believed, was so strong that his clients could not help but be overcome to change. Therefore, therapy largely depended on who the therapist was as a person.

The same can be true for the researcher. To use Whitaker and Bumberry's (1988) concept, is it the existential encounter, the experience of the researcher, that sets the tone for the entire research process, namely, the encounter with participants all the way through their personhood expressed through their writing. The researcher, then, has the responsibility to approach the participant with their own personhood, their ability to be a real human being rather than a researcher. It is the tone of personhood that is important to the experience of the participant and the researcher. That experience does not stop with participants.

The quality of the researcher, their sense of personhood, and their *humanity* are all crucial to the entire process of research. At its essence, I believe, qualitative research is ultimately about people; we are people trying to understand people. That thought is consistent throughout the entire process: formulation of research ideas and questions, interviews, data collection, analysis, and writing results. Consider the following flow of the researcher process that ultimately leads back to our sense of humanity:

The written product comes from our results.
Results come from our analysis.
Analysis comes from our data.
Our data comes from our relationship with our participants.
Our relationship is influenced by the questions we ask.
Our questions stem from our curiosity about the research.
Our curiosity originates from our humanity.

There is a process of continuing to experience your participants throughout the entire research process. The experience of interviewing and collecting data is the essence of the process. The practice of qualitative research in the social sciences, whether the range of topics studied or methods, is largely to gather data through interviews (Potter & Hepburn, 2005; ten Have, 2004). The host–guest concept is extremely important to this initial meeting; it sets up how data is produced. Data, I believe, is an outcome of the relationship between the researcher and the participant. Just like therapy, whatever therapeutic elements come from the process of therapy are outcomes of the relationship between the therapist and client. With this mindset, the researcher's product, then, is data. Their last outcome of their experiences, then, is their writing.

To expound on this process, the modern artist Oliver Lee Jackson believes in his artistic products being complete and made in and of themselves. As he describes, it is not *him* within the painting, but it is a generative process in which he starts with a concept and then lets the painting evolve on its own. Each stroke is the result of the previous, and each stroke tells where the next stroke will go. The entire painting, then, is a process of being present in each stroke and letting the painting evolve on its own. The end product, the painting, is then a product in and of itself.

This is also true for the entire research process, from the inception of the study, to the data collection, to the written results, and even into presenting. The start is the research agenda, or as I like to call it, initial curiosity. How does that initial curiosity grow, how is it molded, and how does it come to fruition? The start of the conversation has been set by the overall research agenda. Each statement of the participant leads the researcher to ask another question, and after each answer, the researcher then provides another "stroke," another question. The research team is also informed by the previous strokes of the data analysis. Within the analysis, the researchers are also informed by each other along the way. Each step of the journey is informed by the previous.

What is important in this concept, parallel to the evolving data, is that the product is never finished. When the interview is done, the process continues. The same presence required to produce data with participants is also required in the analysis and write up.

★★★

End note: The self of the researcher

There is a common practice in therapy where the therapist takes time to reflect on themselves, examine their state of being, calibrate their own personal stresses, and to ultimately be the best therapist they can be for their clients. This practice is similar to self-care; however, it is done specifically for the therapist and their work in therapy. They process and talk with other therapists to work through their stressors in order to be successful in therapy. The researcher can also benefit from such practices.

The entire process of research is maintaining a conversation with participants, but more than that, research is about maintaining a conversation with readers and research itself. Ultimately, research is a curiosity, just like a conversation is rooted in curiosity. We approach conversation with someone from a stance of curiosity, and therefore we approach the entire process of research from that same stance: curiosity. We as researchers are only a part of that conversation, in which we ought to also examine ourselves. Consider the following in researcher examination.

Why do people choose their research topics? Why are people drawn to certain ideas and issues? What is it about complications of the human experience that we are curious about them? I believe the best research to be something the researcher is passionate about; this is not new to academic circles. However, there is a sense of humanity behind research topics and the process of choosing them that the researcher ought to be mindful of. For example, speaking for myself, issues in therapy such as marital conflict, infidelity, and even issues of masculinity are all interesting to work with because those issues hold a place in my heart, and I hold a special place for people that struggle with such issues. My humanity, therefore, is turned into the research process where I want to not only help people in therapy but also to learn about them academically. However my sense of curiosity can be satisfied and however I can learn about people is the root of my curiosity.

As the researcher begins to formulate questions and thinking about research agendas, their sense of humanity, their compassion, and love for people ought to also be examined. There is a responsibility of the researcher to pursue and delve into topics that spark their sense of humanistic curiosity.

It is helpful for the researcher to ask themselves, "What is it about this topic that sparks my curiosity, empathy, sympathy, or need to devote my resources for such a topic?" In searching themselves, I believe, the process of researching can begin. When the researcher knows about why they are interested in a topic, it will organically and generatively evolve.

Formulating questions

Considering the importance of self-examination, there is a lack of transparency in research when it comes to formulating questions. In fact, it is quite rare that the audience or reader sees the questions that were formulated by the researcher. Even though researchers practice reflexivity in disclosing their bias in data analysis and results, reflexivity ought to be practiced through the entire process, especially in the process of asking questions.

This is important because the interview questions are a monumental part of how data is collected. Even though the interview process is where data collection happens, the interview process is initiated by questions. The data collection, then, is potentially in danger of being skewed or biased before it even begins. Therefore, the researcher does their interview participant and their readers a disservice by not disclosing how their questions came to be, from where they were formulated, and from the sense of humanity that drove such questions.

The word *research* bears a heavy connotation. If we are thinking of our participants as data machines (for lack of a better phrase), then we will approach the conversation as such researchers, which that term itself implies something academic, rigorous, even scientific. To also add the component of being a "psychologist" or a "therapist" also adds a level of languaging and interpretations that may not be friendly to the interactions and relationships with our participants.

There is a certain mindset that the researcher ought to have when experiencing the research process. It begins with the initial conversation of research. Be it your institution's institutional review board (IRB) process or the relationship with your dissertation chair or your supervisor, the conversation of research beings within multiple contexts. And it is within these contexts that the mindset of the researcher is established.

If the researcher enters these conversations and multiple contexts with the mindset of anything other than curiosity, the entire process has the potential for being skewed. Granted, there can still be a study, results, and write-ups. However, the entire argument of this book is for the researcher to be mindful of how and who they are. Therefore, each conversation, given whichever context it begins, is rooted in curiosity.

Research, to oversimplify its definition, is essentially curiosity. We are at the root of that curiosity.

References

Anderson, H. (1997). *Conversation, language, and possibilities: A postmodern approach to therapy*. New York, New York: Basic Books.
Clark, R. P. (2006). *Writing tools: 55 essential strategies for every writer*. New York: Little, Brown and Company.
Creswell, J. W. (2016). *30 essential skills for the qualitative researcher*. Thousand Oaks: Sage.
Creswell, J. W., & Poth, C. N. (2018). *Qualitative inquiry and research design: Choosing among five approaches*. Thousand Oaks: Sage.
Goldberg, N. (2005). *Writing down the bones: Freeing the writer within*. Boston: Shambhala.
King, S. (2000). *On writing: 10th anniversary edition: A memoir of the craft*. New York: Pocket Books.
Lamott, A. (1994). *Bird by bird: Some instructions on writing and life*. New York: Anchor Books.
Pinker, S. (2014). *The sense of style: The thinking person's guide to writing in the 21st century*. New York: Penguin Books.
Potter, J., & Hepburn, A. (2005). Qualitative interviews in psychology: Problems and possibilities. *Qualitative Research in Psychology*, 4, 281–307.
Saldaña, J., & Omasta, M. (2018). *Qualitative research: Analyzing life*. Los Angeles: Sage.
ten Have, P. (2004). *Understanding qualitative research and ethnography*. London: Sage.
Whitaker, C. A., & Bumberry, W. M. (1988). *Dancing with the family: A symbolic experiential approach*. Levittown: Brunner/Mazel.
Zinsser, W. (1983). *Writing with a word processor*. New York: Harper & Row Publishers.
Zinsser, W. (2006). *On writing well: The classic guide to writing nonfiction*. New York: Harper Collins.

APPENDIX A

Following is a personal conversation I recorded with Harlene Anderson. The conversation in its entirety was not transcribed, as there are pieces that did not pertain to the overall research conversation. What is detailed are exchanges that only pertain to my curiosities about her views of qualitative research and her practices as a collaborator. The highlighted excerpts are my own reflections on how I conducted my questions within the collaborative language systems model of therapy, or collaborative research. I began with one overall curiosity and allowed the conversation to flow from each statement. From each statement, my own curiosities generated the following set of questions.

Me: Well, I am dedicating an entire chapter to collaborative language systems, but now I feel like I have to change the title because you don't call it that anymore. And it makes sense, I completely understand that the spirit of collaboration does not limit itself to only therapy. It expands beyond that.

Harlene: Well you can mention that I used to call it that. My ideas have moved so far into other areas, and I don't think of myself as a therapist anymore. And not only from my own experiences, as I hear about other people's work, and travel around, there are ICCE [International Culture and Career Exchange] programs, they have therapists and others in their program, whether they be university professors teaching research or whether they work with organizations and communities. One had a heart surgeon and attorney, just a variety of people. So, collaboration is an interest to most people.

With Harlene explaining her vision of collaborative language systems, now called collaborative practices, I took the idea of her vision of collaboration, what it means to her, and how she believed it also pertained to the qualitative researcher. As we were catching up and exchanging informal conversation, my curiosity about her collaborative practices generated the idea of how her expansion of her practice applied to my own curiosities of the researcher. Which led me into my overall curiosity; my one question I had for her and her expertise.

Me: Yes, and it's not just therapy; so, let me backtrack here. I am trying to enter this with *no* agenda. I have a general curiosity that I am looking for, but I am trying to enter this without an agenda, because even the way you conceptualize collaborative practices now, how do you think the qualitative researcher can benefit from the philosophies of collaborative practices?

Harlene: OK, what a question. I think to think of your participants, so to speak, as having expertise that they bring and what they are interested in and how you approach that. It really begins with what you want to *learn*. What do you want to inquire into and for what reason, and how do you communicate this to your participants. And at the same time, for me, invite in the participant's voice – "This is what I'm interested in, is there something that you're [the participant] interested in that might be connected?" Bring in their voice and engage their curiosity in the inquiry, and not to think of it as having a major question with subquestions that need to be answered, but that you are trying to learn something, whether it be a big overall thing or a very specific thing. For me, the questions then come from the conversation.

The idea that sticks out to me is the practice of engaging our participants' curiosity, and therefore not thinking of having an overall major question with subquestions. Instead, we are learning from our participants; big or small ideas are all learning. As Harlene spoke those words, the next question that came to my mind was the "research agenda" and what she thought that meant for the collaborative researcher. Since she thought of not thinking about it in terms of research questions, my next curiosity was how she felt about the agenda overall.

Me: Yes, I love that idea, and I 100% agree with that. And that speaks to the idea of conversation being generative in itself. It generates more questions and curiosities. What, then, does the researcher do then with their research questions? I've been struggling with this for the past several months as I've been writing and thinking about this. I feel like a true postmodern therapist, and therefore researcher, I feel like they run the risk of being too tied to their research agenda, to their questions. Which is a little bit contrary to postmodernism itself. What do you think about that?

Harlene: Well, I have experienced with some doctoral students I've advised who start out with a specific question, but as they take a more

	collaborative approach with their participants, they begin to modify their questions, or sometimes they find that their question has no relevance to the participant as they begin to engage in collaboration. It's being able to hold your overall research question/aim/agenda tentatively. That's the map you start out with, but as you get off on your journey, you take some detours. And you can discuss that in terms of, if you are at all influenced by a collaborative perspective, as you begin asking your questions, the responses that came begin to lead the researcher and the participant in a different direction.
Me:	And I feel like that's how I practice therapy, but my scope and practice is pretty limited to only therapy. So, approaching research that way, I don't know if there aren't many people that practice that.
Harlene:	There aren't many, but you also have to take into consideration the larger context in which you are doing your research inquiry. If that's that context of the university, then what are the university's expectations and requirements of you, particularly if you're doing it towards a degree. So that begins with the conversations you have with your advisor, and to make sure you have an advisor that fits with your own preferences. How to navigate having one foot in one world and another in another world.

I was not expecting Harlene to bring the ideas of contexts within the inquiry or research projects. As she mentioned that, I let myself be fully immersed in what she was explaining about the contextual factors. When she mentioned the role of advisors and supervisors, and navigating collaboration within these relationships, the idea of hierarchy came to mind, which led me to my next question that I had not quite formulated, as you will see.

Me:	Exactly, I agree. You mention having a good advisor, and that brings to my mind the issue of hierarchy; having a research advisor, a therapy supervisor, or even within the research relationship. Especially within a collaborative approach, what do you think about hierarchy ... I don't even know if there's a question in that. If you can, speak to the issue of hierarchy within these different relationships.
Harlene:	The hierarchy is always there. Again, keep in mind the context, and what are the hierarchies within the context. But with the research participant, you are at their mercy. The researcher is. You are basically asking them, for the lack of a better word right now, for a "favor." So really the researcher is asking a favor.
Me:	Fascinating! I have never heard it put that way.
Harlene:	So, if you ask someone a favor, how do you approach it? How do you set the tone for what you're doing, in other words your interest, and why you're talking to them and how they can be helpful to you, and inviting them in.

Me: So, I think this is a common thought in postmodern therapy, the one-down position, leading from behind. I feel like that's a similar idea but using different language. Is that similar?

Harlene: I think of it more as walking alongside. I'm thinking about going on a walk, here to there. And I would like to tell you about my walk and that I would have you join me on my walk ... I'm just making this up as I go along, something like that. But you have to keep in mind the context, different hierarchies, and power differentials in all of those contexts, including the relationship of the researcher in terms of whoever they are beholden to: an advisor, an editor, a publisher, or colleague. There are so many people in that ... and it goes back to conversations, and who should be speaking to whom, when, where, why, and about what. The first conversation starts with the advisor, starts with your publisher, starts with talking with colleagues about your idea, what do they think, what questions come to mind. It's not layers, it's multiple conversations, and each conversation helps inform the next one and the steps that you will take.

Once again, I was not expecting Harlene to mention her ideas of contexts and multiple conversations. The ideas that stood out to me as I listened to her were hierarchy within contexts, all informing the next conversation, which brought about the next couple of questions.

Me: That's a really interesting way to put it, multiple conversations. I agree, the idea of context, and who is directing the researcher, the student, the participant. There are several contexts in which direction happens and steps that need to be followed. But, they're multiple conversations rather than hierarchy.

Harlene: Hierarchy and power may not be appropriate for what the context of research is and especially what you're trying to write and think about. But, maybe it's the notion of influence. It gets complicated unless you think about it from a particular context, and that's one of the things you'll probably want to address. If you're working within an organization, and they have a grant to do a particular kind of researcher, you are beholden to the tradition, the agency, and the funder. Or, a university, and they have rules and degree programs that you have to go through in order to graduate.

Me: And even within the university, you have to get your study approved by IRB [Institutional Review Board], so there is some sort of governance over your project. Again, multiple conversations.

Harlene: Right. How can you address the particular IRB requirements?

Me: And that's where I struggle because IRB will want you to give them a list of particular questions and instruments ...

Harlene: And I would give them a list of questions. If they want to know my primary questions, and then the more specific, the more specific kinds of information you want to obtain, that you're imagining is important to obtain, then you give them the questions.

Me: And of course, that has to happen, there's no way around that. So, I'm piecing together my thoughts, here: I don't think that takes away from the dynamic and relationship between the researcher and participant. These are conversations and contexts we have to be mindful of and hierarchies within each. If I hear you correctly, that doesn't take away from the relationship you have with your participants or the conversations you have with your participants.

Harlene: I don't think it takes away from the hierarchy. Some people do questionnaires, or they have them do question by question. That's just not the way, I think, you get the most important kind of information that comes from talking with people. You have to be able to let them *digress*. This is difficult, even for people that say, "I'm really a social constructionist practitioner." When you really get down to it, and I think what they should be doing in terms of gathering information, they just can't do it. For example, one of the things I think is important, once you talk to your participants, gather your data, and process of your analysis, to go back to your participants after you've looked at everything. Maybe there is something you didn't think about or cover, and you ask that, so you have a second conversation with them. I am also interested in asking what kind of thoughts they might have had after our conversation. Or, since then, because if you're doing research from the perspective that I propose in terms of relationships and conversation with people, it changes along the way.

Before this interview, I had been working on the collaborative chapter and had just read through literature pertaining to the idea of withness. As Harlene was explaining the practice of digressing and allowing participants time to think about an interview, my mind went to a withness question. In the practice of being public, I explain that much to Harlene.

Me: It does, and organic and fluid, and that itself is generative. If you can, and it sounds like your talking – this is on my mind so I might be reading too much into it – it sounds like you're speaking about *withness* that Shotter and Hoffman talk about. I feel like there's a sort of *with* or being with people that allows for that tangential, veering …

Harlene: Carlos, I think it begins with your first contact with your participants, how you introduce yourself, how you meet and greet them, as someone you need and someone that you're trying to sell something to. You really want to think about the relationship from the very beginning. You want to be doing something *with* each other. You want them to have a sense of ownership – if you can imagine that. That this is also mine and I'm helping him by answering his questions and giving him information. Taking the time to get to know your participants a little bit. Some researchers just gather their participants, have them sign the form, and then start off with their questions. "So, you work at the community mental health center there in El Paso. I'm not familiar with this center, tell me a little bit about it and what you do there."

Me: There is a certain amount of, well, we're researching people and we're talking to people. So there is a certain amount of humanity that I feel like this witness calls for. One of my students once said that it's a little bit inhuman to go into a research interview, ask question after question, potentially hard and intrusive questions, and then just leave. It's a little bit inhumane.

Harlene: That's right. You're developing a relationship with your participant. You're inviting your partner/participant and asking them to be in a relationship with you, in conversation with you. If you think about it, like in therapy, you want someone to be your conversational partner. For me, it's the same in research as well. So, you can see that I am much more interested in face to face in terms of talking to people rather than sending someone a questionnaire.

At this point of the conversation, I have completely let go of my original research idea. I have let each of my questions build on the answers and thoughts Harlene has offered. From this point, I am curious about her idea of conversational partners, which sparked in my mind her idea of conversational background and metaphorical space that she writes about.

Me: Yes, it's the conversation, it's the witness. If you can, speak a little bit to conversational background, in research, in interviewing, metaphorical space …

Harlene: The background is the conversation, but the conversation also has a background. The background of the conversation is also cultural discourses, people's everyday life, professional discourses, mostly in their everyday life as well. Each person, the professional and the person you are interviewing or having a conversation with, are having conversations with so many other people that influence their ideas and what you think. In terms of the conversational background, basically, I probably talk these days in terms of space, the type of space you want to create. I mention the notion of metaphorical space, both literal and metaphorical, and what kind of space you want to create. That is part of the background in which the conversation happens.

Me: Speak more to that. I feel like that is a very philosophical and abstract concept. I think it's a little bit difficult for people to conceptually grasp.

Harlene: Maybe we can think of it as the atmosphere, environment that you are hoping to create with and for yourself and another person,

	that is more rather than less inviting of them to join you in, which connection of withness, with another person. There's a very interesting concept call *Ba*. There is an environment in which we want to create, and we invite others into. It's in the Japanese culture, and it's talking about metaphorical space. While I think about it, I have a Taos Institute learner that is interested in coaching, and they are interested in this idea of metaphorical space. But that's what they are interested in; how to create such an environment, how to have that attitude yourself in which people can feel welcomed and open.
Me:	Yes, so that metaphorical space, where two people are mutually involved and engaged in conversation, in dialogue. To sound cheesy, there is something very magical about that space and engagement. I feel like the initial contact is where that space is created. If I hear you correctly, that space starts with the researcher.
Harlene:	I think so, it starts with the person. I am very biased in that way. It begins with the first contact, early on. When you think about the conversational background, what would someone think about their preconceptions about a person who is a therapist or who is a researcher. Not that you will ask them that, but we need to consider it before we enter into therapy and research, and people have all these preconceived notions about what a researcher and a therapist is.
Me:	Yes, you're this big bad researcher who wants to know about my life. That has the potential to have a really skewed or … that produces a certain quality of data if the participants already thinks "this big bad researcher at this fancy university want to know things about me." That sets up a kind of data that is already not what I want.
Harlene:	Right. "And, who will know about this, and what will they know about …" Again, it's about how as a researcher not to be intrusive. *At this point, I have my idea of how a researcher is not intrusive in asking their research questions. However, I am trying to suspend my idea of what it means to not be intrusive. Therefore, I present Harlene with the following question in effort to trust her idea and her insight into that practice, rather than preknow what she means by such advice.*
Me:	Yes! How do you think one does that as a researcher?
Harlene:	I think you're careful about the questions you ask, how you pose them. The relationship is part of the background to those questions. For example, if you're researching someone's history of sexual abuse or something like that, you want to say up front, "I want you to know that I may ask you some questions that are intrusive or uncomfortable, and certainly my hope is not to do that, but if that happens, please let me know."
Me:	Yes, that's really good. I'm doing similar things in my current research projects. And that sounds like a similar idea of host and

	guest. I feel like there is something different with the idea that we are at the mercy of our participants as researchers.
Harlene:	Well, as the researcher, you are the host of your guest, the participant. And at the same time, I find it helpful to think they are hosting me. In other words, they're hosting me in their life. I don't want to be an intrusive guest in their life. So that's how you think about. How do you want to be a welcoming host and a welcomed guest?

Along with her idea of host and guest, from her response the idea of self-disclosure came to mind, and how the researcher can practice it or if it even fits in researcher. In my mind, the relationship in which host and guest is created allows for some self-disclosure.

Me:	That really applies to the process of research, especially in the amount of time the researcher has with their participants, as opposed to therapy where the relationship can be much longer. So, just for a second, you sort of touched on this already, talk about the disclosure and being public, specifically in the researcher process, if that applies here.
Harlene:	Well, I think that would be letting the person know as best you can, why you are interested in this particular topic. I have not had a lot of opportunities for self-disclosure, though, in research. I've had people ask me what I am going to do with the information being gathered, but that's about it.
Me:	I know Yalom talks about self-disclosure in therapy, but he doesn't talk about it in research, not that I know of, at least. I don't know anyone that has written about self-disclosure in research, do you?
Harlene:	No, I don't, but to me, it's not that much of an issue. If you meet someone from the beginning, and you're trying to develop a collaborative relationship with them, then they have a sense that you are present, and open, and they probably won't ask you a lot of questions. Particularly if you ask in a way, "I'm a university student and I am working on my dissertation, and I am in my last year of my program. I'm doing a research ... I wouldn't even call it research. I would say I am trying to learn more about _____. It's about *how* you engage and talk to another person, how you create the Ba, that safe space.

The thought that she wouldn't use the label "research" was fascinating to me. I couldn't help but follow up on that idea and have her expand on that and what it means to research. Again, these last several questions were not planned, but they are were all organically generated by the conversation itself.

Me:	So, you wouldn't even use the word "research"?
Harlene:	I probably would not.
Me:	Does that create too much of a stigma or too much of a power dynamic of some sort? I really like that idea a lot of not even using that word.

Harlene: Well I haven't even thought about it consciously until now when we were talking.

In my opinion, this is the spirit idea of collaborative practices: when ideas become tangible and moldable, sparked by natural curiosity. I was curious about her idea of not using "research," and she responded with something more concrete because she had not thought about it out loud – true generative ideas.

It just seems like "research," oh that heady stuff. First of all, "You're a psychologist? Oh you're going to try to read my mind? Oh, research?" I probably use the language that I'm am trying to *learn* more about. That is what you're trying to do. You want to use, in research and in therapy, more everyday language. I want to learn about this and the way I'm going to learn about it is to ask you some questions.

Me: I think that gets at the heart of collaboration, the everyday language of relationships. There's a normalcy to it. There is not an air of academics. It's just a normal everyday conversation. I like that a lot.

APPENDIX B

This conversation with Dr. Sara Smock Jordan was conducted regarded the solution-focused brief therapy (SFBT) approach and how its philosophies can be used within qualitative research. Smock-Jordan is the editor of the *Journal of Solution-Focused Brief Therapy* and is an accomplished researcher. I sought her opinion regarding the model of therapy and research since she is accomplished in both areas. True to the model of therapy, I entered the conversation with no agenda, letting the conversation organically form. As mentioned in Chapter 6, I listened for answers specifically regarding the model of therapy and qualitative research. Using Listen, Select, and Build, my choices of focus on language and phrases are outlined.

Me: True to the solution-focused form, I have no agenda going into this. Therefore, the first question for you is, what do you think is the most important for the qualitative researcher to know regarding the SFBT philosophy?

Regarding the initial approach to solution-focused brief therapy, where the therapist enters the session asking the question, "What would be the most helpful for us to talk about today that you feel it's a productive session?" I enter this conversation the same way asking a form of that question regarding research and what Dr. Smock-Jordan think is the most important for the qualitative researcher to know about solution-focused brief therapy.

Smock: SFBT is a model that is inductively developed. When we think about qualitative research and SFBT, it's a great pair because both qualitative researchers, even depending on their various methodologies, a qualitative researcher is wanting to gain an experience, wanting to hear about a phenomenon, do ground theory, whatever it might be, they are starting from gathering information and more inductively than a quantitative researcher. A lot of models in the field of marriage and family therapy/couple family therapy, social work, any field that uses systemic models, or even psychotherapy in general, is that those approaches start with a theory. We believe a certain behavior starts "this way," whether it's attachment theory or dysfunction. People say that SFBT does not have a theory or that it's atheoretical. His approach to theory, it's atheoretical. That's true in the sense that Steve de Shazer did not find a grand theory regarding behavior. He wanted to, but he could not come up with one explanation for change in human behavior. That was his original goal. He was fascinated with Erikson's account of change. He started searching and couldn't find anything but was interested and influenced by Wittgenstein in the idea that one should *renounce all theory*. This became clear in his writing: we don't have a theory to explain behavior change. It became known to Steve and those who studied him that SFBT is not rooted in theory. However, we believe, and from his writings, that Steve had what's considered a little t theory. The difference is big T points to one reason, one reason on why things happen. Little t talks about reasons for behavior and change being contextual. That being conversation, language, and context. Even though Steve did not subscribe to a big T theory, he did to a little t theory. And how that applies to qualitative research is that it's the same for qualitative work. *Qualitative work is about the little t. And we believe that. I think qualitative comes from that point.* With my work in microanalysis, it's the detailed moment-to-moment video analysis of conversation, what's going on at the moment-by-moment level. It's also inductive and it's also a mixture of qualitative and quantitative because it's evolutionary. We do count the number if things that happen in a dialogue, which makes it quantitative, but the process is more qualitative. How we design our manual, or rule book, are all developed from a qualitative perspective. They are all inductively based, unique to each study. That's a good fit for SFBT, and with microanalysis, I think qualitative research has a microanalysis aspect.

It all goes back to the idea of little t, there is no big T, that goes back to Wittgenstein. And I think it just all nicely ties together.

At the point, I am interested in Dr. Smock's ideas of theory, specifically how they apply to the qualitative researcher. As I listen, with the intent of finding ways to further the conversation around qualitative research, I select the phrases big T, little t, renounce all theory, and induction. From those words I am curious about how she conceptualizes those ideas and philosophies from SFBT and how it was formulated and how they can translate into practices for the qualitative researcher.

Me: I completely agree, I like that a lot. Let me ask a little bit more of a specific question. I like the idea of big T and little t and the idea of

Appendix B **151**

induction and the process from where the theory evolved: From the notion of big T and little t theory, and the process of accumulation data inductively, for example, the idea of people are not their problems all the time, and the idea of Wittgenstein's philosophy on the verb *to be*, how can the researcher benefit from those SFBT theories with the idea of little t?

Smock: Going back to the evolution of the SFBT model, I believe that there were these key interventions developed inductively from the client. I've heard Steve say before that the miracle question came from a client. For example, the miracle question was inductively created from a client. The client said a miracle would have to happen in order for something to change. So again, it evolved, and it was all about the client, and it wasn't about a big T. We think this is how change occurs and we are going to create this intervention based off this philosophy of change. All this came from the client. All the solution-focused videos, for example, are all titled with language used by the client; *I Want to Want to, I Hear Laughter,* they are all taken straight from the client's language. Therefore, it's all about the client and always has been.

In terms of qualitative researcher, and the idea of Wittgenstein's idea of *to be*, we have really changed from focusing on interventions ... because at the time, it made sense. People were going to Milwaukee and they were working with Steve and Soo [Insoo Kim Berg] and at BFTC [Brief Family Therapy Center], and they were watching things, and trying things and experimenting with things, and things that worked they kept and things that kind of worked they altered. We also talked about and changed to asking pre-session change questions to asking about overall what's changed, which gives the birth of expectations and people aren't their problem all the time. The entire model and process has evolved all based on the clients, from pre-session change, to in-session change, to whatever is working for the client in general.

The development of the model is so focused on language and conversation, and what works for the clients and doing what works, they developed these "interventions" as a philosophy, as a process, to get back to qualitative research.

What is actually going on. Peter [De Jong] and Insoo [Kim Berg] both wrote *Interviewing for Solutions*, and they are asking the question what it is to interview and the process of asking questions. Not so much therapy, but interviewing someone in a solution-focused way. And so, their process of teaching that was called Listen, Select, Build. You listen to what the client says, exceptions, goals, resources. And then you would select those nuggets and pieces of possibilities. Possible solutions, possible places to go. And then you would build off of those. Maybe you would restate what the client says or ask a follow-up question. Maybe you would alter, we've talked about language formulation. That's a restatement of what the other person says. It could be in an altered form, you can delete certain words, you preserve certain words, and you give a summary of what they've said. In this Listen, Select, Build process, it's actually what we do as SFBT therapists. I would debate that all therapists do this, all therapists listen for certain things, have a framework of where they want to go, and they build off of that. And that's how they do therapy. I don't know if other approaches would identify it that way, but that's what they do.

As Dr. Smock is outlining the Listen, Select, Build process, I am internally agreeing with her and how she explains that we all do this, specifically as therapists. I am doing this as she is speaking, focusing on the specific practice of Listen, Select, Build. From that, I am hoping to build on that to ask further questions about the qualitative researcher.

Smock: I would even argue that the qualitative researcher also does this. So, I think there is a parallel between Peters and Insoo's Listen, Select, Build and the qualitative researcher. We are describing the process in quantitative terms, in qualitative processes. Either way, therapy or qualitative researcher, it's an interview. Going to the process of therapy, everyone thought that SFBT was just a bunch of techniques, and that was all wrong. Now we have this shift of researcher that we can capture what's going on with microanalysis. We are trying to quantity co-construction. We are able to operationalize what's going on moment by moment. If we know what's going on moment by moment, we can train qualitative researchers, using the same analysis of language; both therapists and researchers. But the qualitative researcher can especially benefit from the analysis of language.

What words do we use that match our model or theory or wherever we want to go? Things from linguistic literature, how do you phrase a question? What does a formal question even mean? Specifically, with therapists, they are trained in one specific model and they adhere to it and are told what not to do, and that always doesn't translate well into the therapy room. The same is true for the qualitative researcher, studying moment-by-moment analysis, studying language and questioning. There is a lot of literature on linguistics and language that isn't bridged to the research methodologies, quantitative and qualitative.

Building off of her conversation of language and linguistics, and how to ask a question, my thoughts went to the first question the SFBT therapist asks: What would be the most helpful for us to talk about today? I build off of this because the language in that question specifically is such that is allows for the conversation to naturally flow in the direction of solutions. I believe that the same question can be posed in different contexts, like qualitative research, and can be useful for data gathering, like Dr. Smock outlines in the following.

Me: So you're talking about what I've been thinking about, what do you think, how do you think the qualitative researcher can benefit from that approach to interviewing, "What would be the most helpful for us to talk about today"? That kind of process and generative conversation and language. How does the research agenda and the question, "What do think would be the most helpful for us to talk about today?" how does that fit with a research "agenda"?

Smock: My answer would be to start with: every question has embedded presuppositions or assumptions. When you start up an interview, whatever you ask at first, most of the time people start off with a question. That question has an embedded assumption about what you think about the client/participant. The question, What do you think would be the most helpful for us to talk about today? assumes that the client has something to share that is helpful. Or, that the conversation itself that is about to occur can be or has the potential to be helpful. How SFBT can help *qualitative researchers or interviewers is being very aware of their assumptions and what messages they want to put out there in their interview.* We, in our positive and negative choice analysis, we found that what the therapist says has immediate effect on the client. If the therapist uses positive content, the client is more likely to respond in kind with positive. If the therapist is negative, the client is also more likely to respond with something negative. Part of that is the rule of conversation and language. You try to not interrupt, and you try not to challenge or deviate from what the person is asking you. That is just the curious rules of having a conversation. But it's truth. So, what the researcher is asking, from question one, it influences the entire conversation, based on their assumptions. So, if we can train qualitative researchers to be more mindful of the questions they ask, I think that can make a difference in what they get from their data/participant.

Asking a question, not mindful of how we are influencing the conversation, creates a bias. And it's all bias; I want to be very careful about that. However, especially if you are working with at-risk populations, people that have experienced trauma, I think the last thing you want to do is make them feel worse in a qualitative interview. I think you can still get the information that is helpful, for social change or whatever, without having those negative biases. And most of the time, when people ask the question, *they don't think about the assumptions in the question, they just think about "I want this information."* Attorneys do it all the time. They purposefully load the question to be manipulative or place blame. Or it's a question where,

tell me how many times you beat your wife, or something like that … it doesn't matter how they answer it, there's no way to win.
So, the wording of questions, and the assumptions behind them make a huge impact on the response.
With the conversation on language, bias, and how that inevitably drives conversation, my thought went to the research agenda. A research agenda has the potential to be driven by specific language, to ask specific questions, and to ultimately gather specific data.

Me: What, then, happens to a research agenda if we're thinking about these things. Is there a such thing as a research agenda? Is a research agenda already hindering the organic flow of the researcher conversation?

Smock: Everything is biased. Everyone has an agenda whether they think they do or not. The important thing as a researcher is that you acknowledge the agenda. Whether, qualitative or quantitative, there is also bias in quantitative research and process research, but we don't discuss that as part of the results. But there is innate bias there; what we decide to look at, what our rationale for our sample is or for our data set, it's all bias. *So, it's not that we can change the bias, it's that when you're a qualitative researcher, not only being aware of your bias, but also being sure that the questions that you ask reflect those assumptions is very important.* I don't know if that happens. I don't know if qualitative researchers pay that much attention to here is my bias, here is the type of qualitative research I'm doing, and then the questions match up with the assumptions based on my approach. I don't know that that happens.

I have said repeatedly in this book that the way we view the world influences the way we ask questions. Hence the importance of studying epistemology and philosophical assumptions. Dr. Smock is supporting what I have written in terms of the SFBT framework in approaching asking questions.

Smock: I think that is a hole that could be filled, pretty easily. I think about IRB [institutional review board] proposals and submitting research questions. The focus usually from the IRB and the committee is if you're asking ethical questions that can still give you the information you are looking for. I don't think the bias is ever examined.

Me: I don't think so either. Especially with qualitative researchers, I think … well the researchers I've talked to, they ask questions based on their research approach: are these phenomenological questions, are they grounded theory questions. I think that's fair enough, but I don't think that pays special attention to the assumptions and presuppositions. I think there is a small hole there that needs to be filled. If a researcher espouses SFBT philosophies, then, is there even a need for an agenda?

Smock: I would say that as a SFBT therapist, and researcher, my "agenda" is to find out what works for that person in that context through a dialogue. That is my agenda for a conversation. If I was a qualitative

SFBT researcher, I think I would have the same type of agenda. I think my method might be different. I think my assumptions would be the same, though, if I'm coming from the idea that everybody has all the resources they need, some of the major tenets of the model, I think that would show through in my research as well as my practice as a therapist. So, agenda is not a word that, again, we are very careful about language. I wouldn't say I would use the word agenda, I think as a researcher you do, I think the word I would use is *assumptions*. What assumptions does the researcher hold. And how are their interactions and assumptions with their participant conveyed? I would say usually through an interview. That's going to be the main way in which your assumptions are going to be conveyed to the participants. Do your assumptions affect your results? Of course they do. I think that qualitative research does a good job talking about the bias of the researcher. They don't do a good job talking about the process of gathering the information and the biases that is there in terms of how the questions, the words that they use, how they phrase certain things. That is what's needed.

This part of the conversation regarding agenda and assumptions made me think about the postmodern idea of not-knowing. Specifically, how Harlene Anderson and Kenneth Gergen communicate the idea of suspending our knowledge for the sake of the conversation, allowing our conversational partners to lead. In this interview, I am trying to do so, and I am also curious about how Dr. Smock does that in her practices.

Me: I'm thinking of one of the tenets of SBFT, a diagnostic, we don't believe in diagnoses, even that kind of philosophy. How does the researcher put aside, or set aside, or suspend their ideas about the things they are researching themselves?

Smock: We have to use words, for example, "infidelity." I don't think that everyone who does that same behavior would call that thing the same thing. And I think it starts from there. If you're interested in a topic, you have to have parameters as a researcher. Who fits your study? Someone in a committed relationship who has either been, has experienced in some way *mistrust* with their partner. Something very vague. And then you have to have to ask some clarifying questions to find out whether it's an emotional affair or a sexual affair. There are the different variations. But using the word "infidelity" already, in and of itself, puts people into a category; you're either the "victim" or you're the "perpetrator." And you already have lined people up to feel bad. "Cheating, affair, infidelity," those are heavy words. People have a hard time getting past that. Even being part of a study that is being labeled that way, you are already putting your assumptions out there. No matter what your take is on the behavior or the act or experience, if you really want to capture the experience, even recruiting, how do you get these people that have had this experience without labeling it in a certain way? Characterizing it in terms of behaviors, someone who has experienced mistrust with a partner, or something like that, and then you can disqualify them if they don't fit your population. I think that could be a way to lessen the overt assumption in a study like that. And who knows their story? Again, what we would say about diagnosis like depression; Steve said that words were originally magic, he uses the example of depression. When you say you're depressed, I don't know what that means. When you said you experienced infidelity, I have no idea what that means or what happened. Because it's different for everyone. And that's important for sensitive topics like that.

What Dr. Smock is sharing in this point of the conversation is very interesting and pertinent to this book. The question that keeps coming to mind, and that I cannot find a clear answer to, is "how" does one do this. How do we suspend our knowledge for the sake of the conversation? She offers good suggestions for the researcher. My response is only to further the conversation and add to what she is saying.

Me: So, how someone suspends their idea of whatever it is that they're researching, "I have my own definition of ___, but what do you mean by that?" There's a space there, suspending that belief, requires something, and I think the researcher can really benefit from that. …

Smock: It opens up possibilities for people to be more transparent and less judged. It also opens up the richness of the study because you're going to get more of a variety of experience versus those that only participate because they ascribe to that term infidelity.

I would say curiosity. And that fits with SFBT. We are curious. And that is such a great word. It shows the assumption of "I don't know but I want to learn more." In a sense, all science is curiosity. If you're not curious, you're not going to do the work to do the research. It's in a very neutral way, because it takes away the assumption of language. The word "curiosity," to me, is much more respectful word to use and it still captures exactly what we are doing; it doesn't take away from what's going on. So why wouldn't a qualitative researcher's questions reflect that nature of curiosity versus a very blatant, perhaps, question? Again, all questions have assumptions, but assumptions that are detrimental or harmful or not useful to gather the process of information in the spirit of curiosity.

Me: The word that comes to mind is "itemized" questions. You can get data from that, but I don't know if that reflects the true spirit of curiosity.

Smock: The process is just as important as the content, especially in SFBT. I've had conversations in life in general, and it's so off-putting to me that I don't want to answer. I get defensive about it because of the way it's asked. I think it shuts people down. You can also say that it's not ethical. They feel coerced because they already started the interview because they're already consented.

At this point of the conversation, having no agenda, the conversation was reaching a natural end. I had asked several questions about theory, process, research agenda, and how to interview based on the solution-focused brief therapy model. Since I had Dr. Smock, I thought to ask her one last question about the relationship of the researcher and participant in the spirit of self-disclosure.

Me: OK, last question. This is kind of random, but how do you feel about disclosure as a therapist and researcher?

Smock: So, personally and coming from a solution-focused approach, I believe that SFBT does not necessarily ... we tend to focus more on the conversation and not the relationship; it's more about the conversation in therapy. The conversation becomes the relationship. However, I think, this is my personal view, if a client is saying that they are having a specific situation, and it would be helpful for them to normalize, and again, it's more of a gut thing, but *I do it with clients who are asking for it. For me, that is very solution focused.* The same thing with education. Our model doesn't necessarily talk about educating the client, but if the client asks for education, if we didn't give them or provide them that information, that would not be serving our client, that would not be benefiting our client. So, I do the same thing with self-disclosure. The way I do it, if a client asks me point-blank, something that I thought would be helpful to them about myself, that did not compromise the personal/ethical relationship. For example, the question if you have children. If they are asking me that, and it's not of that boundary violation, then sure, I have kids. If that helps them be able to carry on the conversation or co-construct, that's fine. As a therapist you have a boundary and limit. Like anything else, I don't think anything is off limits within ethics and legality. It's about what evolves and what the client is asking for. As long as you keep all of that in perspective, I think you follow the client's lead.

Me: I completely agree. What I've been thinking about is that line: where is it that one crosses that line from following their lead to inserting ourselves. I think, with disclosure, that's a *very* fine line. But, if the conversation calls for it, and they ask you questions ...

Smock: Again, it's about the client. When I train supervisees I say if sharing something about myself is of my own benefit, or for me to, or if it's about me, I don't do it. If it's about the client, then I do it. I don't talk about myself because I want to talk about myself. I mean, we're human beings. I think as a researcher it's more challenging because your role as a researcher is very different, it's a one-time shot, or a few. You're curious, like a therapist, but I think there'd be more of a boundary, perhaps, with self-disclosure as a researcher than as a therapist.

While I listen to Dr. Smock, I focus on her ideas of "doing things within ethical boundaries" and "we're human." I select those because of the nature of the relationship between the researcher and participant. "We're human" begs the thought of self-disclosure, but the boundaries of the relationship might call for something different. Hence my struggle and my next thought I build on.

Me: That's totally fair. I'm having a hard time translating the therapist's practice of self-disclosure to a researcher's practice of self-disclosure because I feel like, for the benefit of the client, yes. But as a researcher, if they disclose, are they doing it for the data? For the agenda?

Smock: If it's chitchat, then OK. I think in an interview, some initial chitchat is OK. But if then the participant turns to the researcher and asks, I think that would be much more boundaried. If you want to use the agenda or curiosity … Here's the difference, this might be helpful: As a qualitative researcher and interviewer, if I am interested in interviewing a participant, I am interested in getting their information. *I am not concerned about the co-construction of our story.* In the therapy session, I am interested in the co-construction of their solutions. It's collaborative. I don't see that the same as a qualitative researcher. I don't think it's a collaborative process. I think that's more informational curiosity gathering. But it is not collaborative. For the most part. I know you have questions as a researcher that builds from their answers, but you're not co-constructing a reality, you're gathering information. And that's the difference between therapy and research.

I did not, and still do not, completely agree with Dr. Smock's thoughts on research not being as collaborative and co-constructive. While I agree with her idea that the co-construction is different for therapy and research, she is arguing they are more different on the co-construction practice than I believe them to be. I think therapy and qualitative research are closer in co-construction than Dr. Smock is inferring. At the same time, while I do not completely agree, I am trying to suspend my ideas of what co-construction of data is so that the idea at hand, the difference in co-construction between therapy and research, can be mutually shared and through the process of asking questions and dialogue.

Me: OK. I like that. One of the phrases I've been wrestling with and thinking about is just that, the co-construction of data. And, I'm still thinking through that. OK that's really helpful.

Smock: Again, I think all conversations are co-constructed; I want to be really clear about that. However, when you're in a therapeutic interview, you go back and forth, you do Listen, Select, Build. I would say, maybe correcting from what I said earlier, I think that the qualitative researcher can learn from Listen, Select, Build in terms of the questions they ask, but the end point is not to *set a goal and not for behavior change*, that's for therapy. For the qualitative researcher you're just gathering information. So, the end is different. The *function* is different. Even though co-construction always happens, because of the nature of the conversation varies, you're going to have difference.

Me: I completely agree. And I am struggling with the idea of self-disclosure, especially for a researcher. That's really helpful, thank you. I don't know, Sara, do you think there is anything else that would be helpful for me to know at this point?

Again, true to the solution-focused therapist, the question of what else would be useful for the therapy session is applied to this interview.

Smock: You know, I think a goal that I would have if you're focusing on qualitative research with solution-focused therapy would be to tie in the language of co-construction, conversation, curiosity, all of those pieces, because those are the commonalities. I think that in general our literature [marriage and family therapy literature] doesn't talk about the communication research at all.

APPENDIX C

The following interview was one I conducted in a research project with a colleague of mine on remarriage in widowhood. We had a set of interview questions, which I loosely followed, but I also created room for conversation, giving space for all our personalities to mesh. The interactions also show efforts in deconstructive questioning, approaching the interview with mindfulness of narratives, and a "way of being" with the participants/co-researchers.

Interviewer: Not so much like you're being grilled or anything like that. Just a few things that we're curious about and that's it. It should be pretty laid back. I don't feel that we tried to make these questions to feel like they're not questions.
Husband: I'm just going to type everything you say (jokingly).
Interviewer: I think that it's important to mention that some of these questions might sound like they're just for 1 person, but they're not. It's a couple question, and so we're not trying to point or single somebody out during these questions. We have the couple in mind, so let's start pretty easily. How did you meet?
Wife: Originally? We were both students here.
Interviewer: Students? Yeah.
Wife: Husband, you want to say something?
Interviewer: Yeah, you can.
Wife: Oh, okay.
Interviewer: I won't put anything, but yeah you can.
Wife: He's 2 years younger, so I was a junior, I guess, when he came here, and then really, after that …
Husband: We knew each other.

Wife: Yeah, we were in the same Brother and Sister Club, kind of thing, but just being that much younger, and me being a junior and then senior year, you're not really too involved in club.

Interviewer: What club were you in?
I am practicing general curiosity in their stories before we get into questioning.

Wife: LOA.

Husband: She was dating Gene Hines … We shouldn't say that.

Wife: Maybe we shouldn't have students transcribe this?

Interviewer: I'll do the transcript, yeah.

Wife: I'll do it (jokingly).

Husband: With people I knew was in the club with so yeah, so we knew each other.

Wife: Yeah, it was kind of just parallel. I knew of …

Husband: We would not have dated in college.

Interviewer: No.

Wife: No.

Interviewer: What club were you in, Husband?

Husband: Kyodai.

Interviewer: Kyodai? Okay. All right.
I wasn't in club when I was here so I'm not really familiar with the clubs.

Husband: Yeah.

Wife: It was what we did back then, so it was … Anyway, so after that we met up at the friend's …

Husband: We got married.

Wife: Mutual friends. Well, he was just asking.

Interviewer: Yeah.

Wife: It was at a friend's birthday party. He had turned 30, and it was right after First Husband had died, and in fact, it was my first outing.

Interviewer: It was fast?

Wife: Yes, it was …

Interviewer: Or soon, I should say. It was soon.

Wife: Yeah, it was. First Husband died in October and that was November 16, or around that time. I don't know the exact date, but that's his birthday, and so we were at a birthday party, and Husband was really not the only person that spoke to me, but the only one that spoke to me about the death, and it was the first time, like I said, that I had done anything by myself. I was always with friends, couples, always, and so because of his dad's death, he knew to say something.

Husband:	I knew to say something.
Interviewer:	It was like an empathy theme or a common experience theme?
Husband:	Yeah, just a, "Sorry about First Husband," because I knew enough to know people will either say ridiculous stuff to try to fix it or they don't say anything else.
Wife:	We just started talking that night.
Interviewer:	It was at that party that y'all met again?
Husband:	Yeah, probably we started getting to actually know each other.
Interviewer:	Okay, and that was years after college, right?
Wife:	Oh man … Because I was almost married for almost 10 years.
Husband:	When did we get married?
Wife:	That was '95.
Husband:	I graduated college in '89.
Interviewer:	Met there. I'm assuming you started to date after, I'm assuming … Or?
	With his sort of question, I am trying to practice the not-knowing stance, trying to show my engagement to their story, and trying not to assume the narrative of a dating relationship.
Wife:	Well, I don't know if dating is the right word.
Husband:	No, we were just friends.
Wife:	It was really we talked that night … Until what? Well, we went to the movies, and …
Husband:	With a group.
Wife:	With a group of people, and later we found out. We never really intended for us to … That was their soul.
Husband:	I was a little bit leery about dating a widow because I was just thinking, "If that doesn't work out, you really look like the bad guy."
Wife:	Yeah, we just had good conversation, and the next day, I was so bored. All of my friends were married, I had absolutely nothing to do, no children, my family doesn't live here, my boss didn't let me go back to work, and so it was kind of … Oh no. I was working by then.
Husband:	You were at work.
Wife:	I was working by then, but it was just I didn't have anything to do at night. Of course, I wasn't sleeping, so the next night I called Husband and said, "Hey, want to go to the movies?" It just kind of became a good little friendship.
Interviewer:	That's cool.
Wife:	Yeah.
Interviewer:	That's cool.
Wife:	Yeah, it was July 1st. I wouldn't have gone if you had asked me though. That probably would have been …

Husband:	I had to fit you in between the other girls I was dating at the time.
Wife:	He's not kidding.
Interviewer:	He's not kidding?
Wife:	He's not.
Interviewer:	That's awesome.
Husband:	Because we were friends, so yeah, it was kind of interesting.
Interviewer:	That's awesome, so it was just like a comfortable thing. It was just kind of slowly progressed to …?
Wife:	I think that …
Husband:	I wasn't really good at being friends with girls, so it was probably good for me that we were just friends.
Interviewer:	Okay.
Wife:	I didn't know how to be anything but married, so that was very … Even on that night when we went to the movie, I went to the bathroom, but I gave him my coat and my purse. I'm like, "Here can you hold these?" Well, that was just reflex to me, and he's like …
Husband:	I was like, "This is bad."
Wife:	Just things that, you know, habit for me.
Interviewer:	Yeah. That's interesting. I like that. I like that. Some of these questions aren't going to be very applicable or some of them you will have already answered just by talking so I'm going to make sure that I ask the most important ones, so what is the first memorable experience that you 2 felt strongly attached to each other? Connected? Bonded? However you want to phrase that. *I am also trying to be public with the questioning, how the process will go, and what they can expect. As I think about the question, I expound on it so that it can be as vague and intentional as possible.*
Wife:	I have about 3. Can I name them all?
Interviewer:	Yeah, of course.
Wife:	When my mom came to town, First Husband and I were supposed to go skiing for Christmas, after Christmas, over the years, and my mom came to town because I had told her that I was going to go on vacation and have, so we were going to go on a cruise and when I was on the cruise, well, when my mom, when she met you, she was like, "Oh, that's going to be bad," because she said, just to me, she just saw glass eyes, and to him, she saw, "Oh, I think he likes her," and mom couldn't imagine, and then so on the cruise she kind of told me that. She's like, "Hey, you need to be …" but it was right after I had realized that I missed you, like the conversation, his companionship.

	The second time was really about the same time we went to that wedding. Remember that girl at work? They sat there, and they said at a wedding in Madison, they were doing the vows, they said, "Until death do you part," and I just started to cry, and he just leaned over and patted me, and for me, that was it. I was like, "I'm okay. This is okay to be with somebody else." Very quickly, but it was okay for me. It was just solidified.
Interviewer:	Makes sense. Yeah. Comforting, yeah. It makes sense.
Wife:	It was like I was given permission at that point. You don't think about letting go.
Husband:	I would say I would guess probably when we went to Amarillo to see my family. She clicked with them and my little nieces and nephews and I've got a sister that, she's always the tough one. She didn't like the girl, it was going to be it's usually obvious. That was a fit.
Interviewer:	Family accepted her. That's important. I know that's big.
Husband:	Oh yeah.
Wife:	I even asked his mom, "Is this okay with you?" Because I knew his mom was a little, my mom, my dad had died a year and a half before, and so I knew what she's probably thinking, the same thing my mom was. "Whoa."
Husband:	I made her go to counseling.
Wife:	Oh yeah, he did. He made me go, and we walked out of counseling and I was like, "You owe me $75," she said, "I am okay."
Interviewer:	That's awesome.
Wife:	I don't think I ever collected, either.
Interviewer:	That's awesome, so there were 3 moments. Do you have your 2? Or just 3?
Wife:	I think it was when my mom had told me.
Interviewer:	Got you.
Wife:	Was probably the beginning of.
Husband:	Yeah, I don't really remember when we went from friendship to …
Wife:	Of course, I went and told his parents, too, so that was a pretty pivotal point to me to say, "I'm going to date somebody. I'm going to date. I'm just going to date 1 person," and it was in the same conversation. It wasn't, "I'm going to start dating again."
Interviewer:	Sure.
Husband:	They just lost the kid, so that's tough. They're good people.
Interviewer:	Family experiences is a common theme that we've been seeing in these interviews as far as the marriage just going well, or smoothly, or comfortably, the family experience is really

important. It really is, but it makes sense. Widowed or not, the family's important, and accepting that other person. I think that that's huge.

Again, being public with the participants, sharing with them the type of data that has been collected thus far and allowing them to see how they are contributing to the process.

Husband: I think that everybody knows, in that situation, the stakes are pretty high, so for the person that's lost someone, so everybody's really careful.

Interviewer: Makes sense, so that was before you were married, then? All of these experiences, right? That's when you all felt connected, attached? Okay. I like that. I like that a lot, so how did you know that you wanted to remarry or slash, marry? Again, that's not just a ... That's a good couple question. That's not just a 1 person question.

Husband: How did I know? I was 29, so I was pretty good at avoiding marriage commitment. That kind of stuff. I think I kind of had to just let myself, but I don't know exactly the time when that happened. It just kind of felt right to just go with it and quit overthinking it because I can talk myself in or out of whatever. I think it was just fun. I had fun hanging out. Everything else, but I think it was we were such good friends, I just never had that component, too.

Interviewer: You can answer if you need to.

Wife: I don't think I ever. I didn't think about it until I went to the wedding and then it was like, "Oh, okay. I can do this again."

Interviewer: Possibility.

Wife: Yeah, and this is who I want to do it with. I had never ... I had several friends who were like, "Well, you want to date so and so, or if you want to go out with us, and want to do this?" and I was like, "No, and well, I have to tell him about my ... Can I tell him about my 10 things?

Husband: Uh-uh.

Wife: He doesn't really like this. It's embarrassing. I made a list. When my friends were telling me, "You're going to have to date soon because you're just kind of a pitiful mess," so I was like, "No, it's okay." Then I said, "Fine. I'm going to make a list of 10 things, and when God brings me those 10 things, I'll date again." Don't dare God. I mean every single last one of those, and it was weird things. I mean, it was almost I kind of was daring God. I wanted someone. Some of the big ones were, "I wanted someone who had seen someone die." I kind of thought I was limiting myself and because the next one was someone who was at the funeral.

	I'm kind of thinking that I'm really narrowing it down to, well apparently, and as we would talk about things, and I had a really good friend who was pregnant, so she was up all night, and she would call me at 3 in the morning, 4 in the morning, when she was getting up to use the restroom, I would tell her, and she's like, "How did you know?" I was like, "Oh, I was sleeping." I wasn't. She knew, and we would talk, and she would say, "How'd the night go? What did y'all talk about?" I'd tell her, and she's like, "Hey, isn't that number 3?" I was like, "Yes it is."
	Then it would be, "Well, wasn't that number 7?" And I'm like, "Yes, it is," and so the more it was … And it was various. They were so specific. It was just kind of apparent that God had told me, "Don't dare me."
Husband:	I really was an answer to prayer.
Interviewer:	Yeah. Literally. Literally, you were.
Wife:	I'm sure you all know. He didn't like that part of it, but it's when I write those things down. I've pulled out the book and just giggled because I think, "Oh wow. You really did. How do you ask for someone who has watched someone die … Because I did?" When he started telling me about his dad. I was like, "You were there?" I wasn't there when my dad died so I don't really know that I assumed, we talked about that, and then just other things.
Interviewer:	But you had an idea of what you wanted?
Wife:	Very sarcastic idea.
Interviewer:	Very sarcastic idea, yeah.
Wife:	Yeah.
Interviewer:	Yeah.
Wife:	I wouldn't typically put … Like on my first lists of a husband, I would put Christian, family, that kind of stuff. This was, "I'm daring you," and so when that came true. When I realized, it was a big thing. It was evident to me that God was. I mean, I felt God around me the whole time, but it was very evident that he was answering.
Interviewer:	This is kind of a subquestion. How much of those expectations, sarcastic or not, how much of those do you think are a result of the previous marriage? If that makes sense? Does that make sense?
	As I try to stay with the interview questions, I am also using their own words, "sarcastic," in efforts to further create the reality they are already sharing. It is my effort to further co-construct this data with them.
Husband:	We're very different. A lot different.
Interviewer:	You and … ? What was his … ?

168 Appendix C

Husband:	First Husband.
Interviewer:	Yeah.
Wife:	Oh yeah. They're absolutely … And First Husband took longer to get ready than I did.
Husband:	He had long hair, earrings.
Wife:	I don't know because they were so … I just wanted somebody who understood me now. I think more what affected it was my father's death. I watched my mother grieve for 18 months, and she lost all of her friendships just because by the nature of it. You're a widow and they do couple things, and so I knew I wasn't going to do that, and so I don't know if it had. I haven't thought about that.
Interviewer:	That's fair. It just seemed like at that point, your expectations were a little bit more refined, and so I was just wondering if that was a result of that experiences in the previous marriage. It was kind of a subquestion, but not really a question. *I am not assuming her narrative of remarriage, repartnering, or any of those labels. Hence some deconstructive questioning here.*
Wife:	I don't feel like it is because I feel like the things that I was asking for, I was daring God to join me, and none of it was … I didn't ask for a Christian spouse. That was just understood. It was not going to be. I was saying, "Somebody who had watched somebody die. Somebody who had been at the funeral. Somebody who was born in a small town," so I didn't have to move from Lubbock, even though you did try.
Husband:	Probably your dad's death had more to do with it. She wasn't over that and so I probably was there for you when your dad, more than with First Husband.
Wife:	Yes, fair enough.
Interviewer:	Anything you want to add to that before we move on? These get a little bit more couple oriented but still past relationship oriented, so for example, if you can recall, how do you both handle a new marriage in widowhood? Or how did you learn how to handle? *This was an effort to be led by the couple while still trying to maintain the questions.*
Husband:	In the marriage?
Interviewer:	Being married to a widow, being a widow, being married again, how did you learn how to handle that kind of relationship?
Husband:	For me, it was really different because she had her life insurance money, she had her bank account. I had my stuff, so it was kind of like that was interesting because I didn't really feel like I

	wasn't trying to get my hands on it. It's kind of like it triggers ... It's really ours, but it was hard to treat it as ours.
Interviewer:	I can see that.
Husband:	Because I was wanted to be sensitive and it was probably being around his family, that was interesting because they're great people but you know they're just thinking, "You're here because my son is not here." They're not saying that but you can see a sadness in their eyes.
Wife:	I forced that. That was something we did a lot. Probably a lot more than ... And you were so ... Because he was so respectful of only being there because their son wasn't. They are such great people. We wanted to see them, and they're still in our lives.
Husband:	I had to go to Christmas family stuff. It's like, "This is terrible."
Interviewer:	That's 1 of these questions. Not the Christmas, but that getting into something else.
Wife:	I think that it took me ... What was it? It was 2 years into our marriage that you had the flu. Every time he moved at night, I would wake up, and he's like, "I'm good. I'm good," and 2 years into our marriage. We're laughing because he had the flu. He's up all night, so I had no knowledge and he just let me sleep because he's like, "That's healing," so for him to be the guy that could recognize that was healing.
Interviewer:	Got you.
Husband:	I was just thinking, "I wanted to you leave me alone?"
Interviewer:	Both of your favorite interpretations.
Wife:	I was so excited when my cold comes.
Husband:	I had the flu and I thought she ...
Wife:	I slept through it? That's fair.
Interviewer:	You think that was his way of being married to a widow. You need this recovery, this rest, this ... ?
Wife:	Yeah.
Interviewer:	That's what I thought, too, when you were saying that.
Husband:	That's how it goes probably just ...
Wife:	I didn't know how not to be married.
Husband:	I didn't ...
Wife:	You didn't know how to be married.
Husband:	I hadn't been married, so it wasn't like a new normal. Marriage was the new normal. Honestly, there's ways with not dealing with baggage of ex-boyfriends or anything like that. We didn't have that.
Interviewer:	That's interesting. I can really see that, though.
Wife:	Yeah, because he was like, "Well, it's not like he's coming back."

Interviewer:	You don't have the chance of running into them at the mall or something. That's interesting. I kind of like that. *Once again, the process of being public, showing my fascination with their experiences and answers.*
Husband:	I was single a long time so I dated a lot of girls. They all had. Everyone's got their own, but just to not have to … That not even be a concern.
Interviewer:	It's relieving, kind of.
Wife:	For me, I didn't think about it because he could have married them, so it didn't matter to me. He married me, so it didn't really …
Husband:	In some ways, it was easier.
Interviewer:	I could see that. I could really see that. That makes total sense to me. Wife, what about you? Handle a new marriage in widowhood?
Husband:	I didn't say it right.
Wife:	It didn't feel like it was. I think because of I knew … It was really … I mean, I wouldn't really call you a gift from God, but it was just a … It was from God. It was an answer to prayer, even as sarcastic as it was … There wasn't really, I didn't ever have a point where I thought …
Husband:	It seemed like it was just 2 different lives. Same person, some of the same people involved, but really, just 2 different lives.
Interviewer:	It sounds almost organic. You said this was an answered prayer, we were friends, we knew each other … It just sounds like everything was just organic.
Wife:	We talked so much in a short … People would say, "How do you really know each other?" I'm like, "You have no idea how many hours we would talk." Hours.
Husband:	I hate talking on the phone.
Wife:	That's why I finally said, I asked him, "Why did you decide whatever that you wanted to get married?" He said, "I just started talking on the phone too long," but that's when I knew that it changed for him. Just different things you could see along the whole way, as he was dating other people when we first started dating. I didn't have … I don't know. It just kind of felt like this was us, and that was us, and it kind of all matched. I think it's because part of who he is that I didn't feel like I had to quit talking about First Husband. I had learned from my mom not to idol, like revere, they're not perfect. They're deceased but they were human, and so I tried never to make comparisons.
Interviewer:	Well, that kind of gets into this next question. Are there any, this says events, but I think it's broader than that. Are there

	any events, things, memories, whatever from your previous marriage that form the style of your marriage today?
Husband:	That's a good question.
Interviewer:	Does it make sense? The style of your marriage?
	"Style" was not a part of the original questions; it was my own ad lib in the moment of the conversation; it seemed to fit.
Husband:	Brought your experiences from being married to this one.
Wife:	It's the same as you bring your showing from dating, everything, you know everything you do. The events.
Interviewer:	Yeah, and that should be broader than that. Events, memories, pictures, anniversaries, Christmases, all those events should be really broad because you were just saying something like, Husband, like you talk about him. Even those things. That kind of stuff too.
Wife:	Can you repeat the question?
Interviewer:	Are there any events from your previous marriage that form your style of marriage today?
	Maybe, I don't know, I'm kind of editing this in my head, right now. Maybe I should ask, "Are there any events in your previous marriage that influence the way you do your marriage today?" Does it make better sense?
	Again, a decision in the moment because of how the conversation felt, how the question sounded the first time, and my being public with "editing" it in the moment.
Husband:	The question makes sense. I get the question. I just think you're so … say weird but it's different. It was really like 2 different lives to where they – your marriage is so different from our marriage, it doesn't mean 1 was good or bad. They were just different.
Wife:	2 really good marriages. I think on that, and I think I watched good marriages. The example from my parents, and his parents, and my grandparents. I think you learn that life is too short after this, so some of the things that might annoy me I'm like, "Yeah, I kind of do that." Things aren't something like that, but there's not …
Husband:	She's that kind of personality though. She's worked a wide range. She's worked for a dentist, she worked at a vocational school, she's taught kindergarten, and she's enjoyed every job she's done. Where I'm kind of like, "Oh God. I need to do something else or whatever." She's whatever moment she's in, she enjoys that. I kind of think that it may play into that was a good marriage, everything was great, I have good relationships. This marriage now … It is interesting because you even your interactions with … They were really close and did a lot with his family.

Wife: We really did every weekend.

Interviewer: Really, you knew them as a couple. Is that right?

I am showing them how I am engaged in their experience, curios about it, and trying to listen for their answers in their "events" that influence their current marriage.

Wife: Yes, which is also one of the things. Well …

Husband: I knew First Husband from school. I didn't really know him well, but I kind of knew her boyfriend before a whole lot better, so we kind of knew each other, and I don't even remember why I went to the funeral. Probably, 2 weeks prior to that there was a Kristina Curry has killed herself. It was a funeral at South Plains. I don't know why I went to that one, but I went to that one.

Wife: She's from Herford.

Husband: She's from Herford, so she knew some family stuff.

Wife: Where she was born.

Husband: Went to that funeral. That's where I kind of saw First Husband and Wife and might have even said, "Hi," and talked for a minute, and then the next thing I know …

Wife: The next week. It's not 2 weeks. It was 1 week.

Husband: The next week, he had died.

Wife: Like she died.

Husband: It was close, too close.

Wife: She died on Wednesday and he died on Tuesday.

Interviewer: Wow.

Husband: I just kind of remember that interaction thinking, and I knew some people that would be there. I should go to that funeral.

Interviewer: I'm kind of ad libbing here because if we're thinking of events from the previous marriage that influence how you do your marriage today, I feel like, really, you have potential to have 2 different views or entry ways of seeing both marriages. Your marriage and then … First Husband was his name?

I am practicing Listen, Select, Build with the words of "events" and how that is forming these current questions.

Wife: Mm-hmm (affirmative).

Interviewer: First husband, so I feel like you can see both marriages, so I'm just wondering how valuable that is?

Husband: Of course, they were very younger. You would have gotten married … How old were you when you got married?

Wife: 22.

Husband: 22, so you were married for 7 years, so I think you go through different things the younger you are, so we were got into that, so it was, when I look at that, and I think that's why I never really felt threatened in some ways because I was different, that

Appendix C   173

	marriage was different, where they were going was different than where we were going, and none of it good or bad. How you ... I can't remember. In y'all's marriage, who managed the money?
Wife:	Me.
Husband:	In our marriage, she did, but my mom kind of did, so there were a lot of things that just kind of happened, but probably we should have investigated more why this was happening and afterwards. You know what? There are some things that I probably just took for granted and didn't question because she'd been married, that kind of worked, and I just kind of went along with it.
Interviewer:	Interesting. Yeah. You had faith in her ability to be married? *This was more of the therapist in me, processing out loud my interpretation of their development in their relationship.*
Husband:	Yeah.
Interviewer:	Or to do marriage?
Husband:	Yeah, how you divide up your stuff or do whatever.
Wife:	Probably, some of it was because during our conversations when we were friends, at first, I'm sure that was all I talked about, was our marriage because one time I remember he was like, "Ugh." I think we were engaged but you were like, "I thought you would never not talk." I was like, "I didn't think that I talked about it very much," so I know I felt bad that it's still there.
Husband:	I probably asked a lot of questions.
Wife:	You're very good at questions.
Interviewer:	Well, this gets into another subquestion. How do those things, allowing the space to still remember, still talk about things, how did those things influence the bond of the marriage? The attachment of the marriage? The closeness of the marriage?
Wife:	Heavy because the fact that I could talk about him is very important to me. Mainly because his parents are there, but that's just part of who I am. I don't think you could understand fully who I am, if you don't know that part of me. I make superficial friends but think my best friend still is went through that experience with me, so I think that really draws you closer from my point of view.
Interviewer:	I totally see that.
Husband:	Well, probably because the focus early on was so much about death whether it was First Husband, or her dad, or my dad, that's what we had in common. Well, when you have that in common, what's kind of important in life, you have in common. You see life differently. You see that this is a very thin veil from life to death, and some of the goofy stuff just melts away.

Interviewer: That's very true and both of you had that together?
Husband: Yeah.
Interviewer: That's the common denominator, glue, whatever you want to call it.
Husband: That was probably the biggest bonding agent that probably was because I've got friends today that they may have lost a grandparent, and we know there's death and it's painful but it leads to other things, and we just worry less about it, so that's probably the most defining part.
Interviewer: I'm almost hearing having the space to just talk about it and both of you explore it freely. However you want to say that.
Wife: There's no jealousy, there's not a … He doesn't …
Husband: We're talking about death and loss. It could be a dad, it could be a husband, it's very different but it's just kind of out there, and it's not a … Because to some people, that might scare them off.
Interviewer: Yeah, big time. I think that's very wise, the fact that people who haven't experienced close loss, it's a far separation between those people and people who have experienced it. A random grandma, so the fact that, so you 2 are connected through that grief experience, I think that's a pretty wise awareness. I think it is.

This comment reflects my sense of "being" with the couple. The tone and demeanor began to be a little more somber with these comments. Therefore, I tried to stay in the moment with my reflection, as opposed to rushing to the next questions.

Husband: To be close enough to seeing parents who lost their son, then you realize that the grief of losing a husband, the grief of losing a father, is different than there's nothing natural about a parent losing a child, even if that child's 30 years old.
Interviewer: Yeah, not at all. That makes sense.
Husband: It's interesting because in that whole deal you're living in a fish bowl. You go to church it's like, "These people didn't talk to me before I started dating her."
Wife: Now everybody wants to get to know.
Husband: Now everybody wants to get to know me.
Wife: He would slide in.
Interviewer: That's funny. Yeah, that makes sense. That makes total sense, so let me see here. I kind of answered a couple of these. Well, this kind of gets to the Christmas thing. How do you all, as a couple, manage those influences from the previous marriage today?
Husband: Do we manage the influences?
Interviewer: Mm-hmm (affirmative). Or just … ?

Wife:	I don't know if there's managing. It was just a healthy … The influences there, we like our kids being around them and so we definitely put our families first. With his parents, we do not … We do Christmas on a different … It's a different random time. It's less than it is with our families. We go see my family in Arizona. We'll go see his family.
Husband:	We never spend Christmas at home.
Wife:	We do not spend …
Husband:	I think part of the factor is there was no kids and I think that allows the 2 different lives … There are less things to carry over.
Interviewer:	That's important. It really is.
Husband:	It would be different.
Wife:	Well, it wouldn't have happened. I would not have asked God for … At that point I would have been dealing with a child. I cannot imagine saying, "Oh, I would like to date." My friends telling me, "You need to date." My friends would have not been telling me that.
Interviewer:	It would have completely different.
Husband:	Your relationship with First Husband's parents, although it was really nice, it may have been even more intrusive.
Interviewer:	Yeah.
Wife:	Yes.
Interviewer:	I can see that, too.
Husband:	I don't know if there's much we …
Wife:	We did used to go to the family Christmas, but it kind of just seems like there's nights that it's not convenient for us.
Husband:	I can do it now and be way more comfortable because …
Wife:	They're just really nice people.
Interviewer:	The lack of kids makes it easier, I bet? I think so. Yeah, I think it's a big one.
Wife:	This would have been probably 2 years down the road, and a lot of … I think you could have loved somebody else's kid. I don't think … If you love that person, it wouldn't have mattered.
Husband:	I probably could have. My willingness to step into it, I have no idea because I would have been really cautious to, "After you get into that and it doesn't work out, what does that do to the … ?"
Wife:	I remember he was dating someone and he said, "I've never met her kid because that's just not …"
Husband:	That's funny because about the time she'd come along, I was dating someone that … Well, dating. Dating as in we have gone out on dates and we're spending time together, but she was older

	but she did have ... She was divorced and had a kid, and yeah, she wouldn't ...
Wife:	But what you respected about her it that she ...
Husband:	I thought it that was cool.
Wife:	She wouldn't let him meet the kid. She's like, "No, you're not meeting my kid. We're not that ... "
Husband:	She was really nice about it. She was just ...
Wife:	I just like that you respected that about her.
Interviewer:	That's funny. I had a really similar experience.
Husband:	Really?
Interviewer:	I dated an older lady. I was 28, I dated an older lady. She had kids, and she's like, "No, I'm not going to let you meet them." *My practice of self-disclosure here was to gain on their storytelling. Since I had shared a similar experience, I assumed my sharing would enhance the conversation, as to suppose a mutual bond in such an experience. I think it went over well.*
Husband:	You're like, "Whew."
Interviewer:	That's funny. Yeah. Seriously. Okay, good. I don't want to. That's funny.
Wife:	Thanks.
Interviewer:	You were 29?
Husband:	Mm-hmm (affirmative).
Interviewer:	I was 31.
Husband:	Really?
Interviewer:	Yeah.
Husband:	We should talk about that because I'm thinking I was a much better husband at 29 than I would have been a father.
Interviewer:	Oh yeah.
Wife:	A kid at 22 is hard.
Interviewer:	Yeah, I didn't know what I was doing when I was 22. I barely knew what I was doing when I was 30.
Husband:	I think you have ... You've got less things to work through when you're older.
Interviewer:	I think that too. Yeah. Yeah, that's interesting. Okay, what has been the most helpful for you 2 in forming this new marriage in widowhood specifically? Who has helped? What has helped?
Husband:	Just having really good people around us. Good family, good friends, you know, because we've gone to school together, we already had this network of people that we kind of knew, and so ...
Wife:	Including the ones that had completely attended for us. I think the conversation, the talking, was what really was. We just had

	so much time. He doesn't really like Rosa's anymore because … We would just go sit and talk and just, you know, it was just very …
Husband:	What was the question?
Interviewer:	What has been the most helpful in forming this new marriage in widowhood? Who? What has helped?
I believe in allowing the interview/conversation take its own course, and allowing it to come back to questions on its own, as it did here.
Husband:	I think, and even in the midst of that, we still make mistakes we have to learn from, but I think with the friendship being in place, and at rough times, stepping out of it really is not an option. Not saying I've even been close, but I mean it is kind of like …
Interviewer:	True.
Husband:	You got to find somebody that you can laugh with.
Wife:	There's never once … I was singing that song the other day, "I never thought once, 'What did I do?'" Even early on, when I would think that most people would say, "You're kind of like this," because honestly, the first marriage on our honeymoon, I was like, "What have I done?" It wasn't about him, it was about, "This is a lot. He's around me all the time." Just different personalities, and more of a high-maintenance personality, and so that was a lot, but even as that grew away from that, I just remember thinking, "I've never thought that," but I think being older and mature just kind of, like I said, I knew I would marry again. I didn't know how not to be married in a good marriage.
Interviewer:	You were 31 when you married Husband? 32?
Wife:	30.
Interviewer:	30. Okay. I feel like that's a good age to get married. 29, 30. That's a good age.
Husband:	Wait until you're done with the last kid.
Interviewer:	Let's see? My wife is … 35 and this is our first, so she's considered geriatric pregnancy.
Wife:	Oh yeah. We were there. I was 38 with the last.
Husband:	You do better care.
Interviewer:	I know. You do, right?
Wife:	33 with the first, and 38 with the last.
Husband:	In today's world, that's not … A lot of people that have kids later.
Interviewer:	It's getting more common. I think it is.
Wife:	I think our friendships helped a lot.
Interviewer:	Friendship?
Wife:	Like I said, I had the friend who was pregnant who I could talk to at any time of the night. I had a couple of those actually. I

	forgot about Amy. My friends were having babies, but they were so willing to just listen.
Interviewer:	That's important.
Wife:	Yeah, just someone ... And really not giving opinions so much. I don't remember that I ever asked their opinion, but ...
Husband:	You decide, in a group of friends, didn't really have to go along with, "Who's this person? Are they just trying to get me?"
Interviewer:	Non-judgmental.
Husband:	That was never even a part of it because they knew both of us.
Wife:	Yeah.
Husband:	Read the question one more time.
Interviewer:	What has been the most helpful in forming this marriage, in widowhood specifically? What's been the most helpful? Who's been the most helpful?
Wife:	I would think friends and conversation. Friends. Our friendship. Our mothers, my sister.
Husband:	Perspective.
Interviewer:	Just a couple more here. We've kind of talked about this, but this gets a little bit more specific. I'll just read this straightforward. I won't try to edit it. How have your experiences in previous marriages affected the way you handle relationships today? Again, that is a couple question. That's not just a widow question. *This effort was trying to be more of a researcher. I feel as if I was being driven by the research agenda, trying to find specific answers to specific questions, too much. As you can see, it did not go over well. This did feel forced, even like I was trying too hard to find an answer.*
Wife:	Can you read it one more time?
Interviewer:	How have your experiences in previous marriages affected the way you handle relationships today?
Husband:	I haven't had any marriages.
Interviewer:	Just the fact that Wife's been married. How has that affected the way that you handle relationships today? Or this relationship today?
Husband:	Okay, one more time.
Interviewer:	How have your experiences in previous marriages affected the way you handle this relationship today?
Wife:	I think it makes me not sweat. Don't sweat the small stuff. I really think we use the same perspective. There is not a whole lot that ... Life is too short, and once you've seen someone die, it kind of changes a lot of things, so I would say that.
Interviewer:	I like that. That's good.

Wife:	Once you witness that, and then birth. You look at things, too, but it's whole, but once you've seen life … Death. It's such fine line. You can't really …
Interviewer:	I totally agree.
Husband:	I think that 1 of the guys I was living with, we went to the same high school, we kind of roomed together, well he, within 6 months, they got married when we did. He married someone that her husband left her, and so they were divorced.
Wife:	Cheated on her.
Husband:	Her husband, so they got married, and then we got married, and you kind of just go, "God used death to give us our common ground." You kind of just … My message to young girls is 1, don't wait to get married to start living, and 2 God will work out whatever He's going to work out, so I guess that …
Interviewer:	That's good.
Husband:	I don't know if that really answered the question but there's kind of a things are going to play out the way they're going to play out.
Interviewer:	That's kind of an existential question, but I think that it's on purpose because it does give a lot of perspective on relationships today, but I like it. I think it's good. I think it's really good. I like the "Don't sweat the small stuff" a lot.
Wife:	It's just really like when you've seen that, and you've seen your dad, you watched your dad die, that was huge.
Interviewer:	Yeah.
Husband:	Probably even, I would guess, to think that you haven't been through that, just the fact that you get to a certain age with hope. You just deal. You don't worry. There's just different stuff when you're 21 years old and married compared to 30.
Interviewer:	Yeah, completely different.
Husband:	Maybe your brain has to finish developing.
Interviewer:	I hope so. Okay, last one here. What advice would you give to someone going through a similar situation as yourselves?
Wife:	Laugh.
Interviewer:	Laugh?
Wife:	Yeah. I think talk. If you can have conversations. To me, that's what drew us so close. That we were able to. Our friendship was first. I think that's what's still the underlying … We have fun together, and so you can go through life's pain, but if you're not friends, it's really not a …
Husband:	I would say don't rush, but it looks like we probably rushed, but we really didn't. We just, there again, in what phase in our life, you know things quicker, and so once you kind of realize that, you kind of take your time.

Interviewer: You all knew each other beforehand too, so …

Wife: Yeah, I didn't have to go through wondering, "Is this a good guy? Does he have good friends?" There wasn't that phase of wondering.

Interviewer: Learning.

Wife: Yeah.

Husband: That probably plays into whatever advice we would give too but that would be different than meeting someone and starting to like them and not having a clue about their history.

Wife: Yeah, because even the night that we went out, I went to that friend's party. That was the biggest thing I thought I was doing that night. I am going to a birthday party all by myself, and my friend's like, "Do we drive you?" I was like, "No. I'm going to drive." It was just something. It was a proud. I was proud that I was there and I actually walked up to the door because I was all alone and there were people there and that wasn't my usual crowd. That wasn't my people, but like in school, I knew them. In church, I knew everybody. That wasn't my best friend or anything like that … They were his friends that I had gone to the party, but I was so excited to go somewhere because none of my friends went out at night.

Because that's what I tell you now. They wouldn't tell us for a long time. They had intentions.

Husband: Me and Bobby we were saying, "Okay, we really don't want to go. We're going to go for 10 minutes. Tell them we're on our way, go in and say, 'Happy birthday,' then leave." I don't know what advice I would give. Just maybe …

Wife: Listen to your head, your heart.

Interviewer: That's good.

Wife: I think …

Husband: Relax and be open to any possibilities.

Interviewer: Yeah. I like that because I think a lot of people put a stigma on widows and widowers, and that closes their possibility, to … to a person. To people.

This interaction shows my efforts in not promoting any sort of "widow" narrative within the conversation and letting the participants (co-researchers) form their own narrative within the questions provided.

Wife: I watched my mom, and I think I just knew that I wasn't going to do it that way. She absolutely lost her … I mean, they didn't say, "We're not going to be your friend anymore." It was just she didn't go eat with them, they would invite her, she wouldn't go, and she wouldn't do anything, and that was hard. Losing friends because you want someone that knew that person, so I think

	that's how that got into the thing, that you had to have known, known him if you were at the funeral.
Husband:	You probably, that's why you see that happen similarly, if someone loses someone, maybe there was a friend then they can open to it.
Interviewer:	What else? I don't know. Just general, important things about being married in widowhood. This is interesting because everyone we've interviewed so far has been quite a bit older. 50s, 60s, and they got married again in their 50s and 60s, so I think you both have been the youngest ones. It's really interesting though. I like this.
Wife:	It's a different ...
Husband:	There's another couple that ... She has kids. Jerry Anne and Scott Morsley. It was interesting. That was about the same time. We all went to high school with them.
Wife:	I think staying true to your own personalities. Like I said, there's 2 different ... I feel like I really have had 2 different lives. I was thinking parts that you marry. Parts of your dad, so I can look at First Husband and see what parts of my dad in him, and then I look at Husband and I think what parts of him, and yet it's just still me, and so it's very interesting to me to see what you choose for a spouse, at what point in your ... We would have not have dated, like we said, in college.
Husband:	She also did have to have a boyfriend so sorry. I would say it's always good to have someone who sees you better than what you see yourself.
Interviewer:	True.
Husband:	Someone who sees what you're capable of. That's what I always liked about you.
Interviewer:	That's a really good advice though. Yeah. It's like we need that a lot. To believe in us. To do better than your spouse.
Husband:	Yeah, because they don't believe in you. It was funny when we, it was 2 years ago, when we told the boys ...
Wife:	Remember when we told Calvin? We were in Dover. I know we were on Hunting and 3rd.
Husband:	It's like, "First Husband could have been my dad?" "No."
Wife:	Then he was like, "I have 2 dads?" "No."
Interviewer:	That's funny.
Wife:	They're very ... And they didn't understand. They called his parents, Nanny and Pop, so it's a close relationship but they didn't understand that at all. They're like, "Well, they're not our grandparents." "Well, they kind of are. They're not." "No. They're not. You have grandmas. You don't have grandpas."

Interviewer:	That's got to be fun telling them.
Wife:	They were just …
Interviewer:	Yeah, that's got to be fun.
Wife:	It was just different, but then they're kind of like, "Okay." They don't really … I think because they're great people. It makes things …
Husband:	It helps them because they don't have granddads on either side, so they want more older guy to care about them is pretty cool.
Interviewer:	I like a lot that y'all both say, "That marriage was that marriage, and this marriage is this marriage, and that's it," and "I was a different person than. 2 different lives." I really like that a lot. I like that idea a lot.
Wife:	It just doesn't … I don't know that I would know any way to do it different.
Husband:	That really had to start in the dating because if there's any comparisons, "Well, First Husband used too …" Go back to him. I have told her if something happens to me, she's not very marketable.
Wife:	Now I have 2 kids and 2 husbands that are deceased. No, I think it's yeah I don't really feel … I don't know. Even the girls that he was dating when we were starting to date, that didn't ever … I think because everybody you date shapes you into who you are now, and good, bad, or whatever it is, but still, if you can look at that, "Okay, yeah." There's some good.
Husband:	Most of them I couldn't see myself being married to, so you think, "Oh, maybe it's just me?" Then later on, it's like, "Okay, I can see myself."
Interviewer:	Totally get it.
Husband:	You're trying to fit a square peg in a round hole and it's just like, "I'm at the age. I'm still don't know. This should be working."
Wife:	I think knowing. When First Husband and I started dating we were seniors.
Interviewer:	In high school?
Wife:	No. Here.
Wife:	Yeah, and we met in a class, and he was such a goof ball in that class, and I was like, "You need some help. I better help you." It was psychological statistics and he was just goofing around and I was like, "You need to get on the ball because you're not going to make this. This is not going to work for you," so we started tutoring, and I started helping him with it, and then so I think when you go from that, and we weren't really friends, really. We started dating pretty quick. I lost my train of thought.
Interviewer:	Square peg, round hole.

Husband:	Probably knowing him and how much different he was, I was thinking, "If she's interested in me, then there wasn't any comparison," because it would be ... You would never have got passed the ball in your hiking boots and earrings, so it was just like he was so different that it never felt ...
Interviewer:	Yeah. I totally get it. 26, 27 year olds, I'm thinking, "Okay, what's wrong here?" I totally get it.
Husband:	I was kind of ... I would have been okay.

INDEX

Note: **Bold** page numbers denote Tables.

Ackerman, N. 7
Adams-Westcott, J. 87
Adler, A. 2–3; *see also* psychoanalysis
Alcoholics Anonymous 102
analyser 45
Anderson, H. 49–50, 56, 57, 61, 84, 91, 114, 130; Ba 145; conversation 68–69; host and guest 117–118; internal dialogue 77; metaphorical space 132; one-down positioning of researcher 122–123; philosophical stance 62; qualitative research and practices 139–147; relational expertise 73; researcher and participant 130; withness 65

Ba 71, 132
Backhaus, K. 104
Bateson, G. 7, 19, 39, 46; therapist as part of family system 48
Bava, S. 75, 76
Beck, A. 6; *see also* cognitive and behavioral therapy
being public 74, 76; *see also* conversational philosophies
Berger, P. L. 52
BFTC (Brief Family Therapy Center) 151
Bion, W. R. 10
Blow, A. J. 46
Bowen, M. 11; *see also* Palo Alto group
Bowlby, J. 10

Bradford, K. 56
bricoleur, methodological 19; *see also* researcher
Buber, M. 57
Bumberry, W. M. 134

case study researcher 24–25; *see also* researcher
Charmaz, K. 21, 65
Clark, R. P. 126
client/therapist relationship 4
cognitive: behavioral therapy 5, 49; therapist 6; therapy 6; *see also* therapist
cognitive and behavioral therapy: Aaron Beck 6; Albert Ellis 5–6
collaborative language systems 56, 61
collaborative researcher 61, 78–79; approach to research 74–78; change through conversation 68–71; conversation 63–64; conversational philosophies 71–74; not-knowing 65, 67–68; philosophical stance 61–63; process of therapy 69; questions 63; Rogerian approach to therapy 63; withness 64–65
collaborative therapist 61
Combs, G. 81, 84, 86, 88, 91
compliments 103; *see also* solution-focused therapist/researcher
constructivism 48; hermeneutics 49–50; and postmodernism 14–15;

see also postmodern therapies and approaches; therapist
constructivist approaches 6–7; *see also* therapist
constructivist therapists 6
continuous evolution 15; *see also* therapist
conversation 63–64; change through 68; conversational background 69–71; conversational partnership 69; dialogical space 68–69; mutual exploration and development 69; *see also* collaborative researcher
conversational philosophies 71; attitude of continuous questioning 71–72; avoiding generalizing 72; being public 74; feminist critique 74; host and guest 71; knowledge and language 72–73; privileging local knowledge 72; relational expertise 73–74; research inquiry 73; *see also* collaborative researcher
Corbin, J. 20, 21
co-researchers 91
counseling 1, 45; modern and postmodern 46–48; therapist 1, **8–9**
countertransference 1; *see also* therapist
creativity at work 12; Sue Johnson 13–14; *see also* therapist
Creswell, J. W. 20, 32, 127
critical paradigm 36–37; *see also* philosophical interpretations
critical theory philosophy 36

Dafforn, T. A. 87
Daly, J. K. 19, 21, 32
data analysis 92–93
Davis, S. D. 7, 10, 46, 56, 87
deconstructive: listening 85–86; questioning 88, 161
Denzin, K. N. 19
Derrida, J. 51
de Shazer, S. 105
Diagnostic and Statistical Manual of Mental Disorders (DSM-5) 51
dialogical: relationship 5; space 68–69; *see also* conversation
discourses 81; internalized discourse 87; subjugated discourses 87–88; *see also* narrative interviewer
Dolan, Y. 105
DSM-5 *see* Diagnostic and Statistical Manual of Mental Disorders

egalitarian hierarchy 96
Ellis, A. 5–6; *see also* cognitive and behavioral therapy
emotion-focused therapy approach 14; *see also* therapist
epistemology 29, 41–42; continuum 30–32, **33**; objectivist 30; subjectivist 31; *see also* epistemology continuum; ontology; philosophical interpretations
Epston, D. 83, 87, 91
ethnographer 24; *see also* researcher
ethnography 24
existential: encounter 56; therapy 3; *see also* therapist
experiential therapy 5; *see also* therapist
externalization 86–87; *see also* narrative interviewer

family: interactions 47; treatment 10
feminist therapy 6
Fife, S. T. 56
first-order cybernetics 47
Fischer, M. M. J. 39
Foucault, M. 51, 81, 87
Freedman, J. 81, 84, 86, 88, 91
Freud, S.; analyser 45; psychoanalysis 121; treatment approach 45
Fromm-Reichmann, F. 10

Gabbard, G. O. 1
Gehart, D. 75, 76
general systems theory 7
Gergen, K. J. 20, 52, 53; co-construction of knowledge 85–86
Gestalt: therapist 4; therapy 4, 45
Goldberg, N. 125
Goolishian, H. 74, 84, 91
grounded theory 21, 23; *see also* researcher
ground theory methods 34

Haley, J. 12, 47, 121
Hare-Mustin, R. T. 81
Harré, R. 52
hermeneutics 49–50
hierarchy 113; debate of 113; expertise in 120–121; feminist critique 114–115; host and guest 117–118; one-down 122–123; participant 119; postmodern 121; researcher 117; therapist 115–117; in therapy 114; *see also* self-disclosure
homeostasis 13

host and guest 71; *see also* conversational philosophies

ICCE (International Culture and Career Exchange) 139
inquiry 86
institutional review board (IRB) 59, 76, 123, 137, 142, 154
internalized discourse 87
interpretation 83–84; *see also* narrative interviewer
interview questions 77
IRB *see* institutional review board
I-thou work 4

Johnson, S. 13–14
Jung, C. 2; analyser 45; concept of wounded healer 2; treatment approach 45; *see also* psychoanalysis

King, S. 127, 129, 130
Kitzinger, C. 114
knowledge, co-construction of 85
Kuhn, T. S. 32, 37

Lamott, A. 126
language 54–55, 99; game 105–106, 107; philosophy of 95–96; *see also* solution-focused therapist
Levy, D. 10
Lewin, K. 10
Lincoln, Y. S. 19
listening 83, 86; deconstructive 85–86
Listen, Select, Build process 106, 108, 151–152; *see also* solution-focused therapist/researcher
Luckmann, T. 52

Madanes, C. 12
Marcus, G. 39
marriage and family therapist 7, **16–17**, 46; modern and postmodern 46–48; *see also* therapist
McGoldrick, M. 12
meaning 40; *see also* ontology
memoing 129; *see also* writing
Mental Research Institute (MRI) 11, 113
method 74
methodological bricoleur 19; *see also* researcher
Minuchin, S. 13, 47
modernism 46–47

modern wave of therapy 47
monologue 69
Moustakas, C. 23
MRI *see* Mental Research Institute

narrative: research 23; therapist 81, 114; therapist's belief 89–90; therapy 81
narrative interviewer 81, 93; alcoholism 89; analyzing stories 92–93; asking questions 83; belief of narrative therapist 89–90; deconstructive listening 85–86; deconstructive questioning 88; discourses 81; externalization 86–87; infidelity 88; internalized discourse 87; interpretation 83–84; interview 91–92; listening 83, 86; not-knowing 84–85; politics of power 83; relative influencing questioning 88–89; research approach 90–93; research questions 90–91; separation of problem from client 86–87; subjugated discourses 87–88
Nichols, M. P. 7, 10, 87
nonsequential writing 129; *see also* writing
not-knowing 65, 67–68, 84–85; humility 67; risk 67; uncertainty 66; *see also* collaborative researcher

objectivist 31; researchers 30, 31
Omasta, M. 129
one-down philosophy 54
ontology 39; meaning 40; social exchange 41; of symbolisms 40–41
opening space 91

Palo Alto group 10, 48; Carl Whitaker 11–12; Murray Bowen 11; Virginia Satir 12; *see also* therapist
paradigms *see* philosophical interpretations
Paré, D. A. 88
Perls, F. 4, 5, 45
person-centered 4; *see also* therapist
phenomenological research 23–24; *see also* researcher
phenomenology 23
philosophical interpretations 32; critical paradigm 36–37; feminist framework 37; positivism 32, 34; postmodernism 37–39; postpositivism 34–35; social constructionism 35–36

philosophical stance 61–63; *see also* collaborative researcher
philosophy 29, 41–42; *see also* epistemology continuum; ontology; philosophical interpretations
Pinker, S. 128
positivism 32, 34; *see also* philosophical interpretations
positivist 34
postinterview 78
postmodern approaches 6–7; *see also* therapist
postmodernism 37–39, 50; social constructionism 52–53; *see also* philosophical interpretations; postmodern therapy
postmodern researcher 38, 110
postmodern therapy 45, 47, 50, 51; constructivism 48; hermeneutics 49–50; language 54–55; metaphor of technocrat 51; modern workings 46–48; non-diagnosing 55–56; one-down philosophy 54; postmodern common factors 54; postmodernism 50; social constructionism 52–53; solution-focused therapy 55; therapist and researcher 56; therapists 14, 56, 47–48; *way of being* 56–57
postpositivism 34–35; *see also* philosophical interpretations
postpositivist 35
Poth, C. N. 20, 32, 127
psychoanalysis 1–2, 49; Alfred Adler 2–3; Carl Jung 2; *see also* therapist
psychoanalyst 2; traditional 46

qualitative research 18, 20, 29, 39, 40, 125; continuum 30; memoing 129; narrative therapy 90; in social sciences 135; *see also* researcher
qualitative researcher 1, 19, 82, 121; narrative therapy 84; nonsequential writing 129; one-down positioning of researcher 122–123; philosophies of re-experiencing 134–136; practice of writing 130; separation of problem from client 86–87; *see also* researcher
questioning: deconstructive 88; relative influencing 88–89
questions 63; asking 83; *see also* collaborative researcher

relational expertise 73–74, 90; *see also* conversational philosophies

remarriage in widowhood 161; *see also* deconstructive questioning
research approach 74, 107; analysis 109; analyzing stories 92–93; asking questions 75–76, 107; being public 76; data analysis 77–78; interviewing and data gathering 76–77, 107–108; interview questions 77; maintaining coherence 76; narrative interviewing 91–92; postinterview 78; research questions 90–91; thought-into-words process 77; quantitative 18; *see also* collaborative researcher
researcher 1, 15, 18–20, **22**, 25, 56, 91; approaches 20; case study 24–25; ethnography 24; externalization 86–87; grounded theory 21, 23; methodological bricoleur 19; narrative research 23; phenomenological research 23–24; qualitative 19; qualitative research 18, 20; *see also* therapist
research inquiry 73; *see also* conversational philosophies
Rogerian: approach to therapy 63; therapist 4
Rogers, C. R. 4, 5, 45

Saldaña, J. 129
Satir, V. 12, 48; *see also* Palo Alto group
Schwartz, R. 13
second-order cybernetics 48
self-disclosure 113, 115–117; expertise 119–120; therapist 116; *see also* hierarchy
semistructured interviews 105; *see also* solution-focused therapist/researcher
separation of problem from client 86–87
Shotter, J. 52, 63, 64; conversation 70
Smock-Jordan, S. 97, 102, 116; bias in research 154; co-construction of data 158–159; curiosity 156; infidelity 155–156; Listen, Select, Build 151–152; self-disclosure 157–158; solution-focused brief therapy 149–159
social constructionism 35–36, 52–53; movement 52; researcher 36; *see also* philosophical interpretations
social exchange 41; *see also* ontology
solution-focused brief therapy (SFBT) 55, 95, 149–159; therapist 96; *see also*

postmodern therapies and approaches; solution-focused researcher
solution-focused question 104; *see also* solution-focused therapist/researcher
solution-focused researcher 95, 96, 109–110; analysis 109; asking questions 107; compliments 103; fixing the broken 99; interviewing and data gathering 107–108; language game 105–106, 107; Listen, Select, Build process 106, 108; miracle question 98–99; normalcy and diagnoses 100–101; philosophy of language 95–96; postmodern researcher 110; problems 101–103; problem talk vs. solution talk 99; question initiating session 103–107; research approach 107; semistructured interviews 105; solution-focused question 104
Spiegel, J. P. 47
Sprenkle, D. S. 46
Sterne, P. 87
Strauss, A. 20, 21
structural family therapy 49
subjectivism 31
subjectivist 31
subjugated discourses 87–88
symbolisms 40–41; *see also* ontology
systems and schizophrenia 7–10; *see also* therapist

Tarragona, M. 75, 76
therapist 1, 25; cognitive and behavioral therapy 5–6; constructivism and postmodernism 14–15; continuous evolution 15; counseling therapist 1, **8–9**; countertransference 1; creativity at work 12–14; emotion-focused therapy approach 14; existential therapy 3; experiential therapy 5; marriage and family therapist 7, **16–17**; Palo Alto influence 10–12; as part of family system 47–48; person-centered 4; postmodern approaches 6–7; psychoanalysis 1–3; self-disclosure 116; systems and schizophrenia 7–10; transference 1; *see also* researcher
therapy 1
thought-into-words process 77
Tomm, K. 90–91
transference 1; *see also* therapist

way of being 56–57; with participants 161
Whitaker, C. A. 11–12, 48, 56, 134; *see also* Palo Alto group
White, M. 49–50, 81, 82, 83, 86, 88, 114; *see also* narrative interviewer
Whiting, J. B. 56
Wilber, K. 51
withness 64–65; *see also* collaborative researcher
Wittgenstein, L. 51, 96, 102, 105, 150
writing 125; analysis 131–132; analysis trialogue 133; editing 130–131; experience of writing throughout 131; first thoughts 125–127; formulating questions 137; memoing 129; philosophies of re-experiencing 134–136; practice 127; research team 133–134; research writing process 127–131; self of researcher 136; starting process of writing 125; transcription 131; written results 130–131

Yalom, I. D. 115; self-disclosure 120

Zinsser, W. 126, 127, 129

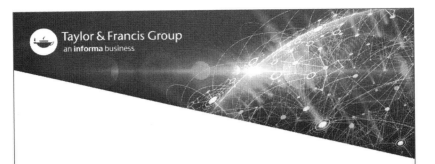